Learning Apex Programming

Property of
ABC Studios - PPS

Create business applications using Apex to extend and improve the usefulness of the Salesforce1 Platform

Matt Kaufman

Michael Wicherski

Doug Luberts
Manager
Technology

ABC Studios
The ABC Building
500 South Buena Vista Street
Burbank, CA 91521
p: 818.460.6104 f: 818.460.6629

doug.w.luberts@abc.com

PUBLISHING

BIRMINGHAM - MUMBAI

Learning Apex Programming

Copyright © 2015 Packt Publishing

First published: January 2015

Production reference: 1270115

Published by Packt Publishing Ltd.
Livery Place
35 Livery Street
Birmingham B3 2PB, UK.

ISBN 978-1-78217-397-7

www.packtpub.com

Credits

Authors
Matt Kaufman
Michael Wicherski

Reviewers
Marco Boerlage
John M. Daniel
Anup Jadhav
Pat Patterson

Commissioning Editor
Edward Gordan

Acquisition Editor
Sonali Vernekar

Content Development Editor
Govindan K.

Technical Editors
Narsimha Pai
Shweta Pant

Copy Editors
Shivangi Chaturvedi
Deepa Nambiar
Neha Vyas

Project Coordinator
Shipra Chauhan

Proofreaders
Simran Bhogal
Maria Gould
Ameesha Green
Paul Hindle
Joanna McMahon

Indexer
Priya Subramani

Production Coordinator
Nilesh R. Mohite

Cover Work
Nilesh R. Mohite

Foreword

Apps, and especially mobile apps, have become the primary path to innovation for most of the companies in the world. Businesses need apps for their employees that solve real problems, and they need apps to help them better connect to their customers and partners. These new apps are being created and are evolving at an amazing pace, and cloud platforms such as Force.com are making this possible.

However, when a modern-day developer sets out to build an app, they have a mind-boggling set of languages and services to choose from. So, it's important for them to understand when and how to use Force.com. We designed Force.com with the guiding principle that there is simply no faster way to build an enterprise application, and once you've built an app on Force.com, it is instantly ready for hundreds of thousands, even millions, of users. It will always be available, mobile, and secure. However, the critical thing to understand is that when we release new features three times a year, your app automatically gets them. It's like having 500 extra developers supporting you, who are working relentlessly to make your apps better, release after release and year after year.

If there's one piece of advice I would offer before you embark on your journey through this book, it's to be sure that you understand this foundational philosophy and why it makes Force.com special. It's a unique platform that can radically change how you think about application development.

Mike Rosenbaum
Executive Vice President,
Salesforce Platform

About the Authors

Matt Kaufman is no stranger to the Salesforce1 Platform, as he is one of the early employees at salesforce.com. Since 2002, Matt Kaufman has worked with hundreds of businesses to improve their efficiency through Salesforce. He is a certified Salesforce Advanced Administrator, Sales Cloud Consultant, Service Cloud Consultant, Advanced Developer, and Advanced Developer Instructor. His extensive experience and knowledge of salesforce.com technologies cause him to regularly be referred to as Mr. Salesforce, Salesforce wizard, Salesforce genie, and other magically endowed names.

Matt is currently the chief technology officer of MK Partners, Inc. (`www.mkpartners.com`), the leading `salesforce.com` implementation partner in southern California. He regularly provides training and talks on cloud technologies and development. He has also written other publications including *Salesforce.com for Dummies* and *Salesforce.com's Service Cloud for Dummies*, Wiley Publishing.

I would like to thank my wife and three children for putting up with me and embracing my passion for technology. I also give special thanks to the dedicated team of experts at MK Partners, who worked hard so that I could get the time to write. Finally, I cannot thank Justin Davis enough, who is the ultimate efficiency expert—without him, this book, and so much more, would not have happened.

Michael Wicherski, for the past several years, has been applying his business sense and knowledge towards designing, developing, and implementing custom solutions for hundreds of Salesforce customers, and has worked with clients of varying sizes—from mom-and-pop shops that are just opening to Fortune 100 companies.

During his time at MK Partners, Michael honed his skills for translating business processes into business logic. He is currently the senior Salesforce developer at The Agency RE, a real-estate firm in the heart of Beverly Hills, where he oversees the day-to-day use of Salesforce; plans, designs, and implements new functionality enhancements; and optimizes those currently in place.

An avid developer and a nerd at heart, Michael is constantly searching for those bleeding-edge technology innovations that can squeeze that extra bit of efficiency into his work.

Michael has also collaborated with peers on other publications related to Salesforce, most notably as the technical editor of *Salesforce.com for Dummies, 5th Edition.*

I would like to thank all those friends and family who have supported me in my endeavors and made sure I never settled and always strived for something more. I would also like to thank Matt Kaufman, Justin Davis, Chris Rodriguez, and the rest of the MK Partners team for their invaluable teamwork over the years, which allowed me to gain and apply the knowledge necessary for writing this book. To all who know me, thank you for embracing my nerd side, without which I would never have written a text about coding.

About the Reviewers

Marco Boerlage is a Dutchman with a varied background in IT. After finishing his study in business informatics, Amsterdam, he started working at Randstad, which was the beginning of his career in international application development. His specialty is to design and build HR and payroll systems, and he has led many projects and departments in that area.

Currently, Marco works at eMerus HR Solutions, which is a fast-growing company that delivers an integrated HR and payroll application in the cloud. eMerus develops on the Force.com platform, provided by Salesforce.com. Marco's activities range from specifying functionalities to testing and deploying Apex and Visualforce code in customer orgs.

John M. Daniel has been working in the technology sector for over 20 years. During this time, he has worked with a variety of technologies and in a variety of roles. Currently, John works for FinancialForce.com. He holds multiple certifications, including the Advanced Developer certification, and is in the process of attaining the Certified Technical Architect certification. John's passions include time with family, swimming, the beach, and working on various open source projects such as ApexUML.

> I would like to thank my wife, Allison, for always giving me the freedom to pursue my interests.

Anup Jadhav is a Salesforce technical architect with over 6 years of experience building applications on the Force.com platform. He is a graduate from the University of Mumbai and has worked with several languages (C, C++, C#, Java, and JavaScript), frameworks (.NET, Struts, Spring, and Visualforce), and integration technologies in his brief career that spans over 9 years. He is passionate about all things related to technology and plays adventure RPGs in his spare time.

He has worked with several Force.com consultancies and helped media clients in the UK such as News UK, Financial Times, and The Daily Telegraph. He is currently working as the "Head of Mobility, UK" at Cloudsherpas where he is architecting and implementing Mobile solutions on the Salesforce1 platform"

Pat Patterson has been working with Internet technologies since 1997, building software and working with developer communities at Sun Microsystems, Huawei Technologies Co. Ltd, and Salesforce. At Sun, Pat was best known as the community lead for the OpenSSO open source project, while at Huawei, he worked on cloud storage infrastructure software. Since joining the developer evangelism team at Salesforce in late 2010, he has worked with all aspects of what is now the Salesforce1 Platform, developing a focus on identity and integration. Describing himself as an articulate techie, Pat has coded everything from Linux kernel drivers to JavaScript web apps, written numerous online articles, and spoken at conferences on five continents.

www.PacktPub.com

Support files, eBooks, discount offers, and more

You might want to visit www.PacktPub.com for support files and downloads related to your book.

Did you know that Packt offers eBook versions of every book published, with PDF and ePub files available? You can upgrade to the eBook version at www.PacktPub.com and as a print book customer, you are entitled to a discount on the eBook copy. Get in touch with us at service@packtpub.com for more details.

At www.PacktPub.com, you can also read a collection of free technical articles, sign up for a range of free newsletters and receive exclusive discounts and offers on Packt books and eBooks.

https://www2.packtpub.com/books/subscription/packtlib

Do you need instant solutions to your IT questions? PacktLib is Packt's online digital book library. Here, you can access, read and search across Packt's entire library of books.

Why subscribe?

- Fully searchable across every book published by Packt
- Copy and paste, print and bookmark content
- On demand and accessible via web browser

Free access for Packt account holders

If you have an account with Packt at www.PacktPub.com, you can use this to access PacktLib today and view nine entirely free books. Simply use your login credentials for immediate access.

Instant updates on new Packt books

Get notified! Find out when new books are published by following @PacktEnterprise on Twitter, or the *Packt Enterprise* Facebook page.

Table of Contents

Preface

Welcome aboard! We're about to take a flight together into the realm of Salesforce1 development. We hope that our engaging banter will keep you on the edge of your seat through our thrilling hands-on exploration of the platform, its capabilities, as and its limitations. Our hope is that upon completing this book, you will walk away with the necessary knowledge to build the best application on App Exchange to date!

We ask that you please remain seated until the back cover has fully closed, lock your chairs in the upright position, and prepare yourselves to code like never before! The following sections will now provide you with an overview of our course and brief you on the features of this paper-bound vessel.

We know you have many choices when choosing a learning partner, and we thank you for the chance to become yours.

What this book covers

Chapter 1, Apex Assumptions and Comparisons, serves to introduce you to the Salesforce1 Platform. The Apex programming language, its similarity to Java, and other core concepts will be covered, as well as how to set up a development environment, which will be used throughout the book.

Chapter 2, Apex Limits, covers the limitations of the Salesforce1 Platform, specifically runtime limitations due to the shared tenant architecture. It also covers optimization methods to ensure that these limits are avoided.

Chapter 3, More and Later, which is an extension to the previous chapter, reviews how to process data asynchronously in bulk—leveraging the increased limits in asynchronous processing.

Chapter 4, Triggers and Classes, explains how to create Apex triggers and their respective Apex classes for database manipulation logic.

Chapter 5, Visualforce Development with Apex, allows you to explore how the Apex programming language can interact with the Visualforce markup language to create user interfaces on the Salesforce1 Platform. The chapter progresses from simple examples to more complex, dynamic interactions.

Chapter 6, Exposing Force.com to the World, teaches you how to create public-facing web services and expose your data to the whole wide world through Apex web services hosted on the Salesforce1 Platform.

Chapter 7, Use Case – Integration with Google Calendar, expands upon the knowledge gained in the previous chapter to consume the Google Calendar web service through Apex in order to create a synchronization process between the Salesforce and Google calendars.

Chapter 8, Creating a Property Management Application, covers how to create a property management application from start to finish, complete with credit card processing through the Authorize.net payment gateway.

Chapter 9, Test Coverage, completes your introduction to Apex programming with a fundamental understanding of Test Coverage, its requirements and limitations, and how to write proper tests.

What you need for this book

Those interested in partaking in this adventure with us will require a computer capable of running either the Eclipse IDE or a Sublime Text editor, preferably Sublime Text 3. We have chosen to demonstrate our examples based on the Eclipse IDE; however, Sublime Text users can also complete the exercises. Depending on your choice, either the Force.com IDE plugin for Eclipse or its open source counterpart, MavensMate for Sublime Text will need to be installed.

In addition to the aforementioned software, those wishing to write the code and test it out on the platform will also need a free developer account available from Salesforce (covered in *Chapter 1, Apex Assumptions and Comparisons*) or a paid license with Apex enabled (either a platform license or Sales Cloud Enterprise or higher).

Who this book is for

This book is intended for developers with prior experience in object-oriented programming development wishing to learn how to develop for the Salesforce1 Platform. It is assumed that you are familiar with the basics of development and do not need to review these concepts before engaging in a discussion about the specifics of the Apex programming language.

Conventions

In this book, you will find a number of styles of text that distinguish between different kinds of information. Here are some examples of these styles, and an explanation of their meaning.

Code words in text, database table names, folder names, filenames, file extensions, pathnames, dummy URLs, user input, and Twitter handles are shown as follows: "This means that it will not be possible to set the `AnnualRevenue` variable to a string or `IsCustomerPortal` to a date."

A block of code is set as follows:

```
trigger accountTrigger on Account (after insert, after update){

    //Use the Boolean attributes to quickly determine where we are
      in the order of execution and what operation occurred.
    if ( trigger.isAfter && trigger.isInsert ){
      for ( Account a : trigger.new ){
        if ( a.Phone != null ){
          system.debug(a.Phone);
        }
      }
    }
    if ( trigger.isAfter && trigger.isUpdate ){
      for ( Integer i=0;i<trigger.size();i++ ){
        if ( trigger.new[i].phone != trigger.old[i].phone ){
          system.debug(
          trigger.new[i].phone +'!='+ trigger.old[i].phone
          );
        }
      }
    }
}
```

When we wish to draw your attention to a particular part of a code block, the relevant lines or items are set in bold:

```
public with sharing class googleAuthorization_Controller {
  public string googleEmail {get;set;}
  //to store our code for dynamic rendering
  public string code {get;set;}
  //to store our user record
  public User u {get;set;}
  public googleAuthorization_Controller() {
    googleEmail = userInfo.getUserEmail();
  }
```

New terms and **important words** are shown in bold. Words that you see on the screen, in menus or dialog boxes for example, appear in the text like this: "Click on the **Setup** link at the top-right of the Force.com GUI. Under the **Customize** section, click on **Users** (these are not in alphabetical order)."

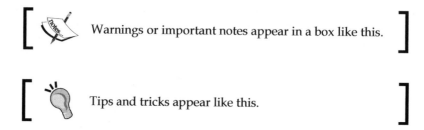

Warnings or important notes appear in a box like this.

Tips and tricks appear like this.

Reader feedback

Feedback from our readers is always welcome. Let us know what you think about this book—what you liked or may have disliked. Reader feedback is important for us to develop titles that you really get the most out of.

To send us general feedback, simply send an e-mail to feedback@packtpub.com, and mention the book title via the subject of your message.

If there is a topic that you have expertise in and you are interested in either writing or contributing to a book, see our author guide on www.packtpub.com/authors.

Customer support

Now that you are the proud owner of a Packt book, we have a number of things to help you to get the most from your purchase.

Downloading the example code

You can download the example code files for all Packt books you have purchased from your account at http://www.packtpub.com. If you purchased this book elsewhere, you can visit http://www.packtpub.com/support and register to have the files e-mailed directly to you.

Errata

Although we have taken every care to ensure the accuracy of our content, mistakes do happen. If you find a mistake in one of our books—maybe a mistake in the text or the code—we would be grateful if you could report this to us. By doing so, you can save other readers from frustration and help us improve subsequent versions of this book. If you find any errata, please report them by visiting http://www.packtpub.com/submit-errata, selecting your book, clicking on the **Errata Submission Form** link, and entering the details of your errata. Once your errata are verified, your submission will be accepted and the errata will be uploaded to our website or added to any list of existing errata under the Errata section of that title.

To view the previously submitted errata, go to https://www.packtpub.com/books/content/support and enter the name of the book in the search field. The required information will appear under the Errata section.

Piracy

Piracy of copyright material on the Internet is an ongoing problem across all media. At Packt, we take the protection of our copyright and licenses very seriously. If you come across any illegal copies of our works, in any form, on the Internet, please provide us with the location address or website name immediately so that we can pursue a remedy.

Please contact us at copyright@packtpub.com with a link to the suspected pirated material.

We appreciate your help in protecting our authors, and our ability to bring you valuable content.

Questions

If you have a problem with any aspect of this book, you can contact us at questions@packtpub.com, and we will do our best to address the problem..

1
Apex Assumptions and Comparisons

Salesforce is the enterprise cloud computing leader. Its **Customer Relationship Management (CRM)** applications were designed from the ground up to use a **Software as a Service (SaaS)** model. Their success revolutionized the technology sector and changed the way software is delivered. Powering their applications is the Salesforce1 Platform, which is a highly scalable, multitenant **Platform as a Service (PaaS)**. This platform is not just for salesforce.com's applications but is available to anyone to build a custom SaaS application. The programming language used on the Salesforce1 Platform is called Apex, and this book will get you started developing with it.

Apex isn't your typical programming language, so this isn't your typical programming book. We assume you already have experience with some other object-oriented programming language and aren't interested in reading about the basic concepts again. Instead, we take a more practical approach and explain what you need to know to start coding right away. We don't waste your time with Hello World code samples, and instead we walk you through writing fully functional code that is useful and serves business purposes.

Before you start

Apex is a proprietary language that can only be compiled and executed by the Salesforce1 Platform. The Salesforce1 Platform is not open source and only runs on servers owned by the salesforce.com company. For these reasons, the purpose of Apex is to extend the Salesforce1 Platform beyond its native features. This might be the most important lesson in this book and can be summarized by two simple rules:

- **Leverage built-in features**: Don't waste your time writing Apex code to do things that the Salesforce1 Platform can already natively do. Built in to the platform are robust features for authentication, reporting, workflow, and more. A good Apex developer is familiar with these features and works with them. Not only will this simplify your development process but also enable system administrators to manage items that frequently change. It will also ensure your projects are future compatible with the long list of feature enhancements salesforce.com delivers with each release.

- **Calculate your ROI upfront**: the Salesforce1 Platform uses a per user subscription model. Before you start developing, determine the costs and benefits of the project. When enhancing an existing application, you should always look for some type of commonality between your existing application and your new one, either in data, users, or administration. A commonality of data might facilitate greater accuracy and better reporting. A commonality of users will reduce costs and improve adoption. A commonality in administration will also reduce costs and hopefully development time. If this is your first use of the Salesforce1 Platform or there are no overlaps, then evaluate the development time, which tends to be much lesser on the Salesforce1 Platform.

These might seem like trivial points, but in our experience working on over 500 projects on the Salesforce1 Platform, the long-term success of any project relies on them.

A gift to our readers

The Salesforce1 Platform is a commercially available service that requires a paid subscription. You might already be a customer of salesforce.com and have access to the platform, but it's OK if you don't. Either way, as a loyal reader of our book, we want to show you how you can register for a free Developer Edition and start coding right away. Don't worry, there's no catch; it's perfectly legitimate. In fact, salesforce. com not only allows anyone to register for a free Developer Edition of its service but actually encourages it. Simply visit `developer.salesforce.com` and click on the **JOIN NOW** button in the top-right corner. Within seconds of registering, you'll receive an e-mail with a link to log in and set your password. Be sure to remember your username and password as you'll need them later in the chapter.

A company that gives away its paid service would not last long; that's why the Developer Edition is built with limits that make it perfect for writing code and experimenting, but not actually running a business. This usage restriction is also spelled out in the fine print, so don't get any ideas.

The Salesforce1 Platform has over 100,000 subscribing businesses with millions of users logging in each day. A subscription can be for as few as one user license or as many as you want. When you log in to the Salesforce1 Platform, your unique username and password are used to identify you and the subscribing organization you are a part of. All of the data, schema, and code specific to your organization are available to other users at your organization but are private for everyone else. The collective term for your unique instance of the Salesforce1 Platform is commonly known as your org. In later chapters, we'll discuss the various ways you can share your code outside of your org. For now, take comfort in knowing that the code in your Developer org is secure and won't be seen by anyone else.

Safety first

Before we go any further, let's talk about safety. Safety is certainly not a normal topic when discussing a programming language, but like we said, Apex is unlike any other language. Apex is intrinsically tied to the Salesforce1 Platform, a platform which businesses use to run their operations and track critical pieces of data. Apex is extremely powerful, and we all know what comes with great power. With this in mind, we want to make sure that while this book might teach you enough to be dangerous, you will pose no danger to anyone.

Writing code directly to an in-use Production environment is not a good idea. At best, you might inconvenience and annoy some users. At worst, you might make an error that brings your company to a standstill. It is for this reason that all paying customers of salesforce.com receive an included Sandbox environment. This Sandbox is an exact copy of your Production org's configuration, code, and other metadata. If you have a complex development process or multiple developers, you can purchase additional sandboxes with your subscription. You can even purchase a Full Sandbox, which not only includes your metadata but also all your data.

To ensure that your code is not destructive, the Salesforce1 Platform does not permit Apex code to be written directly to a paying subscriber's Production org. This means that you must write your code to a Sandbox org or a Developer Edition org. In later chapters, we will discuss the requirements, process, and tools to deploy your code to a Production environment. If you skipped the previous page, go back and sign up for a free Developer Edition of the Salesforce1 Platform. Now, buckle up because we're about to get technical!

The Force.com IDE

The Salesforce1 Platform's GUI includes its own web-based code editor. You can use this tool while on the Web to write Apex code. However, for serious development, programmers turn to a robust **Integrated Development Environment (IDE)**. The Force.com IDE is a software-based tool provided by salesforce.com that is designed to interact directly with Salesforce1 Platform. It includes the ability to read, write, and execute code directly on the server. It can store your credentials, which makes it faster to log in. It can even help you build and run queries against the database. Frankly speaking, the Force.com IDE makes it easier to develop applications for the Salesforce1 Platform, so we will show you how to install and use it.

The Force.com IDE isn't something you just install. It actually consists of three parts that build on top of each other, so you can't skip any of them:

- **Java Runtime Environment (JRE)**: This is the backbone for any Java-based program you want to run on your computer.

- **The Eclipse IDE**: This open source integrated development environment is widely used by developers of different programming languages. It supports code completion, syntax highlighting, version tracking, and more.

- **Force.com IDE plugin for Eclipse**: This plugin extends Eclipse from just editing files on your local computer to being able to connect directly to the Salesforce1 Platform.

Installing the Force.com IDE and its prerequisites can sometimes be frustrating. The simplest path is to follow the latest instructions provided at `https://developer.salesforce.com/` or to search for `Force.com IDE Installation` with your favorite search engine. These downloads are relatively large (around 200 MB total), so make sure that you have enough bandwidth and time.

To start, you will need to install the Java platform, Standard Edition Runtime Environment (JRE), for desktops (not servers). The JRE is the backbone for any Java application you want to run on your computer (such as Eclipse). At the time of writing this book, the JRE is owned and maintained by Oracle and can be found on their website. It is available for free under Oracle Binary Code License and does not require you to register to download. This software is supported on Linux, Mac OS, and Windows and comes in 32- and 64-bit versions. Either version is fine; however, you do need to match the bit version of the JRE with that of Eclipse. After downloading, install the software and reboot if needed. If you already have the Java Development Kit installed, then you should be able to skip this step.

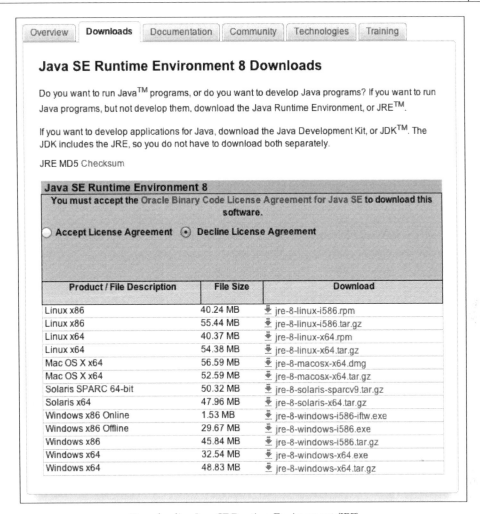

Downloading Java SE Runtime Environment (JRE)

Once you have the JRE installed, it's time to download and install Eclipse. Eclipse is an open source development platform that has existed for over a decade, and it is independent from salesforce.com. It runs on Linux, Mac OS, and Windows (in alphabetical order) and is community driven. It is highly popular among developers and the IDE of choice for Software Development Kit of many other web-based services. There are many packages of Eclipse for different purposes and even some that are branded by various companies. You might want to download the Eclipse IDE for Java Developers; it includes all the prerequisite plugins and some additional ones that you might want to take advantage of. Even if you already have Eclipse installed for some other work, it's a good idea to download a new copy that you will use just for development on the Salesforce1 Platform. Again, be sure to download the version that matches the bit size of the previously downloaded JRE.

Eclipse takes up a lot of disk space and uses a lot of memory, so if you're low on either, you can install the Eclipse Platform Runtime Binary package for a minimal install. You might need to add some missing plugins to use the Force.com IDE or take advantage of some of the features that we will discuss later.

Eclipse does not have an installer. Instead, you just uncompress the downloaded file and move the resulting folder to the appropriate location on your hard drive. Inside the folder, there will be an executable named `Eclipse`, which you use to run the program.

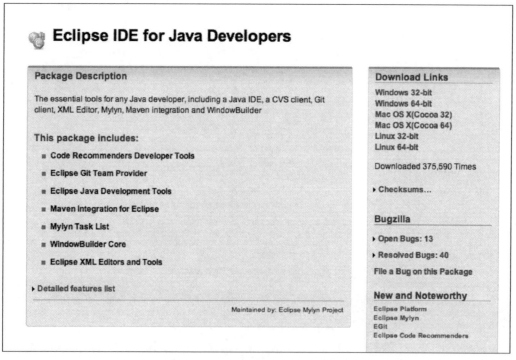

Downloading the Eclipse IDE for Java developers

When you first start Eclipse, you will be prompted to select a workspace. A workspace is a folder on your hard drive where you will store all of the files pertaining to projects you work on. You can create multiple workspaces and change their locations at anytime. So for now, just accept the default location and click on **OK** to proceed. The first time you use Eclipse, you'll be presented with the welcome screen that includes options to view and overview samples, tutorials, and more. These are great resources if you haven't used Eclipse before. When you're ready, you can click the link to go to **Workbench**. You can always return to the welcome screen from the **Help** menu.

Now that Eclipse is up and running, it's time to install the Force.com IDE plugin. Eclipse has a nice built-in tool that makes it easy to download, install, and update plugins from the Web. All you need to do is provide the URL from where the plugin is hosted and Eclipse will take care of the rest. The URL for the Force.com IDE can be found in the installation instructions at `http://developer.salesforce.com`. To install the Force.com IDE from Eclipse, perform the following steps:

1. Click on the **Help** menu and then select **Install New Software…**.

2. Click on the **Add** button to add a new repository.

3. Enter `Force.com` as the name.

4. Paste the URL `http://media.developerforce.com/force-ide/eclipse42`, and then click on **OK**.

   Eclipse will automatically start the process to download and install the software.

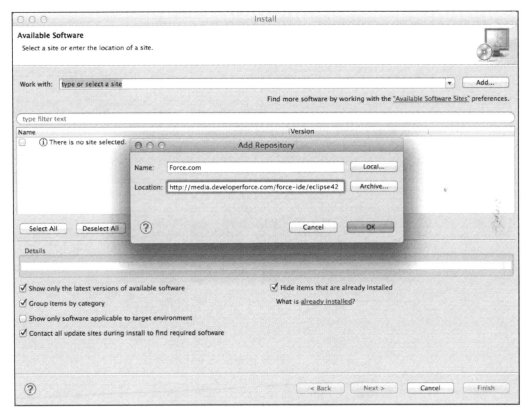

Adding the Force.com repository to Eclipse

5. Check the box to select **Force.com IDE** and click on the **Next** button.

   Eclipse will automatically determine whether there are any other packages required and display a list of everything that will be installed.

6. Click on **Next** again to review the licenses for everything being installed.

7. Select the radio button to accept the licenses and click on **Finish**.

   Depending on your Internet connection, this can take a while.

8. When done, you'll be prompted to restart Eclipse; click on **Yes**.

Take a deep breath; the hard part is over.

Getting comfortable with Eclipse

You finally have the Force.com IDE installed, but there's a few more steps you need to take. It probably doesn't look like Eclipse has changed much, so let's fix that by performing the following steps:

1. Click on the **Window** menu and navigate to **Open Perspective | Other**. A list of available perspectives will appear.

2. Select the **Force.com** option and then click on **OK**.

   The layout of Eclipse should change slightly and also now display **Force.com Start Page**; you're finally home!

The Force.com perspective in Eclipse

Eclipse is highly customizable and has a long list of settings available from the **Preferences** menu available in the **Window** menu (the **Eclipse** menu on Mac). Before we get underway writing code, here are a few tweaks that we recommend you follow, which will help you have a better coding experience:

- **Show line numbers**: This is an absolute must! Navigate to **General | Editors | Text Editors** and check the **Show line numbers** box.

- **Set default perspective**: Ensure that Eclipse always starts out in the Force. com perspective. For this, navigate to **General | Perspectives**, select **Force. com**, and click on the **Make Default** button.

- **Colors and fonts**: You might want to make things easier on the eyes. To do so, navigate to **General | Appearance | Colors and Fonts**.

- **Web browser**: Everyone has a personal preference, but you might want to specify an alternate browser when opening web pages from Eclipse. To set this, navigate to **General | Web Browser** and select your browser.

In addition to these preferences, we also recommend moving the **Outline** view under **Package Explorer**. You can do so just by dragging it to the bottom half of **Package Explorer**. This will increase the size of the editor and make it easier to see more of your code.

If you're like us, you wouldn't like to type things over and over again. Eclipse comes with a Snippets feature that lets you save frequently used code blocks and then use them just by double-clicking on them. You can even use Merge Fields to represent variables that you specify upon use. To get started with your first Snippet, perform the following steps:

1. Navigate to **Window | Show View | Other....**
2. Type in `Snippets` in the filter box.
3. Select the **Snippets** option and click on **OK**. The **Snippets** panel appears in the bottom portion of Workbench.
4. Right-click on the **Snippets** panel and select **Customize....** The **Customize Palette** window appears.
5. Click on the **New** button and select **New Category**.
6. Change the name of your new category to `Apex` and click on **Apply**.
7. Right-click on the **Apex** category in the list and navigate to **New | New Item**.
8. Click on the new **Unnamed Template** item.
9. Change the name of your new item to `System Debug`.
10. Change **Description** to `Outputs to Debug Log`.

11. Click on the **New** button to create a new variable.

12. Click on the new variable name and change it to `Variable`.

13. Set **Description** to **Variable Name or String**.

14. Type `String` in **Default Value**.

15. Type the following line of code in the template:

    ```
    system.debug(${Variable});
    ```

16. Click on **Apply** and then **OK**.

You just created your first Snippet. You can't use it just yet but go ahead and put a sticky on this page so that you can come back later and create more Snippets with useful code. In later chapters, when we are writing code, we'll use this Snippet.

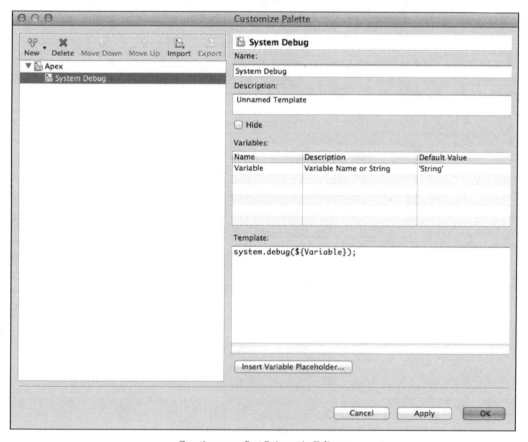

Creating your first Snippet in Eclipse

Linking Eclipse to the Salesforce1 Platform

Before you can write any code, you'll need to set up a new project in Eclipse. You'll need your Sandbox or Developer Edition org credentials to do this. If you don't have either, go back to our earlier section on how to register for a free Developer Edition.

When you log in to the Salesforce1 Platform via your web browser, you use a username and password and use e-mail or SMS for two-factor authentication. When you log in programmatically via a tool (such as Eclipse) that leverages the Salesforce1 Platform's APIs, you need a third credential called a security token. This security token is generated by the platform for each user and is automatically reset anytime a password is changed. To obtain your security token, you will need to first log in to the Salesforce1 Platform via your web browser. Once logged in, you can click on the drop-down menu at the top of the window labeled with your full name. Select the **My Settings** option and then expand the **Personal** section on the left. Click the **Reset My Security Token** link to read more about how the security token works, and then click the **Reset Security Token** button. Your security token will be generated and e-mailed to you. We recommend starring this e-mail to make it easy to find later.

> Instead of using a security token, you can whitelist your IP range from **Setup** | **Administer** | **Security Controls** | **Network Access**. Doing so will simplify the login process while you are in the IP range, but make it more complicated when you are not. Check with your IT policies prior to whitelisting any IPs and always make sure that they are static and will not change.

Now that you have your username, password, and security token, you can create a new project in Eclipse. Navigate to **File | New | Force.com Project** and a **New Force.com Project** window will appear. Give your project a name. We recommend including a date in the name as well. This will allow you to create multiple projects for the same org over time; this is a low-tech way of backing up your code right inside Eclipse. Enter your username, password, and security token. If you are using a Developer Edition, keep the **Environment** as **Production/Developer Edition**. If you are using a Sandbox, change it to **Sandbox**. When complete, click on the **Next** button to have Eclipse authenticate and retrieve a list of your existing metadata.

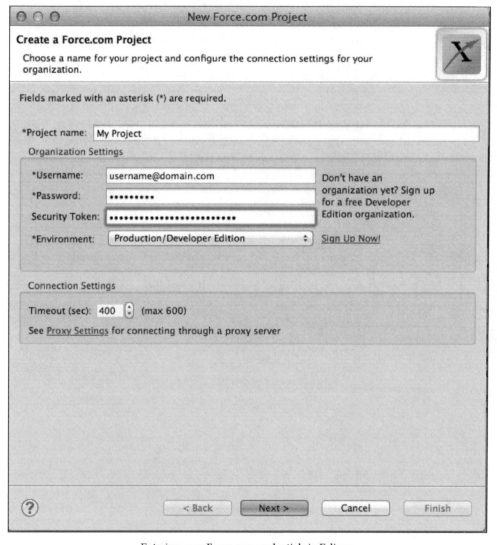

Entering your Force.com credentials in Eclipse

After authenticating, you will be prompted to select which metadata you want to download into Eclipse. The default option is only Apex and Visualforce, which is perfect for the purposes of this book. You can also select from all possible metadata components or choose to work with a blank slate by selecting the **None** option. Click on the **Finish** button to have Eclipse download your metadata into text files in your workspace organized into folders by type. You're ready to start coding, so let's take a more in-depth look at the Salesforce1 Platform and its Apex programming language.

Under the hood

You definitely don't need to understand how the Salesforce1 Platform works in order to write Apex code. You might find it interesting though, and it might answer some of your questions about Apex's behavior. For several years, salesforce.com has been called *the most innovative company in the world*. While its growing number of customers might be the interest of financial analysts, in our opinion, the real innovation is behind the scenes with Apex. Apex was the first multitenant, on-demand programming language. It is compiled and executed **Just In Time (JIT)** by Force.com platform servers.

The Salesforce1 Platform is designed to scale, so multiple threads of your code won't impact performance. In fact, roughly 50 percent of all transactions on the Salesforce1 Platform are programmatic and not performed via a **Graphical User Interface (GUI)**. It has taken years for the other major players on the Web to start developing their own programming languages, and it's no surprise that they have a striking resemblance to Apex. Despite being proprietary, Apex continues to be at the forefront of web development and evolves at a very rapid pace. salesforce.com produces three major releases each year while still maintaining backward compatibility for previous versions. These releases include community-driven features and typically simplify the development process.

Apex is a class-based **object-oriented programming (OOP)** language originally modeled after Java. It is often referred to as being Java-like, and at first glance, you might even think that it is Java. However, since its original design, concepts and methods of other programming languages have been incorporated into Apex, making it easier for non-Java programmers to adopt it. Regardless of your programming language of choice, Apex is the only language for you to choose if you want to run code on the Salesforce1 Platform.

The Salesforce1 Platform is powered by a myriad of technologies, but its core is Java. However, Apex code is not compiled into Java; it's actually stored as a series of instructions in metadata. This metadata also includes any nonprogrammatic configuration changes or customizations made via the Salesforce1 Platform's GUI. One of the biggest selling points of the Salesforce1 Platform is the ease in which a nonprogrammer can make declarative changes to the behavior and design of the application. While this was a true game changer in the industry, the more astounding feature is that custom instructions compiled from your code are executed along with (as opposed to after) the standard ones. Essentially, the Salesforce1 Platform considers your code to be just as important as the core code that powers built-in functionality.

The primitives we use in Apex are not Java primitives. The smallest unit of processing in Apex is an object. This primitive is the most generic data type in Apex and all other data types (including tables defined via the GUI) are inherited from it. The following is a list of Apex primitives, each of which has their own characteristics and methods. For a complete list of their methods, refer to the **Force.com Apex Code Developer's Guide** located at http://developer.salesforce.com.

- Blob: This is a single object that consists of a collection of binary data. These are commonly used for file bodies and with web services.

- Boolean: Unlike other languages, an Apex Boolean is null unless set to true or false.

- Date: These are typically constructed using a static method on the built-in Date class. Apex Date does not include time (see DateTime). They also cannot be used with arithmetic, but have methods to facilitate such operations.

- DateTime: These are typically constructed using a static method on the built-in DateTime class. Apex DateTime cannot be used with arithmetic, but have methods to facilitate such operations.

- Decimal: This is the most commonly used number data type; it includes a decimal point and represents any number fields created via the GUI.

- Double: This is a 64-bit number that includes a decimal point. (It is a large Decimal value.)

- ID: This is an 18-character string only set by the platform that is used to uniquely identify a record in the database.

- Integer: This is a positive or negative whole number (without a decimal point).

- Long: This is a 64-bit number that does not include a decimal point. (This is a large Integer value.)

- Object: This is the smallest unit of processing from which all other data types are inherited. (It is a singularity from which all of Apex is derived!)

- String: Any characters found between two single quotes.

- **Time**: This is typically constructed using a static method on the built-in Time class. Apex Time does not include dates (see DateTime). They also cannot be used with arithmetic, but have methods to facilitate such operations.

All statements in Apex must end with a semicolon. Apex as well as queries against the database are not case sensitive. Apex is statically typed, which means you must specify the data type for a variable before using it. Apex is also described as being strongly typed; however, it does include methods that return a value as an alternate data type and supports casting. While some other languages might be more flexible, these rules do ensure accurate interpretation by the platform (and your colleagues). There are methods to convert variables from one data type to another, and you can cast variables to another data type as well. When declaring variables, you do so with syntax similar to Java demonstrated as follows. However, note that the initial value of a variable is null unless otherwise specified:

```
String stringExample = '10'; //Looks like a number but is a string
Integer integerExample = integer.valueOf(stringExample);
system.assert(integerExample == 10);
Date d = date.newInstance(2014,1,1); //Happy New Year
Time t = time.newInstance(0,0,0,0); //Midnight
DateTime dt = dateTime.newInstance(d,t);
Boolean nullBoolean;
nullBoolean = false;
```

In this code sample, we construct a String variable that consists of the numbers 1 and 0 (also known as the number 10). We then construct an Integer variable from that string using the valueOf() method on the built-in Integer class. We then prove that the integerExample variable really is the integer 10 using the system.assert() method. Next, we construct the Date, Time, and DateTime variables using the newInstance method on their respective built-in classes. These methods are overloading and available with different input parameters. Next, we construct a Boolean variable without setting its value, and then we set the value of Boolean from null to false.

To ensure that your code performs efficiently and does not exceed the platform's limits, Apex heavily relies on collections. Collections are one or more objects grouped into a single unit. Collections can hold any data type including primitives, classes, and even collections. In fact, collections can be nested inside other collections up to five levels. As we'll see later in the book, it's a best practice to always group your objects and write methods that operate on these groups. Apex includes three types of collections, each with their own unique methods:

- **List**: This is the most common collection data type. It can be declared and functions very closely to an array in other languages. It includes a sort() method, so we use lists whenever we need something to be ordered.

- **Set**: This automatically enforces uniqueness. We use it constantly to prevent duplicates in our code. In exchange for this super power, sets are unordered.

- **Map**: This is a complex collection that consists of key-value pairs. Keys behave like a set (which is unique), while values typically behave like a list. The correlation of the two allows us to keep track of objects based on their keys rather than just their positions in a list. This is shown in the followind code:

```
List<Integer> myIntegerList = new List<Integer>();
myIntegerList.add(100);
myIntegerList.get(0);

String[] arrayLikeNotation = new String[10];
arrayLikeNotation[0] = 'Item 0'
system.assert(arrayLikeNotation.size() == 10);

Set<Date> uniqueSetOfDates = new Set<Date>()
uniqueSetOfDates.add( system.today() );
uniqueSetOfDates.add( system.today() );  //This overwrites the
    first instance of today's date and does not result in two items
    being in the Set.
Map<Date,String> dateStringMap = new Map<Date,String>();
dateStringMap.put(system.today(),'Monday');
dateStringMap.put(system.today(),'Tuesday');  //This overwrites
the first key-value pair.
system.assert(dateStringMap.get(system.today)=='Tuesday');
system.assert(dateStringMap.size()==1);
```

This code demonstrates how to create and work with all three types of collections. For a complete list of methods unique to each type of collection, refer to **Force.com Apex Code Developer's Guide** located at http://developer.salesforce.com.

Primitives and collections serve as the building blocks for the majority of our Apex code. Although we don't use it as often, Apex also includes support for enums or enumerated lists. This is a special data type that you can define in your code to have specific constant values. As we'll see in later chapters, the Salesforce1 Platform uses enums internally for all sorts of things, but you can also use them to enforce your constant values.

Data and metadata

Since its release, one of the biggest selling points of the Salesforce1 Platform is the ease at which anyone can make configuration changes through the platform's GUI. Naturally, when Apex was first developed, a key requirement was the ability to easily interact with these objects and their data in the database. The folks at salesforce.com took an innovative approach to this and tightly coupled Apex with the metadata of the Salesforce1 Platform.

The data stored on the Salesforce1 Platform has the sObject data type. This data type can be used to refer to the generic concept of any record regardless of the object type. Each of the built-in tables and custom tables you create on the Salesforce1 Platform automatically have their own unique data type that is inherited from the generic sObject data type.

When you write Apex code, you can refer to any of the metadata on the Salesforce1 Platform. The data type of that metadata is automatically known by a compiler and the Force.com IDE. This allows you to reference sObjects and their fields without having to cast them. It also makes the IDE's code complete functionality extremely useful as it provides you with all the attributes and methods you need at the touch of your fingers.

Even more amazing is that the Salesforce1 Platform is aware of the metadata you reference in your Apex code. When you reference a sObject or field in your code, the platform automatically protects those components from destructive changes. This amazing attention to detail ensures that once your code can rely on sObject and fields as existing and being of the same data type, not just upon compilation but every time it is executed in the future. Given the ease at which someone can make changes to sObjects and fields, this is a critical feature which is shown as follows:

```
Account newAccount = new Account();
newAccount.Name = 'Acme';  //This is a string field
newAccount.IsCustomerPortal = true; //This is a boolean field
newAccount.AnnualRevenue = 10000000; //This is an integer field
List<sObject> myList = new List<sObject>();  //This is a List that can
hold multiple sObjects regardless of table.
myList.add(newAccount);
insert myList;  //This creates a new record in the database
```

In this code, we first construct a new instance of an `Account` sObject. This is a standard sObject that is included in the Salesforce1 Platform, and it is typically used to track a company. We're able to reference all the fields on the `Account` table by name and the data types of those fields are automatically known by Apex. This means that it will not be possible to set the `AnnualRevenue` variable to a string or `IsCustomerPortal` to a date. Next, we constructed a list of sObjects (in this case, we could have constructed a list of `Account` objects and been limited to adding only objects of the `Account` data type). We then use the `.add()` method to add our newly constructed account to the list. Finally, we insert the entire list of sObjects into the database. We'll discuss all of these concepts in greater detail later, and you can always read more about the specific methods in **Force.com Apex Code Developer's Guide** located at `http://developer.salesforce.com`.

Writing code

If you're familiar with object-oriented programming, then it's fairly easy to start writing Apex code. The rigid structure of the language provides easy-to-follow rules to ensure that your code is valid. In fact, the compiler even prevents you from saving code that is syntactically invalid and provides easy-to-understand error messages that include line numbers. On top of this, all transactions are monitored by the platform and will be automatically terminated if an exception is thrown or a limit is exceeded. Essentially, you can write code in your Developer Edition without having to worry about breaking anything.

Irrespective of whether you are using the Force.com IDE or the web-based editor, there are only two places in the Salesforce1 Platform where you can store Apex code: triggers and classes.

Just like all of Apex, triggers are compiled into a set of instructions stored as metadata. However, what makes triggers unique is that these instructions can only be invoked by the platform itself. Each trigger is tied to the operation on records of a specific sObject type in the database. The individual operation (insert, update, and so on) for the data type can also be specified. Triggers allow you to modify the default behavior of the platform when a record is saved.

As triggers are only called by the platform, classes end up being the main stomping ground for Apex code. Classes aren't limited to being called by the platform. You can interact with them from other classes and triggers, call methods on demand from **Execute Anonymous** (similar to a command line editor), and even expose them outside as web services.

Classes can be instantiated just like any other object. However, as the Salesforce1 Platform is a multitenant service, we typically use a lot of static methods to avoid creating a bunch of short-lived instances. These methods can be called directly without first instantiating a class. The built-in Apex classes include a lot of static methods, and the best practice is for your code to do the same as it will use fewer resources and this reduces the chances of hitting the platform limits. This is shown in the following code:

```
public class myClass{
public void myInstanceMethod(){
  system.debug('This is my instance method');
}

public static void myStaticMethod(){
  system.debug('This is my static method');
}
}

//Construct an instance of myClass and call a method
myClass instanceOfMyClass = new myClass();
instanceOfMyClass.myInstanceMethod();
//Call a static method without instantiating the Class
myClass.myStaticMethod();
```

We'll discuss triggers and classes in detail in *Chapter 4, Triggers and Classes*. For now, you just need to be familiar with their names and general use.

Summary

That's it for the first chapter. In this chapter, you've already learned a lot about the Salesforce1 Platform and basic Apex concepts. What you should remember from this chapter is that Apex is the proprietary Java-like language of the Salesforce1 Platform. It is strongly typed, case insensitive, and uses single quotes. All statements must end with a semicolon in order to compile. Apex is different from other languages in that it is metadata aware and requires unit testing to be distributed and used in Production environments. Finally, we're sure you won't forget that the Force.com IDE is the preferred tool to develop Apex code and that everything about Apex is documented in **Force.com Apex Code Developer's Guide** on the Web.

In the next chapter, we'll discuss the limits of Apex and the Salesforce1 Platform. You'll learn about the best practices to avoid them and start working on some code.

2
Apex Limits

When you stay at a friend's house, you behave a little differently than when you're at home. You wipe your shoes before you enter, you don't put your feet on the coffee table, and you even use a coaster for your drink. The same holds true for the Salesforce1 Platform. While you might be paying rent, your code isn't running on your own server, so you have to follow the house rules. In Apex, these rules are referred to as the governor limits and they dictate what your code can and can't do when executed.

It doesn't make sense to write a whole chapter on Apex governor limits. Salesforce releases three major upgrades a year. These upgrades typically include classes and methods that correspond to the various new features available in the Salesforce GUI. Sometimes though, they also include a reduction in the Apex governor limits. In fact, this happens often enough that documenting the limits today would most likely render this chapter obsolete within a year from when we wrote it. This puts us in a tricky situation. If we don't write about the limits, we're ignoring a huge aspect of Apex, but if we do write about them, we're giving this book a short shelf life. Instead, we compromised and decided to discuss the concepts of the limits, how they affect us, and how we get around them. We have not discussed the specific quantities except for the ones used in examples. Only time will tell how we have fared.

Exceptions prove the rule

Like other programming languages, Apex includes a built-in class for exceptions. When your code exceeds a limit, an exception is thrown. For this reason, you really need to understand how exceptions work in Apex before we can go any further on limits. When the Salesforce1 Platform throws an exception, all statements that have been executed within that transaction are rolled back causing your entire attempt to execute code to fail. It's not fun to get an exception; it means that an end user is upset and you have more work to do.

Apex includes a generic exception class as well as over 20 types of specific exceptions for when various rules are broken. A lot of these specific exception types are easy to avoid such as don't divide by 0 when doing math, don't refer an index of a list that is out of bounds, and don't construct an account and then add it to a list of contacts. You get the picture. When your code does cause one of these exceptions, you can usually avoid it with an `if` statement. The following screenshot displays the exception types included in Apex, but you can learn more from **Force.com Apex Code Developer's Guide** at http://developer.salesforce.com:

Exception	Description
AsyncException	Any problem with an asynchronous operation, such as failing to enqueue an asynchronous call.
CalloutException	Any problem with a Web service operation, such as failing to make a callout to an external system.
DmlException	Any problem with a DML statement, such as an `insert` statement missing a required field on a record.
EmailException	Any problem with email, such as failure to deliver. For more information, see Outbound Email.
InvalidParameterValueException	An invalid parameter was supplied for a method or any problem with a URL used with Visualforce pages. For more information on Visualforce, see the *Visualforce Developer's Guide*.
JSONException	Any problem with JSON serialization and deserialization operations. For more information, see the methods of System.JSON, System.JSONParser, and System.JSONGenerator.
ListException	Any problem with a list, such as attempting to access an index that is out of bounds.
MathException	Any problem with a mathematical operation, such as dividing by zero.
NoAccessException	Any problem with unauthorized access, such as trying to access an sObject that the current user does not have access to. This is generally used with Visualforce pages. For more information on Visualforce, see the *Visualforce Developer's Guide*.
NoDataFoundException	Any problem with data that does not exist, such as trying to access an sObject that has been deleted. This is generally used with Visualforce pages. For more information on Visualforce, see the *Visualforce Developer's Guide*.
NoSuchElementException	Used specifically by the iterator.next method. This exception is thrown if you try to access items beyond the end of the list. For example, if iterator.hasNext() == false and you call iterator.next(), this exception is thrown.

NullPointerException	Any problem with dereferencing null, such as in the following code:
	`String s;`
	`s.toLowerCase(); // Since s is null, this call causes`
	`                // a NullPointerException`

QueryException	Any problem with SOQL queries, such as assigning a query that returns no records or more than one record to a singleton sObject variable.
RequiredFeatureMissing	A Chatter feature is required for code that has been deployed to an organization that does not have Chatter enabled.
SearchException	Any problem with SOSL queries executed with SOAP API search() call, for example, when the searchString parameter contains less than two characters. For more information, see the *SOAP API Developer's Guide*.
SecurityException	Any problem with static methods in the Crypto utility class. For more information, see Crypto Class.
SerializationException	Any problem with the serialization of data. This is generally used with Visualforce pages. For more information on Visualforce, see the *Visualforce Developer's Guide*.
SObjectException	Any problem with sObject records, such as attempting to change a field in an `update` statement that can only be changed during `insert`.
StringException	Any problem with Strings, such as a String that is exceeding your heap size.
TypeException	Any problem with type conversions, such as attempting to convert the String 'a' to an Integer using the valueOf method.
VisualforceException	Any problem with a Visualforce page. For more information on Visualforce, see the *Visualforce Developer's Guide*.
XmlException	Any problem with the XmlStream classes, such as failing to read or write XML.

If you like to play it safe, you can take advantage of Apex's exception handling abilities. You can use a `try-catch` block around your code as an insurance policy against exceptions. This will allow your code to continue to run after the exception is thrown by the Salesforce1 Platform so that you can handle the error gracefully. This is shown in the following code snippet:

```
//Try breaking a rule
Integer x = 10;
try {
  x = x/0;
```

```
} catch ( MathException e){
  system.debug('Go back to school!');
} finally {
  system.debug(x);
}
```

The previous code block demonstrates how to use a `try-catch` block with the optional `finally` statement.

The most common exception type is the dreaded `NullPointerException`. It is thrown anytime you reference an object as if it wasn't null, but it really is. This happens anytime you write code expecting a certain situation, but instead the unexpected occurs. It doesn't matter whether your business requirements dictate that a value should exist, you always need to write your code to avoid this exception. This is shown in the following code

```
//Here's what not to do
Integer x;
Integer y = 5+x;  //You can't divide by null

//Do this instead
If ( x != null ){
  y = 5+x;
}

String z;
System.debug(z.length());  //You can't call a method on null

//Do this instead
If ( z != null ){
  System.debug(z.length());
}

List<String> stringList;
System.debug(stringList[0]);  //You can't reference a nonexistent
object

//Do this instead
if ( stringList != null && stringList.size() > 0 ){
  system.debug(stringList[0]);
}

Boolean myFlag;
if ( myFlag == true ) {
system.debug('This Boolean isn't set yet');
}
```

```
//Do this instead
if ( myFlag != null && myFlag == true ){
  system.debug('Wow, you read this book');
}
```

This example demonstrates just some of the extremely common situations that lead to NullPointerException and how you can easily avoid them with the use of a single if statement. It's only one additional line of code to avoid NullPointerException, that's a great deal!

Embracing an exception

The Exception class includes various methods that help you better understand why an exception was thrown. You can even find out the type of exception, what line of Apex code caused the exception, and even get the entire stack trace. In addition to the built-in exception types, Apex includes the ability to create your own exception types. This allows you to catch a system exception, evaluate it, and throw your own custom exception. Although it involves slightly more work, a custom exception type can be the difference between frantically debugging code in the middle of the night and sleeping like a baby. Imagine writing code to integrate with an outside system. There are times where that process will fail (like when the other system is under maintenance). If you proactively throw your own exception, you'll immediately know why it failed. The following code will show you how to define a custom exception type:

```
//Define our custom Exception type
Public class myCustomException extends Exception{}

//Try calling out to our outside system
try {
httpRequest req = new httpRequest();
//You have to whitelist the endpoint in Setup|Remote Site Settings
req.setEndpoint('http://www.madeUpUrl.net');
req.setMethod('GET');
//Set the timeout to 1 millisecond to force an exception
req.setTimeout(1);
httpResponse res = new http().send(req);
} catch ( Exception e){
if (e.getTypeName() == 'System.CalloutException' &&
  e.getMessage() == 'Read timed out'){
  throw new myCustomException('Go Back to Sleep', e);
} else {
  throw e;
}
}
```

An exception to end all exceptions

As we mentioned earlier, when you break an Apex limit, the Salesforce1 Platform throws an exception. It's actually a special type of exception called `LimitException`. A `LimitException` is a fatal one that you cannot handle gracefully with a `try-catch` block. When `LimitException` is thrown, all processing immediately ceases. The exception is appended to the debug log and an e-mail is sent out to the developer of that Apex class. Have faith though, it might not be possible to catch `LimitException`, but it is very possible to avoid it.

Apex includes an entire class dedicated to listing and measuring limits. It's no coincidence that the name of this class is `Limits`. It includes two methods for every limit in Apex. One method is to get the maximum number allowed for a limit, and the other method is to get the number that has already occurred. You can use the combination of both of these types of methods to ensure you never exceed the actual limit. The best part is by using this pattern, your code will easily adjust itself when the limits are relaxed in the future! This is the following code snippet:

```
//This query will never exceed the limit on QueryRows
Integer queryRowLimit = limits.getLimitQueryRows();
Integer rowsAlreadyQueried = limits.getQueryRows();
Integer rowsRemaining = queryRowLimit - rowsAlreadyQueried;
List<Account> accountQuery = [
Select Id
From Account
Limit :rowsRemaining
];
//Neither will this condensed one
List<Contact> contactQuery = [
Select Id
From Contact
Limit :( limits.getLimitQueryRows()-limits.getQueryRows() )
];
```

The previous code block demonstrates how easy it is to avoid hitting `LimitException`. However, in doing so you might cause other issues in your code. In this example, it's possible that the first query results in the maximum number of rows causing the second query to have a limit of 0 and not resulting in any number!

Obeying the speed limit

Everyday Salesforce.com publishes the number of transactions that take place on their servers, and the average speed in which all those transactions take place at `http://trust.salesforce.com`. For years, the average speed has consistently been well under 300 milliseconds. This extremely fast speed has remained the same despite the number of transactions growing to nearly 2 billion (with a B) per day! In general, the page load time for web pages is usually calculated in seconds and not in milliseconds, and the same is true for pages on the Salesforce1 Platform. It doesn't take a rocket scientist to figure out then that for every page that loads in, say 3 seconds (a published best practice), there's got to be a very large number of transactions that are occurring in well under 300 milliseconds to balance it out. It's these extremely fast transactions that we care about because they are happening via Apex not through web page loads. It doesn't really matter how fast they are occurring. We do know that they are much faster than the published average, and they seem nearly instantaneous to the human eye.

The average transaction speed is a big selling point of the Salesforce1 Platform and a big source of pride for Salesforce.com and their technical staff. When Apex was first released, it was revolutionary and nothing like it had been done before. There was no way of knowing the effect of letting anyone run their own code. Customers rely on the Salesforce1 Platform to run their businesses, so the folks at salesforce.com couldn't risk anyone negatively impacting performance. The solution was clear; all Apex transactions had to stay within strict limits. These limits governed our usage of Apex and restricted the number of operations that could be performed, the number of records that could be operated on, the number of script statements that could occur, the amount of memory that a transaction could use, and much more.

> Amazon's EC2, infrastructure as a service, was released in 2006, slightly prior to Apex. However, virtual servers and platform as a service are different offerings. More importantly, the hardware and software behind the Salesforce1 Platform is very different than that of Amazon's. So any published data at the time would not have been a reliable source of estimates for the likely effect of Apex utilization on the salesforce.com servers.

Those of us who programmed in Apex in the early days would often spend more time rewriting our code to avoid the governor limits than it took to write the original version. The limits were so severe that we were forced to use clever techniques to get around them. For one client, the only way to avoid hitting the limits was to have the trigger perform only half the operation, and then use Apex to send an e-mail to a custom Email-to-Salesforce e-mail address that invoked the second half of the process. This type of juggling was common, but is no longer needed.

More limits

Before we get too far into the Apex execution limits, we do need to bring up some other limits that you need to keep in mind. As we mentioned in the previous chapter, Apex is not a general programming language. It is specifically designed for use with the Salesforce1 Platform. While it might be technically possible to write code and build an application that behaves like the latest social networking website, a group coupon website, or even search engine, you shouldn't.

We're often approached by companies who want to copy an existing website or application. They select the Salesforce1 Platform for the backend because they know applications can be built on it very rapidly. What they don't know is that Salesforce and the Salesforce1 Platform are purchased on a per user subscription basis. It is much too cost prohibitive to purchase a license for every person in the world to access your service. We always try to break the bad news gently rather than take on the project. While we might have crushed someone's dream, we saved them a lot of money and future frustration.

Data storage is also an often overlooked consideration. The most popular sites on the Web consume vast amounts of data. On the Salesforce1 Platform, each user license includes a set data allocation. Each record you create takes up exactly two **kilobytes (KB)** of your allocated storage space. This number is calculated based on the cost associated with storing your data, replicating it across redundant hardware, and backing it up for disaster recovery. Regardless of whether a record has one field populated or 500 fields populated, it will only use up two KB of data storage. Given the ability to create multiple long-text area fields on a single sObject, this arrangement is usually a great deal for customers, even without taking into account the replication and backup. In addition, for each sObject there can be supporting tables for sharing and field history that use up a lot of data, but are not counted against your storage allocation.

The data storage allocation included with your licenses is more than enough to run the average business, but it's definitely not enough to catalog every picture and video of a cat on the Web and all their attached comments. This is an important factor to keep in mind before starting development of your code. If your legitimate business application requires a lot of data, you can purchase additional storage from salesforce.com or purchase additional licenses.

 All of the limits, including the Apex governor limits are cataloged in detail in the Salesforce limits quick reference guide located at http://developer.salesforce.com. This downloadable document is updated three times a year with every major release. The limits include everything from valid date ranges for date fields to the maximum number of characters in an Apex class and everything in between.

Edition limits

Customers of salesforce.com subscribe to a specific edition of the service. These editions exist across the various core applications (marketed as clouds) as well as the Salesforce1 Platform offering. The lowest priced edition always has the most restrictions. As you move up in price, these restrictions are reduced, but still exist. As a result of these restrictions, when you build an application on the Salesforce1 Platform, it's always a best practice to have as small of a footprint as possible so that any customer, regardless of the edition, can install your app.

Subscribers of the Salesforce core applications can install and execute code that references any of the objects included in those applications, such as opportunities, assets, or cases. Subscribers to just the Salesforce1 Platform don't have access to those objects and therefore can't install or execute code that references them. If you are building an application for the AppExchange app store, it's critical to determine ahead of time which of salesforce.com's customers you are building it for. Including the wrong object in your package could prevent your ideal customer from being able to install your application.

> AppExchange is salesforce.com's app store where anyone can publish an app for the Salesforce1 Platform. Many of the apps are free to install and use. Best of all, you can install an app in a Developer or Sandbox environment, so there's no risk to trying it out. You can find AppExchange at `http:www.appexchange.com`.

One of the most important limits to be aware of is the custom objects limit. Each edition has a limit to the number of sObjects that can be created (though at the high end it's in thousands). If you are a subscriber to one of the lower-priced editions, this will impact you as you build the schema for your business. While you can create hundreds of custom fields per sObject, you might be limited to creating as few as 10 custom objects. Complex processes with multiple many-to-many relationships can easily exceed this limit. As always, there are workarounds, you can reuse sObjects, store data as JSON in long text fields, or leverage code to determine relationships. In the end, it might be easier to just pay the piper and upgrade to a higher edition.

API limits

The Salesforce1 Platform includes multiple robust APIs which can be utilized by external systems to integrate with Salesforce. These APIs include all the operations available in Apex such as querying record, inserting records, updating records, and so on. When developers new to Apex struggle with the limits, they often revert back to coding in other systems and calling one of the APIs. While this approach can certainly get the job done, it's typically not our preference and often results in future problems.

There is a limit on the number of inbound API calls that can be made to your Force. com org. This limit is partially based on the edition you are subscribed to and partially based on the number of licenses in your subscription. The minimum per 24-hour period is currently 5,000. There are 1,440 minutes in the day, so at first glance, it looks like you can synchronize with the Salesforce1 Platform every minute and still have plenty to spare. In reality though, it's much more complex.

Let's say that your outside system is syncing new sales orders with opportunities in the sales cloud application on the Salesforce1 Platform. In order to even start the process, the outside system will first need to authenticate using the `login()` method; that counts as one API call. Once authenticated, you can use the resulting session ID to query for the `Account` record for the customer; that counts as your second API call. If the record is not found, you'll need to insert it; that's three. Now you can insert the primary contact at the account; that's four. Finally, you can insert the opportunity record; that's five. But wait, you might not be done yet; you might want to insert an opportunity line item, opportunity contact role, asset, or a contract. Each synchronization could easily take up well over five calls. While you can batch process records, the frequency at which you can synchronize will likely be spread out further and further as the complexity of the process increases.

As if that wasn't reason enough to learn Apex, many of the third-party tools and applications built for the Salesforce1 Platform also use an API. The calls made by these tools also count toward your inbound API request limits. In fact, every time you even use the Force.com IDE, you are using your API requests. So not only do you need to factor in all of your outside integrations, but also any external tools or applications used by any of your users.

One day, two of my colleagues and I decided to build an e-commerce application in a brand new Developer Edition org. The three of us split up the parts of the application we would each work on and started coding away in the Force. com IDE. All three of us are obsessive about saving our work as we type to prevent loss and view any errors reported by the Apex compiler. After only a few hours, we all came to a sudden halt and couldn't save anymore. We had collectively saved our code so many times that we had hit the 5,000 API call daily limit just while writing the code!

E-mail limits

From the beginning, salesforce.com has made it clear that they do not want their name associated with spam in any way. For this reason, there have always been limits on the number of mass e-mails you can send from the Salesforce1 Platform. However, a user can always send as many single e-mail messages (which can have multiple To, CC, and BCC recipients) as they can via the standard e-mail interface in the Salesforce GUI.

The mass e-mail limits vary based on the edition of your subscription. They are calculated in a rolling 24-hour period. This means that once you have sent the maximum number of mass e-mails allowed, you will have to wait a maximum of 24 hours before you can send more mass e-mails.

Apex includes the ability to send both single or mass e-mail messages. But since Apex can be used to programmatically send multiple single e-mail messages, the Salesforce1 Platform counts e-mail messages sent via Apex in your daily limit. Remember, the people behind Apex are very innovative, so they've already figured out what you and I would do to get around the limits and built with that in mind. You can test it out yourself with the following code block:

```
//Construct a list of email addresses to use later
List<String> toAddresses = new List<String>{
   'mattkaufman@thisbook.com',
'justindavis@thisbook.com'
};

//Construct a list of email messages that we will send
List<Messaging.SingleEmailMessage> emailsToSend =
   new List<Messaging.SingleEmailMessage>();

//Loop through 1001 times
for ( Integer i=0; i<1001; i++ ){
   Messaging.SingleEmailMessage email =
     new Messaging.SingleEmailMessage();
   email.setToAddresses(toAddresses);
   email.setReplyTo('noreply@thisbook.com');
   email.setSenderDisplayName('Apex Code');
   email.setSubject('Too many emails!');
   email.setPlainTextBody('This will not work, nice try!');
   email.setHtmlBody('This will <b>not</b> work, <i>nice try!</i>');
   email.setUseSignature(false);
emailsToSend.add(email);
}
```

```
try {
  messaging.sendEmail(emailsToSend);
} catch (exception e){
  system.debug(e.getMessage());
}
```

Based on the current e-mail limits, the previous code block will always result in an exception. If you want to send more e-mails, you'll need to do it manually via the GUI, use a third-party service, or leverage the (non-Apex) workflow feature including with the Salesforce1 Platform.

Time and relative limits in space

We readily admit that this section header is a stretch (if you're not familiar with it, try searching for TARDIS on the Web), but there are only so many phrases related to time travel that can be replaced with the word limit. One of the amazing features of Apex is that it allows you to program back in time. Despite the fact that Apex and the Salesforce1 Platform are updated three times a year, Apex is fully backward compatible. In fact, you can write your code today under the current Apex limits, and then with a few keystrokes magically send your code back in time to a previous API version with historical limits.

Part of every Apex class is a bit of metadata that defines under which API version the code should run. This value stays set unless you modify it. That means that if your code behaves correctly today, it should continue to behave the exact same, even as the Salesforce1 Platform continues to be updated over time. This metadata is accessible in both the Force.com IDE and the Force.com GUI. In the IDE, it looks like the XML code as follows:

```
<?xml version="1.0" encoding="UTF-8"?>
<ApexClass xmlns="http://soap.sforce.com/2006/04/metadata" >
  <apiVersion>31.0</apiVersion>
  <status>Active</status>
</ApexClass>
```

Limits tend to be relaxed over time, so you probably wouldn't ever roll back an API version to increase limits, but sometimes it can be useful. We'll discuss this more in later chapters. In reality, you're much more likely to increase the API version of your older code to take advantage of new features. Keep in mind though, if your code isn't broken, then there's no need to change it, although keeping up with three releases a year can be great job security.

You want me to process how many records?

We'll talk about triggers more in a later chapter, but for now you just need to know that a trigger is code that is automatically executed whenever a record is operated upon (meaning inserted, updated, deleted, or undeleted). When you first start programming in Apex, it tends to be trigger-related. These are usually simple scenarios such as when an account phone is modified, update the phone for all of the contacts on that account. This is shown in the following code:

```
//This code has a potentially fatal flaw in it
public static void updateContactAddresses(){
List<Contact> contactList = [
Select Id, Phone, AccountId, Account.Phone
from Contact
];
for ( Contact c : contactQuery ){
  c.Phone = c.Account.Phone;
}
update contactQuery;
}
```

Did you spot the flaw in the previous code block? If you tried it out in your Developer Edition org, it probably worked exactly as described. The problem doesn't lie in the syntax or logic.

A common mistake of new Apex developers is to assume that your code will only be executed when a user interacts with a record via the Force.com GUI. In that scenario, most likely only one record will be operated at a time and your code will execute without exceeding any limits. However, Apex is actually designed to operate on multiple records at a time, not just one. In fact, an Apex trigger will operate on upto 200 records at a time. It's not hard to test this out either. The Salesforce1 Platform includes a free ETL tool called the Apex Data Loader that you can use to interact with large numbers of records at a time. There are other ways to interact with multiple records at once such as via Apex, a Visualforce page, web service, or an API.

If you were to update multiple accounts at once and for each account the previous code block was executed, you would probably exceed at least one Apex governor limit and your day (and possibly night) will be ruined. The following is a screenshot of the Apex transaction limits at the time of writing this book. Keep in mind they will change over time.

Description	Synchronous Limit	Asynchronous Limit
Total number of SOQL queries issued[1]	100	200
Total number of records retrieved by SOQL queries	50,000	
Total number of records retrieved by `Database.getQueryLocator`	10,000	
Total number of SOSL queries issued	20	
Total number of records retrieved by a single SOSL query	2,000	
Total number of DML statements issued[2]	150	
Total number of records processed as a result of DML statements, `Approval.process`, or `database.emptyRecycleBin`	10,000	
Total stack depth for any Apex invocation that recursively fires triggers due to `insert`, `update`, or `delete` statements[3]	16	
Total number of callouts (HTTP requests or Web services calls) in a transaction	10	
Maximum timeout for all callouts (HTTP requests or Web services calls) in a transaction	120 seconds	
Total number of methods with the `future` annotation allowed per Apex invocation	10	
Total number of `sendEmail` methods allowed	10	
Total number of describes allowed[4]	100	
Total heap size[5]	6 MB	12 MB
Maximum CPU time on the Salesforce servers[6]	10,000 milliseconds	60,000 milliseconds
Maximum execution time for each Apex transaction	10 minutes	
Maximum number of unique namespaces referenced[7]	10	

How many times and how many things

While we cannot stress enough that the limits we are discussing will change in the future, we still want to discuss the types of limits we tend to see in Apex. Since the reason behind the limits is to ensure equal performance for all customers on the server, there tends to be limits on how many times you can perform some operations and how many records you can perform on.

To date, there has always been a limit on the number of records that can be returned by queries, the number of records that can returned by searches, and the number of records you can save in any Apex transaction. Limiting the number of records you can operate on ensures that you write your code to only operate on the records that need to be operated on. This greatly improves the overall performance because you can't write inefficient code that operates on all records every time it is executed. The following code block further elaborates on the previous example to ensure that we only operate on contacts with a phone that needs to be updated:

```
//This code is better but still not great
public static void updateContactAddresses(){
  List<Contact> contactQuery = [
  Select Id, Phone, AccountId, Account.Phone
  from Contact
  limit :( limits.getLimitQueryRows()-limits.getQueryRows() )
  ];
  List<Contact> contactUpdates = new List<Contact>();
  for ( Contact c : contactQuery ){
    //limit to just the records that need it
```

```
    if ( c.Phone != c.Account.Phone ){
      c.Phone = c.Account.Phone;
      contactUpdates.add(c);
    }
  }
  update contactUpdates;
}
```

Limiting the number of times you can do something ensures you write your code to only perform operations when necessary. This also forces you to write your code, to be more efficient. You shouldn't do the same thing over and over in a single transaction. Instead, group those items together and perform a mass operation. In the following code block, we will further elaborate on the previous code again. This time, we will pass in the entire list of accounts that have been modified, as well as the prior version of those records so that we can determine whether we even need to update any contacts. Before the query and update, we will also make sure that we have something to query or update. This is demonstrated in the following code:

```
//This pattern is common in Apex
public static void updateContactAddresses(
List<Account> priorVersions,
List<Account> updatedVersions
){
  Set<Id> modifiedAccounts_Ids = new Set<Id>();
  for ( Integer i=0;i<updatedVersions.size();i++ ){
  if ( updatedVersions[i].Phone != priorVersions[i].Phone ){
    modifiedAccounts_Ids.add(updatedVersions[i].Id);
    }
  }
  if ( modifiedAccounts_Ids.size() > 0 ){
    List<Contact> contactQuery = [
    Select Id, Phone, AccountId, Account.Phone
    from Contact
    where AccountId in :modifiedAccounts_Ids
    limit :( limits.getLimitQueryRows()-limits.getQueryRows() )
    ];
  List<Contact> contactUpdates = new List<Contact>();
    for ( Contact c : contactQuery ){
      //limit to just the records that need it
      if ( c.Phone != c.Account.Phone ){
        c.Phone = c.Account.Phone;
        contactUpdates.add(c);
      }
    }
```

```
        if ( contactUpdates.size() > 0 ){
          update contactUpdates;
        }
    }
}
```

This last version of our code would probably work for most situations and meet our business requirements. By passing in a list of accounts, we can ensure that we do not exceed the number of queries that can be performed as a result of saving a large number of accounts. By limiting our contact query to the number of records that can be queried, we also ensure that we do not exceed the limit on the number of records that can be queried. However, there still are a few unexpected situations that we need to consider.

The first outside possibility is that the number of contacts on the accounts that have been modified exceeds the current limit. In this scenario, we won't cause LimitException; however, we would be breaking our business rule. Only a subset of the contact records would be updated and thus we would leave data inaccuracies in our database causing confusion among our users. The solution for this situation would be to call a batch Apex class that can work on large datasets without exceeding limits. We'll discuss batch Apex in a later chapter.

The second outside possibility is that the number of contacts that need to be updated exceeds the limit for the number of records that can be processed as a result of a DML operation. This is a serious problem that would throw LimitException and cause our code to fail. Again, a long-term solution would be to use batch Apex to process the large dataset. A short-term solution would be to limit the number of records that can be added to the contactUpdates list shown as follows:

```
for ( Contact c : contactQuery ){
//limit to the number of records we can operate on
  if (
  c.Phone != c.Account.Phone &&
  contactQuery.size() < limits.getLimitDMLRows()
  ){
    c.Phone = c.Account.Phone;
  contactUpdates.add(c);
  }
}
```

Techniques to avoid query limits

If you have ever been responsible for code to meet business requirements, then you probably know that decision-makers change their minds and requirements change over time. For this reason, it is a best practice to store your constant variables (or should we call them not so constant) as data rather than hardcoding them in your Apex classes. In order for your code to access those constants, you would have to query them. Let's suppose that our code needs to know the phone number for the company we work for, as well as our company's parent company. We could write code to query the Account records as shown in the following code block:

```
Account ourCompany = [
Select Id, Phone
from Account
where Name = 'Acme National'
limit 1
];
Account ourParentCompany = [
Select Id, Phone
from Account
where Name = 'Acme International'
limit 1
];
```

While the previous code is simple enough to write, it uses two of our allowed queries and doesn't follow our best practice of being as efficient as possible. Instead of using the equals operator, we can use the IN operator to get both the pieces of information in a single query, as shown in the following code block:

```
Account ourCompany;
Contact ourCompanyCEO;
Account ourParentCompany;
Contact ourParentCompanyCEO;
Set<String> accountNames = new Set<String>();
accountNames.add('Acme National');
accountNames.add('Acme International');

//Query for Accounts whose name is in the Set
for ( Account a : [
Select Id, Name, Phone
from Account
where Name IN :accountNames
limit 2
]){
```

```
  if ( a.Name == 'Acme National' ){
    ourCompany = a;
  } else
  if ( a.Name == 'Acme International' ){
    ourParentCompany = a;
  }
}
```

By taking the time to compile our values (in this case a set) ahead of time, we are able to reduce the number of queries we need to perform. This is an extremely common pattern in Apex and the one you definitely want to master. In this case, we were able to consolidate our queries because the information we needed was on records of the same sObject type. Let's expand our business requirements to say we also need the names of the CEOs of each of the two companies. We can try to solve this new requirement by adding the following query to our earlier code:

```
Contact ourCompanyCEO;
Contact ourParentCompanyCEO;
for ( Contact c : [
Select Id, Name, Account.Name
From Contact
Where Title = 'CEO' and Account.Name in :accountNames
Limit 2
]){
  if ( c.Account.Name == 'Acme National' ){
    ourCompanyCEO = c;
  } else
  if ( c.Account.Name == 'Acme International' ){
    ourParentCompanyCEO = c;
  }
}
```

While we might have efficiently queried for the two contacts with a single query, we're still doing one query for accounts and then a second one for the contacts. Whether you're already familiar with the schema included with the Salesforce1 Platform or not, you can clearly see that there is a relationship between contacts and accounts in the database. Similar to SQL, **Salesforce Object Query Language (SOQL)** includes the ability to perform nested queries. In this case, the Contact records are directly related to the Account records that we previously queried. So we can join these two queries into one and thus make our code even more efficient, as follows:

```
Account ourCompany;
Contact ourCompanyCEO;
Account ourParentCompany;
Contact ourParentCompanyCEO;
```

```
Set<String> accountNames = new Set<String>{
'Acme National',
'Acme International'
};

//Query for Accounts (and their CEO) whose name is in the Set
for ( Account a : [
Select Id, Name, Phone,
(Select Id, Name from Contacts where Title = 'CEO' limit 1)
from Account
where Name IN :accountNames
limit 2
]){
  if ( a.Name == 'Acme National' ){
    ourCompany = a;
    if ( a.Contacts != null && a.Contacts.size() == 1 ){
      ourCompanyCEO = a.Contacts[0];
    }
  } else
  if ( a.Name == 'Acme International' ){
    ourParentCompany = a;
    if ( a.Contacts != null && a.Contacts.size() == 1 ){
      ourParentCompanyCEO = a.Contacts[0];
    }
  }
}
```

These aren't the queries you're looking for

There are times when you need to store a lot of constants in the database and they aren't related to each other or maybe have nothing to do with accounts, contacts, or any other sObject. Again, we don't want to perform multiple queries and we definitely don't want to hardcode these variables into our Apex classes. Instead, we can leverage an Apex trick called custom settings to get data out of the database without performing a query that counts against our execution governor limits.

Custom settings are similar to other sObjects, but are cached for faster access. You can create custom fields on them, but only on certain field types. The more complex field types such as picklists, long text area fields, formula fields, and so on are not allowed. You can create multiple custom setting sObjects and records, but are limited to a small amount of data compared with your overall data storage limits. Custom setting records are only accessible via the Force.com setup screens, and do not have their own tab. You can however interact with them via Apex code and Visualforce pages. Your Apex code can query them just like any other sObject, but if you want to be more efficient, you can use special custom setting methods to get data out of your custom setting records without even performing a query.

Let's revisit our earlier example, where we needed the phone number and CEO name of our company and our parent company. Instead of storing this information in accounts and contacts, we could store them in a custom setting. Let's assume that we created a custom setting called `My Custom Setting`. The Name field will hold the name of the company, and we have created two fields to store the phone number and CEO name. Our uber-efficient code could look something like this:

```
//Use the Custom Setting method to get data without doing a query
My_Custom_Setting__c ourCompany = My_Custom_Setting__c.
getInstance('Acme National');
String ourCompanyPhone = ourCompany.Phone__c;
String ourCompanyCEO = ourCompany.CEO__c;

My_Custom_Setting__c ourParentCompany = My_Custom_Setting__c.
getInstance('Acme International');
String ourCompanyPhone = ourParentCompany.Phone__c;
String ourCompanyCEO = ourParentCompany.CEO__c;

//Just to prove that we didn't do any queries
system.assert( limits.getQueries() == 0 );
```

Visualforce limits

Visualforce is the markup language of the Salesforce1 Platform. The logic and data for the custom pages you create using Visualforce are controlled by Apex classes. Salesforce.com includes page load times of your custom pages in their overall performance metrics. So, as you might have guessed, the Apex code used by your custom pages must adhere to the same governor limits as all other Apex code.

In addition to the Apex limits, Visualforce has a few other limits too. When you interact with a Visualforce page, the Salesforce1 Platform keeps track of the state of everything on the page. When you fill in the `FirstName` field, it keeps track of that value. If the page displays a list of data, it keeps track of that list.

All little things that are being tracked are part of what is called the page's view state. In order to ensure that the page can load quickly, there is a limit on how much information can be stored in a page's view state. That limit has been 135 KB for quite some time, and will probably stay that way for quite some time too. Unlike data storage on the Salesforce1 Platform, **View State** is not calculated at 2 KB per record. This can make it difficult to calculate your view state usage and figure out why you're hitting the limit. Built into the Force.com GUI is a developer console that includes a feature to view your **View State** to help you troubleshoot, as shown in the following screenshot:

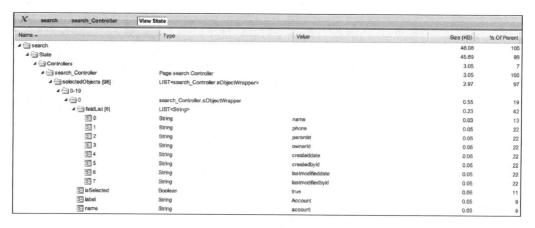

If you look at the previous screenshot, you'll notice that each field referenced counts towards our view state. For this reason, it's important to make the queries used by Visualforce pages as specific as possible. While it's tempting (and often less of a headache) to just query all fields, it definitely is not efficient for the server to do so. The best practice is to just query fields and records you need. If you do that you'll probably never need to worry about view state anyway. We'll discuss Visualforce and techniques to avoid the view state limit more in a later chapter.

Summary

My goodness, what have you gotten yourself into? You thought this book would teach you how to program in Apex, and we just spent a whole chapter telling you what not to do! Worry not dear reader, for knowing what not to do will make you a better Apex coder and help you avoid embarrassment. We can't tell you how many times we've looked at someone else's code and cringed from all the mistakes they made. Besides, this was only the second chapter, stick in there, we're about to get to the good stuff!

3
More and Later

The difference between a game and a business application is the data. Most games don't need to store information about everything you've ever done; some games don't even bother to store your high score! Business applications rely heavily on data and lots of it. For example, a simple sales deal might involve:

- An account record for the business
- Some contacts for key people who work there
- An opportunity record to represent the potential sale
- Multiple quote records for the various estimates you put together
- Multiple quote line items on each of those quote records
- Opportunity line items synced with the most recent quote
- Pricebooks and product records that store the definitions and prices of what you sell
- Opportunity contact roles to distinguish which contacts are decision makers
- Sales team records to list you and your colleagues working on a deal
- User records that represent you and your colleagues
- Activity history for all of your calls, e-mails, and meetings
- Don't forget the field history for all of these records tracking every change you make!

What might seem like a simple sales deal is actually an ever-increasing set of relational data all nicely displayed in the Force.com GUI. With all this data, you can start to see how our Apex governor limits can sometimes make things difficult for us Apex programmers. In this chapter, we'll look at some Apex features that can be used to stretch your code past the limits.

Chain reactions

By definition, the unexpected is hard to prepare for. When given business requirements, it's always for the expected use case. Rarely is one told what should happen when rules are not followed. Less often are you given requirements that take into account the code from previous requirements or possible future ones. You could spend all your time refactoring your code, but most of us have deadlines and other responsibilities to meet. Add in possible changes of staff, pressure from management, and too many late nights and you'll take the easy way out and just write code to meet the current requirements.

We've worked with many clients who have large code bases that are not documented, not understood, and sometimes not even used. Excess code is not a good thing, especially as our Apex governor limits restrict how much can happen in any given transaction. Let's say that you already have at trigger that updates contacts when an account is updated (similar to the one we worked on in the previous chapter). Then, one day you receive a new business requirement that says accounts need to be updated every time a contact is updated. It sounds like an easy task; after all, it's nearly the same code but just in reverse. After having successfully completed the first trigger, you can confidently give a small estimate to meet this new requirement. Unfortunately, you're playing with dynamite; if not properly implemented, these triggers can cause each other to run repeatedly until you hit the maximum stack depth limit. Take a look at the two abbreviated methods in the following code blocks; you'll see what we mean:

```
//Called by a Trigger after an Account is updated
public static void updateContactPhones(
List<Account> priorAccounts,
List<Account> updatedAccounts
){
  List<Contact> contactUpdates = new List<Contact>();
  ...  //Code to compile Contacts
  if ( contactUpdates.size() > 0 ){
    update contactUpdates;
  }
}
```

```
//Called by a Trigger after a Contact is updated
public static void updateAccounts(
List<Contact> updatedContacts
){
  List<Account> accountUpdates = new List <Account>();
  ... //Code to compile Accounts
  if ( accountUpdates.size() > 0 ){
    update accountUpdates;
  }
}
```

Before you frantically revise all the estimates you've given out, take a deep breath and relax. By the time you've finished reading this book, you'll be programming well-written Apex code and won't face these problems. You'll also have read this chapter and know some tricks to deal with these types of situations.

Where we're going, we don't need roads

In *Chapter 2, Apex Limits*, we looked at how to write a method in Apex that will update contact numbers when the phones on their account records are modified. Then, we modified our code to operate efficiently on just the records that need to be operated upon and also added in statements to ensure we don't exceed our Apex governor limits. However, the only way to stay under the limits was to cap the number of records we operated upon, possibly leaving some records untouched. While business requirements can vary, I think it's safe to assume that no one likes it when code works only sometimes. If you need a refresher, here is the method we wrote:

```
//A common pattern for triggered operations in Apex
public static void updateContactPhones(
List<Account> priorAccounts,
List<Account> updatedAccounts
){
  Set<Id> modifiedAccounts_Ids = new Set<Id>();
  for ( Integer i=0;i<updatedAccounts.size();i++ ){
    if (updatedAccounts[i].Phone != priorAccounts[i].Phone ){
      modifiedAccounts_Ids.add(updatedAccounts[i].Id);
    }
  }
  if ( modifiedAccounts_Ids.size() > 0 ){
    List<Contact> contactQuery = [
    Select Id, Phone, AccountId, Account.Phone
    from Contact
    where AccountId in :modifiedAccounts_Ids
    limit :( limits.getLimitQueryRows()-limits.getQueryRows() )
```

```
      ];
//The above query uses limits methods to calculate the number of
records we can query, thus never exceeding the Limit.
      List<Contact> contactUpdates = new List<Contact>();
      for ( Contact c : contactQuery ){
//limit to just the records that need it
        if (
        c.Phone != c.Account.Phone &&
        contactUpdates.size() < limits.getLimitDMLRows()
        ){
          c.Phone = c.Account.Phone;
        contactUpdates.add(c);
        }
      }
      if ( contactUpdates.size() > 0 ){
        update contactUpdates;
      }
    }
  }
```

As discussed in *Chapter 2, Apex Limits,* this method can be used to update the Phone field on contacts when the Phone field on their parent account is updated. The method exhibits best practices to efficiently run code and avoid our limits. However, when used with large datasets, our safe pattern can do more harm than good and result in inconsistent data. In order to ensure that no contact is ever missed, we need to find a way to go beyond our Apex governor limits. One technique we can use is to call an asynchronous method anytime we reach a limit. Asynchronous Apex methods are treated as unique transactions from the ones that call them, and as such have their own set of governor limits. You can denote a method as an asynchronous one by using the @future annotation above it.

These @future methods do have some restrictions though. If you look back at the previous chapter, you will notice that there is a limit on the number of @future methods that can be invoked at a time. The @future methods can only have primitive data types (or collections of them) for their input parameters. As they run at a future time from when they are called, they have nowhere to return a response and thus can only return a void type. Other than these few differences, they look and behave like any other method.

The following method performs the same operation as the earlier code block, but is rewritten to run asynchronously using the @future annotation:

```
@future
public static void updateContactsLater(Set<Id> contactIds) {
  List<Contact> contactUpdates = new List<Contact>();
```

```
   for ( Contact c : [
   Select Id, Phone, Account.Phone
   from Contact
   where    Id in :contactIds
   ]){
     c.Phone = c.Account.Phone;
     contactUpdates.add(c);
   }
}
```

We can modify our existing code to call the previous `@future` method when we have more contacts than DML operations allowed in a single transaction. This will create a second transaction that has its own set of limits. By doing this, we double the number of records on which we can perform a DML operation. In order to make this work, we will have to keep track of contact IDs that we are not able to operate on and pass them into the `@future` method, as shown in the following method:

```
public static void updateContactPhones(
   ...   //Code skipped for brevity
List<Contact> contactUpdates = new List<Contact>();
Set<Id> contactIds = new Set<Id>();
for ( Contact c : contactQuery ){
//limit to just the records that need it
  if (
  c.Phone != c.Account.Phone &&
  contactUpdates.size() < limits.getLimitDMLRows()
  ){
    c.Phone = c.Account.Phone;
    contactUpdates.add(c);
  } else
  if (c.Phone != c.Account.Phone ){
    //we are above our limit!
    contactIds.add(c.Id);
  }
}
if ( contactUpdates.size() > 0 ){
  update contactUpdates;
}
if ( contactIds.size() > 0 ){
  //Call our @future method
  updateContactsLater(contactIds);
}
}
}
```

I fought the law and won

A few extra lines of code and we easily enabled our code to operate on twice as many records as allowed. If you look back at the limits in the previous chapter, you'll notice that we can query five times as many records as we can process with the DML statement. This means that twice as many records is not enough; we really need to be able to operate on five times as many. Over the years, many of the clients we work with came to us because their requirements well exceeded the Apex governor limits. You can always resort to using an external system and the Salesforce1 Platform's SOAP API, but we like to push Apex to the very edge, then cross our fingers and hit *Enter*! While it might be overkill, the following code block turns the dial up to 11 (literally) and allows us to blow our limits out of the water:

```
public static void updateContactPhones(
List<Account> priorAccounts,
List<Account> updatedAccounts
){
  Set<Id> modifiedAccounts_Ids = new Set<Id>();
  for ( Integer i=0;i<updatedAccounts.size();i++ ){
    if (updatedAccounts[i].Phone != priorAccounts[i].Phone ){
      modifiedAccounts_Ids.add(updatedAccounts[i].Id);
    }
  }
  if ( modifiedAccounts_Ids.size() > 0 ){
    List<Contact> contactQuery = [
    Select Id, Phone, AccountId, Account.Phone
    from Contact
    where AccountId in :modifiedAccounts_Ids
    limit :( limits.getLimitQueryRows()-limits.getQueryRows() )
    ];
    List<Contact> contactUpdates = new List<Contact>();
    Set<Id> contactIds = new Set<Id>();
    for ( Integer i=0;i<contactQuery.size();i++ ){
      if (
      contactQuery[i].Phone != contactQuery[i].Account.Phone &&
        contactUpdates.size() < limits.getLimitDMLRows()
      ){
        contactUpdates.add(contactQuery[i]);
      } else
      if (
      //Our limit has been exceeded
      contactQuery[i].Phone != contactQuery[i].Account.Phone
      ){
        contactIds.add(contactQuery[i]);
        if (
        contactIds.size() == limits.getLimitDMLRows() ||
          i+1 == contactQuery.size()
        ){
```

```
        //Pass the Ids to our @future method
        updateContactsLater(contactIds);
        //Clear the Set so that we can keep going
        contactIds.clear();
    }

  }
  if ( contactUpdates.size() > 0 ){
    update contactUpdates;
  }
 }
}
```

The previous code block is somewhat more complex than the original. Within a single execution, we will perform one synchronous update of contact records and up to ten asynchronous ones (although we know there will only be up to five, given the current query row limit). Using two different code blocks to perform the same operation takes more time to program, more time to test, and is likely to lead to inconsistencies in the future. Although it's not ideal, it will get the job done and without having to leverage any external systems.

 As the @future methods run asynchronously, you might not notice whether an exception is thrown during execution. We recommend using a try-catch block that sends an e-mail anytime an exception is thrown. If you want to take your code to the next level, you can create a custom object to log exceptions and other issues and then leverage workflow, reporting, and all the other declarative features on the Salesforce1 Platform.

Besides working on larger amounts of data, one of the most common uses of @future methods is syncing with outside systems. Callouts are time-consuming operations. As we mentioned earlier, ensuring the speed of the Salesforce1 Platform is important. For this reason, callouts can only occur under special annotations. We'll look at how to make callouts in a later chapter, but for now we'll show you the changes you'll need to make to the code in order to do so.

Even though it occurs asynchronously, the @future annotation by itself won't enable a callout to occur. Instead, you must also use a special callout annotation with @future aptly named callout. The code is as follows:

```
@future (callout=true)
public static void calloutLater(){
  //Callout code goes here
}
```

The callout annotation can also be set to false if you want to ensure that regardless of what happens during the transaction, a callout should not occur.

Please sir, I want some more

As customers use the Salesforce1 Platform for more business purposes, their license count increases. An increase in license count means an increase in allotted storage, which will ultimately result in an increase in records. More records means more worrying about hitting an Apex governor limit. The `@future` annotation is a valuable tool to have in your coding arsenal, but it is still bound by limits. As we just saw, we can find clever ways of exceeding beyond these limits, but we can't operate on an unlimited amount of data.

Fortunately for us, and you, Apex includes a `Database.Batchable` interface that is designed to process very large data sets. It works by breaking up your large data set into smaller batches and treating each batch as a unique transaction with its own set of limits. Based on the current Apex governor limits, our previous code that repeatedly calls the `@future` method will not be able to update more than 110,000 records (assuming we can even query that many). However, using the `Database.Batchable` interface, we can technically operate on up to 50 million account records with 10,000 contacts each. That's a total of 500,000,000,000 contacts!

The `Database.Batchable` interface includes three methods:

- `start()`: This method is run only once at the beginning of your batch process. It is typically used to determine the complete set of objects to be operated on in your batch process. Most of the time, this is just compiling a query string.

- `finish()`: This method is run only once at the end of your batch. It is typically used to notify you of completion or log the results of the entire batch process. You can use a variation of the code block in *Chapter 2, Apex Limits*, that sent out e-mails.

- `execute()`: This method is run once per batch and is where all of your logic goes for the operation(s) you are performing on all of your objects.

There are two implementations of the `Database.Batchable` interface. The more commonly used one has the `start()` method that returns a `Database.QueryLocator` object. This object is a representation of all records that need to be broken up into batches and processed by your code. The less commonly used implementation has the `start()` method returning an iterable object. This object defines the list of objects to be processed and how to iterate through them. Iterables are useful for processing complex objects that are not defined by a single sObject. In exchange for this ability, an iterable is limited to the normal SOQL query row limit, which currently is only 50,000 records (which is why the `QueryLocator` query is more prevalent). The following code block is the basic framework for the `Database.Batchable` interface:

```
//Apex Class that implements the Batchable interface
global class myBatch implements Database.Batchable<SObject> {
```

```
global Database.QueryLocator start(Database.BatchableContext
  ctx){
//Return a QueryLocator by passing in a queryString to the
Database.getQueryLocator() method
return Database.getQueryLocator(
'Select Id from Account'
  );   //This will work as long as you don't have more than
    50,000,000 Account records.
}

global void execute(
Database.BatchableContext ctx,
List<SObject> sobjects
){
  //Code your processing logic here
}

global void finish(Database.BatchableContext ctx){
  //Log an activity, send an email or do something when done
}
```

Combining forces

As it's a prebuilt interface, leveraging the `Database.Batchable` interface is simple enough. There's very little required for you to take advantage of the Apex magic. On the surface, it seems like we could simply call our existing method from within the `Execute()` method and be done. However, it's important to remember our rules and ensure that we code as efficiently as possible. This means we need to ensure that we only operate on the records that need to be operated upon. To do this, we need to modify our code to query just the contacts that need to be updated.

Salesforce Object Query Language has the ability to include a `Where` clause in our query string. However, unlike SQL, it does not allow this `Where` clause to compare values of two different fields against each other. To do this most efficiently, we need to take off our programmer hats and put on our database administrator hats. Instead of writing code to determine whether a contact needs to be updated, we can create a custom formula field that denotes whether the contact's phone differs from the account phone.

To create the custom field, perform the following steps:

1. Click on the **Setup** link at the top of the Force.com GUI.
2. Navigate to **Build** | **Customize** | **Contacts** | **Fields**.

3. Click on the **New** button.

    The **New Custom Field** screen is displayed with type options.

4. Select the **Formula** field type option and then click on the **Next** button.

5. In **Field Label,** enter `Update Phone`.

6. Select the **Checkbox** option and then click on the **Next** button.

    The **Enter Formula** screen is displayed, as shown here:

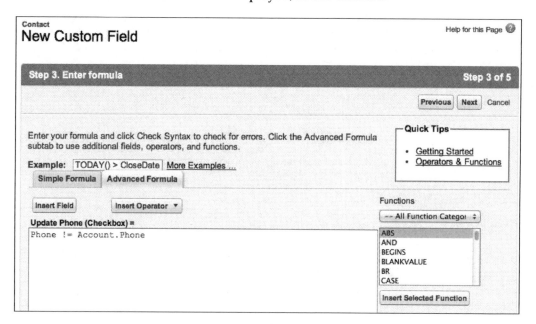

7. Click on the **Advanced Formula** tab.

8. Enter the following formula into the formula box and then click on the **Next** button:

    `Phone != Account.Phone`

    The field-level security selection screen is displayed.

9. Click on the **Next** button. The page layout selection screen is displayed.

10. Click on the **Save** button to save your new field.

The Salesforce1 Platform will automatically ensure that our new formula field is set to TRUE whenever the contact's phone is out of sync with its account phone, and it is set to FALSE when they are the same. No coding is required on our part to make this happen, and there's no chance that an exception or any other issue causes this field to not be automatically updated.

Now that we have created a field to track which contact records need to be updated, we can proceed with writing our implementation of the `Database.Batchable` interface:

```apex
//Apex Class that implements the Batchable interface
global class contactBatch implements Database.Batchable<SObject> {

global Database.QueryLocator start(Database.BatchableContext
  ctx){
  return Database.getQueryLocator(
  'Select Id, Phone, Account.Phone from Contact where
    Update_Phone__c = TRUE'
  );
}

global void execute(
Database.BatchableContext ctx,
List<SObject> sobjects
){
  List<Contact> contacts = (List<Contact>)sobjects;
  for ( Contact c : contacts ){
    c.Phone = c.Account.Phone;
  }
  update contacts;
}

global void finish(Database.BatchableContext ctx){
  //Log an activity, send an email or do something when done
  Messaging.SingleEmailMessage email =
    new Messaging.SingleEmailMessage();
  email.setTargetObjectId(userInfo.getUserId());
  email.setReplyTo('noreply@thisbook.com');
  email.setSenderDisplayName('Apex Code');
  email.setSubject('Too many emails!');
  email.setPlainTextBody('This will not work, nice try!');
  email.setUseSignature(false);
  email.setSaveAsActivity(false);
  messaging.sendEmail(
  new List<Messaging.SingleEmailMessage>{email}
  );
  }
}
```

Great! So now we have the ultimate code that can handle our extremely large data set, now what? Programming the code is just half the problem; getting it to execute is the other half. Apex includes the following method to cause your batch class to be executed:

```
//Call the below line to queue your batch process
Id batchProcessId = Database.ExecuteBatch(contactBatch);
```

After executing the previous statement, our batch process will be queued to run in the near future and ensure that our business requirements are met. I don't think any programmer wants to be responsible for logging in and executing code on a daily basis though. It will make much more sense to call the previous line of code whenever our previously written method encounters the situation of having more contacts than can be processed, shown as follows:

```
//Same method as before but calling the Batchable interface instead of
@future
public static void updateContactPhones(
List<Account> priorVersions,
List<Account> updatedVersions
){
  Set<Id> modifiedAccounts_Ids = new Set<Id>();
  for ( Integer i=0;i<updatedVersions.size();i++ ){
    if ( updatedVersions[i].Phone != priorVersions[i].Phone ){
      modifiedAccounts_Ids.add(updatedVersions[i].Id);
    }
  }
  if ( modifiedAccounts_Ids.size() > 0 ){
    List<Contact> contactQuery = [
    Select Id, Phone, AccountId, Account.Phone
    from Contact
    where AccountId in :modifiedAccounts_Ids
    limit :( limits.getLimitQueryRows()-limits.getQueryRows() )
    ];
    List<Contact> contactUpdates = new List<Contact>();
    for ( Integer i=0;i<contactQuery.size();i++ ){
      if (
      contactQuery[i].Phone != contactQuery[i].Account.Phone &&
        contactUpdates.size() < limits.getLimitDMLRows()
      ){
      contactUpdates.add(contactQuery[i]);
      } else
      if (
      contactQuery[i].Phone != contactQuery[i].Account.Phone
      ){
```

```
        if ( contactJob.size() == 0 ){
          Id batchProcessId = Database.ExecuteBatch(new
            contactBatch());
        }
      }
    }
  }
}
```

Wow, that looks much better than that crazy code we wrote to call our @future method so many times. See, you're already programming in Apex better than before! Now, when our code is triggered and more contact records are queried than the limits allow us to operate on, we queue up our batch process and let it take care of it.

Bigger, better, and batchier

The Database.Batchable interface can be a lifesaver when dealing with large datasets. As there is a limit on the number of callouts that can occur in a single transaction, the Batchable interface is often used to sync data with outside systems. In order to perform a callout from an implementation of the Database.Batchable interface, you need to make a small tweak to your class definition. In addition to implementing the Database.Batchable interface, you must also implement the Database.AllowCallouts interface, shown as follows:

```
//Apex Class that implements the Batchable interface
global class contactBatch implements Database.Batchable<SObject>,
  Database.AllowCallouts {
  ...
}
```

Your code to perform callouts can occur in the start(), execute(), and finish() methods. The exact number of callouts allowed is specified in **Salesforce Limits Quick Reference Guide** located at https://login.salesforce.com/help/pdfs/en/salesforce_app_limits_cheatsheet.pdf. At the time of writing, the limit is 10 callouts each for the start() and finish() methods. These 10 callouts can also be made each time the execute() method is called per batch. The default batch size for the Database.Batchable interface is 200 records. If the system you are making a callout to doesn't handle data in batches of 200, then you might need to have more than 10 callouts to make it work. Fortunately, you can override the number of records per batch and specify any other number from 1 through 2,000 when calling the Database.ExecuteBatch() method, shown as follows:

```
//Run my batch process on groups of 10 records at a time
Id batchProcessId = Database.ExecuteBatch(contactBatch, 10);
```

Often, at the end of your batch process, you will want your finish() method to notify you of the number of records that were processed. Believe it or not, but this ability to notify is not included in the Database.Batchable interface. After some pleading though, the folks at salesforce.com did us a favor and granted us the ability to keep track of variables from start() through finish(). To enable your batch class to store variables throughout its execution, you also have to implement the Database.Stateful interface in the class definition, as follows:

```
//Apex Class that implements the Batchable interface and stateful
global class contactBatch implements Database.Batchable<SObject>,
Database.Stateful {

    global Integer counter;

    global Database.QueryLocator start(Database.BatchableContext
        ctx){
        counter = 0;
        return Database.getQueryLocator(
        'Select Id, Account.Phone from Contact where Update_Phone__c =
            TRUE'
        );
    }

    global void execute(
    Database.BatchableContext ctx,
    List<SObject> sobjects
    ){
        for ( sObject s : sobjects ){
            counter++;
        }
    }

    global void finish(Database.BatchableContext BC){
        system.debug(counter);
        //now send an email with this number
    }
}
```

At the end of execution of the previous code block, the counter variable will be set to the total number of records queried by our batch process. We can use the same concept to keep track of errors, the number of batches, or anything else we need to log in our finish() method.

Dyna batch

Sometimes, after you write your code, you realize that you need to execute it slightly differently now and then. You could make a second version of your class, but what if there were three or four different situations? Remember, we don't like to write the same code twice; that's inefficient. If the only difference between your use cases are the records that need to be queried but the actual logic is the same, then you can easily add some flair to your implementation of the `Database.Batchable` interface and make it more dynamic!

```
//Apex Class that implements the Batchable interface
global class dynaBatch implements Database.Batchable<SObject> {

    String queryString;

    global dynaBatch (String otherQueryString){
        queryString = 'Select Id from Contact';
        if ( string.isNotBlank(otherQueryString) ){
            //override the default queryString with one passed in to
            //the constructor
            queryString = otherQueryString;
        }
    }

    global Database.QueryLocator start(Database.BatchableContext
        ctx){
        return Database.getQueryLocator(queryString);
    }
    ...
}
```

More than meets the eye

If you want to be clever (and we do), you can even write a single class that operates on different sObjects. The query string passed into your constructor can be on any sObject you want. In fact, if you look at our batch process earlier in this chapter, you'll see that we had to cast our list of records from the generic sObject type to the contact sObject type anyway. The ID field is the only field that is common to all sObject types. Some standard sObjects do have fields with the same API name though, such as `FirstName` and `LastName` on leads, contacts, and users. So, if the various objects you need to process all have the same fields, you might be able to avoid casting and operate on them as generic sObjects. More likely though, they will differ and you will need to use an `if-else` statement. We've demonstrated how to do both in the following `execute` method:

```
global void execute(
Database.BatchableContext ctx,
```

```
    List<sObject> sobjects
  ){
    for ( sObject s : sobjects){
      if (
      s instanceof Contact ||
      s instanceof User ||
      s instanceof Lead
      ){
        //access a field value using the get() method
        System.debug( s.get('firstname') );
      }
    }
    //operate on the entire list of sobjects based on its type
    if ( sobjects instanceof List<Contact> ){
        fixContactsMethod(
        (List<Contact>)sobjects
        );
      } else
      if ( sobjects instanceof List<Lead> ){
        fixLeadsMethod(
        (List<Lead>)sobjects
        );
      } else
      if ( sobjects instanceof List<User> ){
        fixUsersMethod(
        (List<User>)sobjects
        );
      }
    }
  }
```

Building skynet

Triggers that call batch processes are fairly common, but like we mentioned earlier, it's not a good practice to have two sets of code that perform the same function. Sometimes, it's just easier to have your batch process run nightly (or on some other regular basis). This ensures that you start the day fresh with a clean slate and a database full of accurate data. A fairly new method in Apex is now available that lets you schedule the execution of a batch class called System.scheduleBatch(). The System.scheduleBatch() method has four input parameters:

- **Apex class**: This is the Apex class that implements the Database.Batchable interface.

- **Job name**: This is a string you use for easy reference.

- **Minutes from now**: This represents an integer that specifies in how many minutes your batch process should start.

- **Batch size**: This represents the size of each batch processed by the execute() method. This parameter is optional and will be set to the default value of 200 if not specified.

Calling the System.scheduleBatch() method is as easy as calling the Database.executeBatch() method:

```
system.scheduleBatch(
  dynaBatch,
  'My dynamic batch process',
  60,
  10
);
```

One of the greatest features of the Database.Batchable interface is the ability to call the system.scheduleBatch() or database.executeBatch() method from your batch class' finish() method. This means that you can write a virtually never-ending process, and if you leverage dynamic features, it can be smart and take different actions based on the state of your data in the Salesforce1 Platform. Take a look at the sample finish() method as shown:

```
global void finish(Database.BatchableContext BC){
  Integer badLeads = [
  Select Count()
  From Lead
  Where State = null and PostalCode != null
  ];
  Integer badContacts = [
  Select Count()
  from Contact
  where Update_Phone__c = TRUE
  ];
  String jobName;
  String queryString;
  dateTime nextMidnight = dateTime.newInstance(
  system.today().addDays(1),
  time.newInstance(0,0,0,0)
  );
  //Figure out how many minutes until midnight
  Integer runLaterMinutes = (
  nextMidnight.getTime() - system.now().getTime()
  ).intValue()/60000;
```

```
    if ( badLeads > 0 ){
      jobName = 'Update Lead States';

      //Set our query string for the leads batch process
      queryString = 'Select Id, State, PostalCode from Lead where
        State = null and PostalCode != null';

      //There are records to fix, so run right away
      runLaterMinutes = 1;
    } else {
      jobName = 'Update Contact Phone';

      queryString = 'Select Id, Phone, Account.Phone from Contact
        where Update_Phone__c = TRUE';

      //Run now if there's anything to fix, otherwise try again at
        midnight
      if ( badContacts > 0 ){
        runLaterMinutes = 1;
      }
    }
    //Dynamically schedule our dynamic batch process
    system.scheduleBatch(
    dynaBatch(queryString),
    jobName,
    runLaterMinutes;
  );
  }
```

We're taking efficiency to a new level with the preceding code block. Not only does our process reschedule itself, but it will take into consideration whether it has any work to do before doing so.

If you have long-running batch processes, you will probably want a way to monitor their progress and ensure that they are running properly. You can do this with code, but the Force.com GUI actually includes a nice page in setup that does it for you. You can view the page in the Force.com GUI by navigating to **Setup | Monitor | Jobs | Apex Jobs**. The **Apex Jobs** page will show you a list of jobs, their current status, total number of batches, whether they are still running, and the current batch number. You can also abort a running job or view the completion date of one that is done.

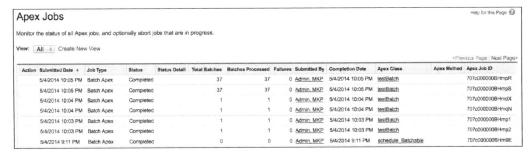

Action	Submitted Date ↑	Job Type	Status	Status Detail	Total Batches	Batches Processed	Failures	Submitted By	Completion Date	Apex Class	Apex Method	Apex Job ID
	5/4/2014 10:05 PM	Batch Apex	Completed		37	37	0	Admin, MKP	5/4/2014 10:05 PM	testBatch		707c000000BHmpR
	5/4/2014 10:05 PM	Batch Apex	Completed		37	37	0	Admin, MKP	5/4/2014 10:05 PM	testBatch		707c000000BHmpS
	5/4/2014 10:04 PM	Batch Apex	Completed		1	1	0	Admin, MKP	5/4/2014 10:04 PM	testBatch		707c000000BHmdX
	5/4/2014 10:04 PM	Batch Apex	Completed		1	1	0	Admin, MKP	5/4/2014 10:04 PM	testBatch		707c000000BHmqN
	5/4/2014 10:03 PM	Batch Apex	Completed		1	1	0	Admin, MKP	5/4/2014 10:03 PM	testBatch		707c000000BHmp1
	5/4/2014 10:03 PM	Batch Apex	Completed		1	1	0	Admin, MKP	5/4/2014 10:03 PM	testBatch		707c000000BHmp2
	5/4/2014 9:11 PM	Batch Apex	Completed		0	0	0	Admin, MKP	5/4/2014 9:11 PM	schedule_Batchable		707c000000BHm9E

Monitoring your Apex jobs

If you ever need it though, here is the code you can use to monitor your batch jobs and even abort a running one:

```
//If you have the AsyncApexJob Id from database.executeBatch()
AsyncApexJob a = [
Select Id, JobItemsProcessed, NumberofErrors, Status,
  TotalJobItems
from AsyncApexJob
where Id = :myExistingId
Limit 1
];

//Abort a job that is queued or processing
system.abortJob(a.Id);
```

More scheduling options

Talk about automation! Not only did we write a dynamic implementation of the `Database.Batchable` interface, but our code is also able to schedule itself and can even determine which process to run next. Cool and scary at the same time! Remember, the Salesforce1 Platform is on the cloud; there's no plug you can pull out to terminate it, so don't program it to destroy the human race.

Sometimes, the process you want to schedule doesn't need batch processing, or maybe you've watched a lot of sci-fi and feel better with more human control over the scheduling of your code. Well, Apex also includes a `Database.Schedulable` interface that you can implement. The `Database.Schedulable` interface only has one required method, `execute()`. Unlike the `Database.Batchable` interface, this `execute()` method only runs once. The code is as follows:

```
global class myScheduler implements Schedulable {
  global void execute(SchedulableContext SC) {
    //your code goes here
  }
}
```

Another benefit of the schedulable interface is that it is bound by a higher set of limits denoted as the asynchronous limits in **Salesforce Limits Quick Reference Guide** located at `https://login.salesforce.com/help/pdfs/en/salesforce_app_limits_cheatsheet.pdf`. We saw earlier how the `Database.Batchable` interface can reschedule itself but the schedulable interface can actually be set to run on a recurring schedule up front, without the need to reschedule after each execution. This is an ideal use case for processes that need to occur on a regular basis like a monthly commission calculation process or quarterly territory alignment process. Best of all, the Salesforce1 Platform includes an easy-to-use page for system administrators with no programming experience to manage a schedule (like a kill switch for skynet). To schedule a class that implements the schedulable interface, perform the following steps:

1. Click on the **Setup** link at the top of the Force.com GUI.
2. Navigate to **Setup | Develop | Apex Classes**.
3. Click on the **Schedule Apex** button. The **Schedule Apex** page appears.
4. Now, enter a name for your scheduled job.
5. Select the Apex class that implements the `Database.Schedulable` interface.
6. Select the frequency at which the process should run. Select the **Daily** and **one of the day** options for daily processes.
7. Enter the start and end dates. If you want it to run forever, put a date really far in the future.
8. Select a preferred start time and then click on **Save**, as shown in the following screenshot:

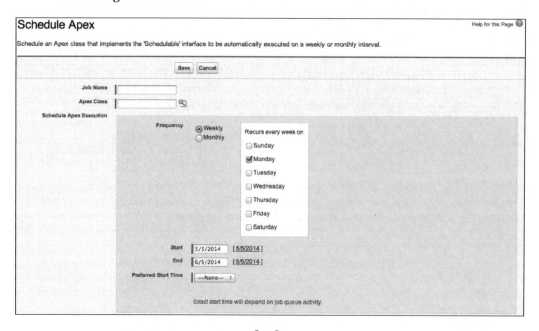

See, that's pretty easy and nontechnical, and this is why the schedulable interface is so popular. Why should anyone need to execute code to turn on and off a schedule when a system administrator can do it so easily?

Master control

If your scheduling needs are more complex, you need to be ultra-specific; you might not be able to easily use the **Schedule Apex** page. Let's say you need a process to run once a quarter or just once a year. Instead of trying to hack together some creative schedule, you can just use a CronTrigger. A CronTrigger represents a scheduled job and is similar to a cron job on UNIX systems. CronTriggers can be set with a very specific expression through the System.schedule() method. You can specify the schedule by seconds, minutes, hours, day of month, month, day of week, and year. There are options for using a range, intervals, and all possible numbers. Basically, if you can think of a schedule, you should be able to write a CronTrigger for it such as follows:

```
//Scheduling a Schedulable Apex Class
myScheduler cls = new myScheduler();
String cronExpression = '0 59 11 * * ?';   //Nightly at 11:59pm
String jobId = System.schedule('Job Name', cronExpression, cls);
```

Summary

Writing code to process large data sets is not your typical day. The Database. Batchable and Database.Schedulable interfaces are exceptions to the rule. Most of your code will be transactional and based on a DML event that occurs due to a user's action. Now that you're familiar with the limits of Apex and how to surpass them, we can focus on the code that will take up the bulk of your time. Get your trigger finger ready because the next chapter will focus on triggers and classes.

4
Triggers and Classes

As we mentioned in the first chapter, this book is not an introduction to **object-oriented programming (OOP)**. If you've read this far, we assume that you are already familiar with OOP and understand the concept of classes. Classes exist in Apex just like in other languages. There are, however, some differences between how classes are written in Apex and in other languages and this is what we will focus on in this chapter.

The majority of Apex code that you will write will be in a class; however, Apex also includes triggers. While you might be familiar with the concept of triggers already, Apex triggers are unique to the Salesforce1 Platform, so we will explain everything you need to know to start writing them.

A brief history of triggers

Years before the introduction of Apex, the SOAP API was introduced to the Salesforce1 Platform. The SOAP API was a huge accomplishment and well received by customers. Finally, they could apply their external business logic to data stored on the Salesforce1 Platform. With the SOAP API, you can programmatically access all your data on the platform. You can perform queries, create, update, and delete records, and more. All of your business requirements and custom logic can be executed by calling into the Salesforce1 Platform. The calls are well documented and there are even toolkits for popular languages.

Once customers started taking advantage of the SOAP API, it wasn't long before they wanted more. Calling into the platform every hour to poll for new records and make updates is cumbersome. It also means that users sometimes have to wait an hour before their records are updated with information from outside systems. There had to be a way to initiate the process from the Salesforce1 Platform and not have to constantly poll for records. That's when workflow was introduced to the Salesforce1 Platform.

Workflow allows a system administrator to define automated actions such as field updates, task record creation, sending e-mails, and outbound messages. These automated actions can then be configured to execute when a record is saved and meets the defined criteria. By sending an e-mail or outbound message from the Salesforce1 Platform, you can have the platform initiate your process and notify your external system that it has to do something. The combination of the SOAP API and workflow seemed to be the perfect solution that would make every customer happy.

As you might have guessed, it wasn't long before customers wanted even more. Some customers had business requirements that needed to prevent a user from saving a record. This couldn't be accomplished with an asynchronous process. Instead, the user was able to save a record and then get notified later that they shouldn't have. This made for some very frustrated customers. Other customers just needed to cross-reference information between a record being saved and other records already stored on the Salesforce1 Platform. It didn't make any sense to have to set up a server and web service just to facilitate communication between the Salesforce1 Platform and itself!

That's when it all changed. In 2007, Apex was introduced as the world's first on-demand programming language. With Apex, customers could programmatically access all their data, just like with the SOAP API. Not only can Apex store and execute your custom logic, but it also includes a key feature called triggers, which can initiate your code when a record is saved. Thus, customer requirements were met and no outside servers were needed, making everyone happy.

Trigger happy

The simple definition of an Apex trigger is code that is executed when a record is saved. In reality though, triggers are much more complex than this. Triggers are programmatic event handlers for the Salesforce1 Platform (unlike workflow, which is declarative). As Apex is stored and executed on the Force.com servers, triggers only run server side, not client side. Accordingly, the only events that triggers can handle are **Database Manipulation Language (DML)** operations. The only DML operations on Salesforce1 Platform are insert, update, delete, and undelete. In the Force.com documentation, you might occasionally see references to a merge or clone operation; however, for the purposes of triggers, a merge operation is really a combination of the update and delete operations and a clone operation is merely an insert operation.

It is possible to use Apex code to handle non-DML-related events such as the clicking of a button or selecting a value in a drop-down menu. For these types of user interface events, you typically have to use a combination of Visualforce and Apex. See *Chapter 5, Visualforce Development with Apex*, for more information on Visualforce.

We already looked at some code blocks in earlier chapters. Triggers are mechanisms we use to have the platform execute our code so that we don't have to do so. Without triggers, we will either have to leverage an outside system and the SOAP API or spend a lot of time hitting the *Enter* key on our keyboards.

Pulling the trigger

By now, you have hopefully logged in to your Developer Edition of the Salesforce1 Platform and created some sample data. You might have noticed that in order to create a new record, you must fill out any required fields. You might have already played with the workflow feature we mentioned earlier, which can modify a record upon save. If you're really eager, you can even experiment with validation rules, which can prevent a record from being saved if it does not meet your preset criteria. All of these various features make the simple act of saving a record a very complex process. To make things more complex, triggers are executed in two places in this process.

The first place in the process where a trigger is executed occurs before a record is committed to the database. Triggers that execute at this time are commonly referred to as **before triggers**. They are used to intercept a record that is being sent to the database. This is the perfect time to validate the record against your business logic. You can ensure that the record is filled out completely or that the values entered are valid. Before triggers are also perfect tools to augment records. You can fix spelling mistakes and ensure that data is entered consistently. The main downside to before triggers is that in the context of a before trigger, a newly created record does not have an ID yet, which makes it impossible to relate other records to it.

The second place in the process where a trigger is executed occurs after a record is committed to the database. Triggers that execute at this time are commonly referred to as **after triggers**. At this point, a new record has already been saved to the database and thus has an ID that can be related to other records. For this reason, after triggers are typically used to create or augment other records than using the one that was saved. As an after trigger occurs post-save, in order to modify the record that was saved, you will have to perform an additional DML operation against the record. This is a risky undertaking as you can cause an endless loop and hit a limit. This is another reason why a before trigger is typically used to augment the record that is being saved.

Although a single trigger can execute in both places, you can actually specify which of the two it should be executed under. When you define your trigger, you must not only specify which DML operations it is for, but also whether it should be executed in the before step, the after step, or both. This granular level of definition ensures that your trigger only executes when you want it to so. You don't have to write extra code to ensure that it's the right time.

Execution time

Let's take a step-by-step look at the order of execution when you edit an existing record:

1. A copy of the original record prior to the edit is loaded.
2. Required fields on page layouts, data formats, and value lengths are evaluated (whether the record was saved via a standard screen in the GUI).
3. Triggers that operate on the before event of an operation are executed.
4. Both system validations and custom validation rules are performed.
5. The record is saved to the database but not committed yet.
6. Triggers that operate on the after event of an operation are executed.
7. Declarative assignment rules are executed.
8. Declarative auto-response rules are executed (applies to leads).
9. Declarative workflow rules are executed.
10. If the workflow rules update the record, the before and after triggers are executed again to operate on the updated record.
11. Declarative workflow flow triggers are executed.
12. Declarative escalation rules are executed (applies to cases).
13. If the roll-up summary fields or cross-object workflow exists, they are executed, and this record's parent record is updated and goes through this same process.
14. If the roll-up summary fields and cross-object workflow exist on the parent record, they are executed, and this record's grandparent record is updated and goes through this same process.
15. Declarative criteria-based sharing rules are executed.
16. The operation is finally committed (no turning back).
17. Post-commit operations occur (sending of queued e-mails, queuing of @future methods, and so on).

Wow, talk about complexity! Fortunately, most of these steps relate to declarative features that are configured by a system administrator via the Force.com GUI. While we highly encourage you to understand each step and how it can affect your use of the Salesforce1 Platform, this book is about programming in Apex. We won't get into the details of what an assignment rule is or the difference between workflow and auto-response rules, or anything like that. In fact, for the purpose of this book, we can summarize these steps in about half as many as the previous steps:

1. A copy of the original record prior to the edit is loaded.

2. Triggers that operate on the before event of an operation are executed.

3. Both system validations and custom validation rules are performed.

4. The record is saved to the database but not committed yet.

5. Triggers that operate on the after event of an operation are executed.

6. Declarative features might update the record and cause our before and after triggers to execute again on this record.

7. Declarative features might update a parent and/or grandparent record and cause them to go through this same process.

8. The operation is finally committed (no turning back).

9. Post-commit operations occur (sending of queued e-mails, queuing of `@future` methods, and so on).

This isn't so bad, I think we can handle this shorter list of steps. So, let's talk about them in greater detail:

- **Step 1**: The original copy of the record is loaded into memory. This is critical as the only way we can determine the nature of a change to a record is by comparing its previous version to its new state. As we'll see later in the chapter, both states of the record are available to us inside a trigger. Using a simple `if` statement, we can determine whether the situation is such that our code needs to run and execute it accordingly. Remember, we want to be as efficient as possible, so always determine whether your code needs to run; don't just run it every time a record is saved.

- **Step 2**: Before triggers are now executed. As you can see from the order of execution, the record has not yet been saved to the database, so it's your chance to fix any data issues.

- **Step 3**: The record is evaluated against system and custom logic. This is an important step to be aware of. Your code might work perfectly, but if a system administrator introduces a conflicting validation rule, not only will users not be able to save records, but your test coverage will drop significantly too. We'll talk more about test coverage in a later chapter, but for now, know that you must keep an eye on any validation rules for sObjects on which you have written triggers.

- **Step 4**: The record is saved to the database. The record is not committed though, so the platform can revert back to its current state if any exception is thrown and not caught by a `try-catch` block. An ID is assigned to the record and is automatically available on it in future steps.

- **Step 5**: The after triggers are then executed. If you modify another record in your code, that record will go through this whole process at this point. As a result of that record going through this process, another record can be modified, and it too will go through this process. This cycle will continue until either all resulting modified records have completed through this process or an exception is thrown. Only once the cycle has completed on all resulting modified records will we move on to the next step for the originally saved record.

- **Step 6**: If declarative features have been configured, and their evaluation criteria is met, they will execute and possibly update the record that was originally saved.. The update that occurs as a result of these declarative features is a DML operation and as such causes this whole process to run again. Fortunately, in this second instance of the process, the platform skips declarative updates, preventing declarative features from causing an endless loop. However, it is still possible for your code to cause one. We'll talk about how to avoid this later in this chapter.

- **Step 7**: If declarative features have been configured to do so, they will execute and possibly update a record related to the one that was originally saved. Just as before, this update is a DML operation and causes the whole process to run on those records.

- **Step 8**: Assuming an exception has not been thrown or a limit hit, the originally saved record is finally committed and the synchronous process is complete. At this point, the record as well as any other records modified as a result are in its new state and cannot be reverted back.

- **Step 9**: Now, asynchronous operations are queued. This includes the sending of e-mails and the `@future` methods.

Earlier, when looking at the order of execution, we presented it in an overly simple fashion. In fact, we omitted a very important detail. The order of execution does not just occur on one record at a time, but rather occurs on all records that are saved as a result of a single transaction. As we mentioned earlier in the book, it's easier to think of our code as executing when a user goes to a page and edits a single record. However, when it comes time to writing your Apex triggers, it's critical to take into consideration that multiple records might be passing through your triggers and not just one.

Inside the mind of a trigger

We know that triggers are executed when a DML operation occurs on an sObject record and that they can be executed at two points in the order of execution. All of these details have to be specified in the trigger definition, because triggers can only be executed by the platform itself. There is no way to call a trigger directly and force it to execute. Instead, you will have to write code to perform a DML operation and the Salesforce1 Platform will take care of the rest.

Let's stick with our previous business requirement of keeping the phone field on contact records in sync with the phone field on their respective accounts. To do this, we will start by creating a new trigger. As the trigger will be for DML operations that occur on an account sObject, we will follow the best practice of starting the name of the trigger with the name of the sObject. To keep things simple, we'll just call this new trigger `accountTrigger`. We can create the new trigger from the Force.com IDE as follows:

1. Right-click on your project in the Force.com IDE and navigate to **New | Apex Trigger**.

   The **Create New Apex Trigger** window appears as shown:

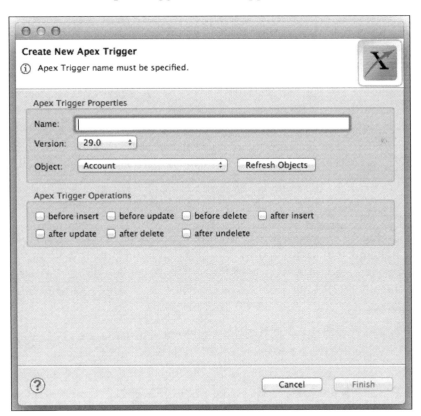

2. Enter the name for your new trigger. For this example, use `accountTrigger`.

3. Select the appropriate sObject that you want your trigger to be on. For this example, select **Account**.

4. Place a check in one or more of the **Apex Trigger Operations** checkboxes. For this example, select **after insert** and **after update** and click on **Finish**.

   A progress bar will appear followed by your new trigger.

While the trigger that we just created is empty, it is valid and will be executed every time an `Account` record is inserted or updated in the database.

All for one and one for all

Triggers are defined for one and only one sObject. They can, however, operate under multiple operations: insert, update, delete, and undelete. There are two schools of thought when it comes to creating triggers. One school of thought believes that it is acceptable to have a single trigger on an sObject that is executed under multiple DML operations. The other school of thought believes that each DML operation on a given sObject should have its own trigger. We are not going to declare one school of thought as the correct one. However, as you will soon see, the triggers we write tend to have very little code in them. Hence, we feel there is little harm done in having a single trigger on multiple DML operations.

> No matter who you ask, everyone agrees that you should always avoid having multiple triggers on a single sObject for the same DML operation. Not only will this increase the likelihood of hitting a limit, but it will also introduce chaos into your code execution. When you have two triggers on the same sObject for the same DML operation, there is no way to know which trigger will be executed first. Under most circumstances, this will probably be harmless, but if the two triggers operate on the same fields or perform the same functions, it can have disastrous results.

When you do have a single trigger on multiple DML operations, you typically will write `if` statements to determine the operation that occurred and whether you are at a point in time before or after saving to the database. While this can be determined programmatically by looking at the sObject record itself, triggers include the following context variables to make it easier for you:

- `trigger.isBefore`: A `Boolean` variable that specifies we are at step 2 in our process, before the records are saved to the database

- `trigger.isAfter`: A `Boolean` variable that specifies we are at step 5 in our process, after the records are saved to the database

- trigger.isInsert: A Boolean variable that specifies whether the DML operation that occurred is an insert operation
- trigger.isUpdate: A Boolean variable that specifies whether the DML operation that occurred is an update operation
- trigger.isDelete: A Boolean variable that specifies whether the DML operation that occurred is a delete operation
- trigger.isUndelete: A Boolean variable that specifies whether the DML operation that occurred is an undelete operation

As you can imagine, these attributes save you from having to write code just to figure out what is going on. Instead, you can focus on evaluating the state of the records and the logic of your business rules. Triggers include some additional variables that can help you with that too, which are as follows:

- trigger.new: This represents a list of sObject records that were operated upon.
- trigger.newMap: This represents a map of ID to the sObject record for records in trigger.new.
- trigger.old: This represents a list of the state of the sObject records prior to the operation that occurs. This list is in the same order as the records in trigger.new. For insert operations, this is null.
- trigger.oldMap: This represents a map of ID to the sObject record for records in trigger.old.
- trigger.size: This represents the number of records in trigger.new and trigger.old.

Now that you know what variables are included in a trigger, let's take a look at how we can use them with the trigger we created earlier:

```
trigger accountTrigger on Account (after insert, after update){

    //Use the Boolean attributes to quickly determine where we are
      in the order of execution and what operation occurred.
    if ( trigger.isAfter && trigger.isInsert ){
      for ( Account a : trigger.new ){
        if ( a.Phone != null ){
          system.debug(a.Phone);
        }
      }
    }
    if ( trigger.isAfter && trigger.isUpdate ){
      for ( Integer i=0;i<trigger.size();i++ ){
        if ( trigger.new[i].phone != trigger.old[i].phone ){
          system.debug(
```

```
        trigger.new[i].phone +'!='+ trigger.old[i].phone
      );
    }
  }
}
}
```

As you can see, the built-in attributes of Apex triggers allow us to focus our efforts on business logic instead of why the trigger was executed.

Class is in session

As we mentioned before, when we write triggers, the majority of code goes into our Apex classes, not the triggers themselves. As only the platform can execute the code in a trigger, any code you put in there is inaccessible to you. This means that if you ever need to reuse the same logic, you'd have to rewrite it in a class. If you're going to have it rewritten anyway, you might as well just start off correctly and put it in a class to begin with.

We can create a new Apex class from the Force.com IDE as follows:

1. Right-click on your project in the Force.com IDE and navigate to **New | Apex Class**.

    The **Create New Apex Trigger** window appears as shown:

2. Enter the name for your new Apex class. For this example, use `accountMethods`.

3. Leave the **Template** option as **Default**.

4. Click on the **Finish** button.

   A progress bar will appear followed by your new Apex class.

Currently, there are only three template options available when creating a new Apex class from the Force.com IDE:

- **Default**: This is an empty class that declares the most common keywords.

- **Inbound Email Service**: This is a template that implements the built-in `Messaging.InboundEmailHandler` interface. This interface is used to write code to receive inbound e-mails sent to the Salesforce1 Platform.

- **Test Class**: This is a template with the appropriate annotations needed to write Apex test methods.

There haven't been any new templates added to the Force.com IDE in years. Eclipse is an open source project though, so if you'd like to become a hero to your fellow developers, see if you can figure out how to make one and share it with the rest of us.

Inner space

Let's take a look at the empty shell of the class that we created earlier in the Force.com IDE:

```
public with sharing class accountMethods {

}
```

When we created our Apex class, we just specified the name and used the **Default** template. This template creates the outer shell of our class, which is commonly referred to as an outer class or top-level class. An outer class can have a nested class inside it, which is typically called an inner class. Both your outer and inner classes can have methods and variables and be instantiated as an object. However, inner classes cannot have other inner classes nested inside them because in Apex, you can only nest an inner class one level deep.

The default class template set up our class as being declared `public`. Although, the Salesforce1 Platform is a multitenant environment, `public` in this case, it does not mean that it is accessible to the world. In this case, `public` serves as an access modifier that determines whether or not other code can access this class and its contents. In Apex, the following access modifiers are used on classes, methods, and variables:

- `private`: The `private` access modifier can only be used inside an outer class. It limits access to the item to only within its outer class and cannot be referenced elsewhere.

- `protected`: The `protected` access modifier can only be used inside an outer class. It limits access to the item to only within its outer class and classes that extend its outer class.

- `public`: The `public` access modifier is the most commonly found one. It allows access to all other code you create directly in your Force.com org. Code installed via a package will not have access to public items.

- `global`: The global access modifier allows your code to be accessed outside of your namespace. This is typically used when building application packages that will be installed by others from the AppExchange; however, it's also required if you are going to expose your code as a web service via the Force.com API.

You have to use either the `public` or `global` access modifier in your outer class definition. The methods, variables, and classes inside your outer class can use any of the previously mentioned access modifiers. If you do not specify an access modifier, then that item will be considered to be `private` and available only within its outer class. It's a good idea to be explicit and always specify an access modifier to avoid any potential confusion.

Share and share alike

When we discussed triggers, we mentioned that the code inside them is executed by the platform. For many business requirements, this is ideal; your business logic can execute as if it was built-in to the application itself regardless of who is currently interacting with it. The Salesforce1 Platform includes a robust data sharing model though, and there might be times where you want to limit your code to accessing only the data that the current user has access to. It's for this very reason that Apex classes can be defined with a keyword to determine the data access to be used during execution.

If you look back at our outer class shell, you can see `with sharing` after our access modifier. The `with sharing` keyword ensures that all code that executes within the class will do so with respect to the data shared with the current user. Many programmers work for years with Apex and never really need to distinguish whether their code respects the sharing model or not. One of the benefits of using a centralized database is that you can easily share data, so a lot of customers don't restrict sharing.

One day though, you might work for a company that does business with the government, tracks personal information, or just likes keeping secrets. If you were to write code to perform a search for `Account` records, you'd want to ensure that an end user cannot use your code to access any records that they cannot normally view. This would be the perfect time to use the `with sharing` keyword and leave the details of configured the sharing rules to a system administrator.

In case you're wondering, the opposite of the `with sharing` keyword is the `without sharing` keyword. It is used to explicitly state that the data sharing model should be ignored during the execution of any code in a class. If you don't specify a sharing keyword, the default behavior is the same as `without sharing`, so it's not necessary to use the `without sharing` keyword, but we always encourage making things obvious, so you probably should.

Staying classy

Whether you are implementing a built-in interface, controlling a Visualforce page, or facilitating a trigger logic, classes are the solution. While classes are often used as templates for objects that you construct, most of the examples we've shown so far leverage static methods in these classes. It's actually a best practice to call static methods stored in classes from your triggers, as they are more efficient on the server. There are times though where you want to do more than just call a single method, so let's take a look at some more complex functionality in classes.

When you plan on instantiating your class as an object, you often want to set some default values. If you are going to create multiple instances of this object, then you'll be writing the same code over and over. This is where having a default constructor can be useful, shown as follows:

```
public class sampleOuterClass {

  public String myString;
  public Integer myInteger;

  public sampleOuterClass(){
    myString = 'hello';
```

```
        myInteger = 1;
    }
}
```

Using the previous constructor, we can now create an instance of our class without having to specify the values of myString or myInteger, which saves us two lines of code for each instance:

```
sampleOuterClass obj1 = new sampleOuterClass();
system.assert( obj1.myString == 'hello');
system.assert( obj1.myInteger == 1);
```

Without setting the values in our default constructor, this assertions would not only fail, but the reference to myString and myInteger would also result in the dreaded NullPointerException (queue menacing music). Of course, there might be times where you want to be able to specify the values of your variables and don't want to use an additional two lines of code. Well, Apex supports overloading methods and constructors, so you can have the best of both worlds! The code for this is as follows:

```
public class sampleOuterClass {

    public String myString;
    public Integer myInteger;

    public sampleOuterClass(){
        myString = 'hello';
        myInteger = 1;
    }
    public sampleOuterClass(String inputString){
        myString = inputString;
        myInteger = 1;
    }
    public sampleOuterClass(Integer inputInteger){
        myString = 'hello';
        myInteger = inputInteger;
    }
}
```

In the previous version of the class, we overloaded our constructor twice. Now we can construct our class and preset the values of our variables. One downside to this pattern is that if you're doing more than just setting variables in your constructors, such as performing calculations or comparisons, you'll have to modify each constructor to ensure that they operate correctly. Well, by now you probably realized that we like to go the extra mile, so take a look at the following updated version of this class to see how to efficiently overload your constructors:

```
public class sampleOuterClass {

  public String myString;
  public Integer myInteger;

  public sampleOuterClass(){
    this.sampleOuterClass(null,null);
  }
  public sampleOuterClass(String inputString){
    this.sampleOuterClass(inputString,null);
  }
  public sampleOuterClass(Integer inputInteger){
    this.sampleOuterClass(null,inputInteger);
  }
  public sampleOuterClass(String inputString, Integer
    inputInteger){
    //logic goes here
    myString = inputString;
    if ( String.isBlank(myString) ){
      myString = 'hello';
    }
    myInteger = inputInteger;
    if ( myInteger == null ){
      myInteger = 1;
    }
    //more logic goes here
  }
}
```

The previous code block overloads the constructor three times, but our custom logic only exists once. We're able to do this using the `this` keyword to facilitate constructor chaining, which automatically calls the correct constructor based on the signature. So, regardless of the parameters included when we instantiate our class, the same logic will be used. We firmly believe that efficiency and consistency go hand in hand and make for better code; the previous class is the perfect example of this.

Wrap it up

As we mentioned before, Apex code is designed to work with your data. However, sometimes your data structures don't really match what you're trying to accomplish in your code. When Apex was first introduced, we often created hidden sObjects and fields just to facilitate our code logic. Not only was this foolish, but it also really wasn't fair to customers of lower-priced editions of the Salesforce1 Platform who are limited to a smaller number of custom objects.

In the following sample code block, our business requirement is to provide metrics on the number of `Account` and `Contact` records grouped by state. However, we don't have an sObject that represents the concept of a state and the record counts. Here is how we can accomplish this task:

```
public class sampleOuterClass(){
    private static Map<String, Integer> contactsByState =
        new Map<String,Integer>();
    private static Map<String, Integer> accountsByState =
        new Map<String,Integer>();

    public static void calculateMetrics(){
        for ( Account a : [
        Select Id, BillingState
        from Account
        where BillingState != null
        limit 5000
        ]){
            Integer thisState = 0
            if ( accountsByState.containsKey(a.BillingState) ){
                thisState = accountsByState.get(a.BillingState);
            }
            accountsByState.put(a.BillingState, thisState+1);
        }
        for ( Contact c : [
        Select Id, MailingState
        from Contact
        where MailingState != null
        limit 5000
        ]){
            Integer thisState = 0
            if (contactsByState.containsKey(c.MailingState) ){
                thisState = contactsByState.get(c.MailingState);
            }
            contactsByState.put(c.MailingState, thisState+1);
        }
    }
}
```

While the two maps in the previous code are certainly useful to store our calculations, they cannot be returned as a result of calling the method. Apex methods are limited to returning a single object. In order to enable this method to return our calculations, we must wrap the maps into a single object such as the following class:

```
public class mapWrapper(){
   public Map<String,Integer> accountMap;
   public Map<String,Integer> contactMap;
}
```

This class can either be created as its own outer class or as an inner class. However, we think this code can be improved upon. Our business requirement is to provide two numbers per state, so we need to ensure that if a state is returned, a number is returned for both the count of the Contact and Account records. So, we're going to rewrite our outer class to include a new inner class and use this to store our calculations. While we're at it, we're also going to leverage the aggregate functions in SOQL to reduce the number of code statements, as shown:

```
public class sampleOuterClass(){

   //Our inner class that does not exist outside of runtime
   public class stateWrapper {
      public String stateName;
      public Integer contactCount;
      public Integer accountCount;

      //Default constructor for innerClass
      public stateWrapper(
      String stateName,
      Integer contactCount,
      Integer accountCount
      ){
         this.stateName = stateName;
         this.contactCount = contactCount;
         if ( contactCount == null ){
           contactcount = 0;
         }
         this.accountCount = accountCount;
         if ( accountCount == null ){
           accountCount = 0;
         }
         //the 'this' keyword denotes that we are talking about
         //the variables outside the constructor and not
         //the input parameters by the same name.
      }
```

```
        }

    public static Map<String,stateWrapper> calculateMetrics(){
      Map<String,stateWrapper> stateMap =
        new Map<String,stateWrapper>();
      for ( AggregateResult ar : [
      Select Count(id) cnt, BillingState state
      from Account
      where BillingState != null
      group by BillingState
      ]){
        //AggregateResult values are generic objects that need
        //to be casted to specific primitive types
        stateWrapper sw = new stateWrapper(
        (string)ar.get('state'),
        (integer)ar.get('cnt'),
        null
        );
        stateMap.put(sw.stateName,sw);
      }
      for ( AggregateResult ar : [
      Select Count(id) cnt, MailingState state
      from Contact
      where MailingState != null
      group by MailingState
      ]){
        stateWrapper sw = new stateWrapper(
        (string)ar.get('state'),
        null,
        null
        );
        if ( stateMap.containsKey(sw.stateName) ){
          sw = stateMap.get(sw.stateName);
        }
        sw.contactCount = (integer)ar.get('cnt');
        stateMap.put(sw.stateName,sw);
      }
      return stateMap;
    }
  }
```

The previous class combines the use of inner class instances with a static method to efficiently calculate and return the metrics required by our business requirements. The concept of a wrapper can be used with sObjects or on their own. We'll see in a later chapter that wrappers are extremely useful for integrating with outside systems.

No libraries, no problem

Unlike Java or other languages, Apex doesn't have a concept of a library. You can't use an `import` statement to import packages into your Apex classes. Fortunately though, you don't need to. All of the built-in classes on the Salesforce1 Platform and the custom classes that you create are automatically accessible in Apex. You don't need to use any special statements or annotations to access instances of a class, methods, or variables. You just use the appropriate names of the classes and their methods or variables, and you can access them just as if they were in the current class you're working on. It's even possible to install packages of classes that have been uploaded at `www.appexchange.com`. If the classes in these packages have been configured to be accessible by their installers, then you can access them by prefixing the class names with a unique namespace prefix. The namespace prefix allows you to distinguish between two classes with the same name: one that you installed via a package and one that you created yourself in your org's default namespace.

When you're given a new requirement, it's always worthwhile to search for existing packages that might do what you need. There's no point reinventing the wheel and you might learn a few things too. It's also a good idea to familiarize yourself with the long list of classes that are built-in to Apex. There are too many built-in classes to list in this book, so the following are some of our favorites. The following list grows with the three major upgrades each year, so be sure to check out the latest version in **Force. com Apex Developer's Guide** located at `http://developer.salesforce.com`:

ApexPages	Approval	Blob	Boolean	BusinessHours
Cookie	Crypto	Database	Date	Decimal
Double	EncodingUtil	Exception	Http	HttpRequest
HttpResponse	Id	Integer	JSON	JSONGenerator
JSONParser	Limits	List	Long	Map
Matcher	Math	Messaging	Page Reference	Pattern
RestContext	RestRequest	Rest Response	Schema	SelectOption
Site	sObject	System	Test	Time

It's best practice to ensure that you do not name your custom Apex classes the same as any other class or object on the Salesforce1 Platform. It might be tempting to create a class named Test, but doing so is not be a good idea. Any references to the methods or variables in your class can be confused with an attempt to reference the built-in Test class and might cause your code to fail or not even be compiled. In general, we recommend using a descriptive class name that makes it very clear what its use is for. Definitely, do not start your classes with a prefix such as cls; it eliminates your ability to sort your classes alphabetically.

Rinse, lather, and repeat

Putting your logic in a class can help you avoid hitting a limit due to recursion. Remember, every time a record is saved, the order of execution can cause an update to occur to that same record or to other records, which in turn can cause other updates and so on. All of these updates are part of a single transaction governed by the same limits. If you have a complex environment with a lot of triggers and declarative features in use, you can avoid recursion through the use of static variables in a class. The following code is a sample trigger and class that begins with a really poor design:

```
trigger accountTrigger on Account (after update){
   accountMethods.afterUpdateMethod(trigger.new);
}

public class accountMethods {

   public static void afterUpdate(List<Account> newList){
     //Hundreds of lines of complex logic
    update newList;
   }
}
```

In the previous code block, you can see that our trigger calls a method in our class, which then performs an update on the same records and causes an endless loop until a LimitException is thrown by the platform. I don't think anyone would ever do this on purpose, but this type of situation can happen in a complex environment. Fortunately, we don't have to rewrite all of our logic to fix the situation. Instead, we can keep track of things using a static variable and a few extra lines of code and make the problem go away, as shown in the following code:

```
trigger accountTrogger on Account (after update){
   accountMethods.afterUpdateMethod(trigger.new);
```

```
  }

  public class accountMethods {

    static Boolean hasExecutedAlready = false;

    public static void afterUpdate(List<Account> newList){
      if ( hasExecutedAlready == false ){
        //Hundreds of lines of complex logic
        hasExecutedAlready = true;
        update newList;
      }
    }
  }
```

The reason this code block works is because static variables stay in memory for the duration of the entire execution thread, regardless of the number of times their class is referenced. So, the very first time our trigger executes, we call the `afterUpdate()` method and perform our complex logic. Before doing our update though, we set the `hasExecutedAlready` variable to `true` so that future executions of this method in the same execution thread will not perform another update.

Static variables neither persist beyond a single execution thread nor do they exist across two of them that can occur at the same time. If you need to reference a value across threads, you will need to commit that value as data. Depending on your requirements, it might make sense to create a new custom object to store these variables or maybe even a custom setting. We'll discuss both options in a later chapter.

Put your hands together

Now that we know about triggers and classes, it's time to revisit our business requirement again and complete the process to synchronize the phone field on contacts with accounts. We'll start by taking our outer class shell and inserting our `updateContactPhones()` method from *Chapter 3, More and Later*, as shown:

```
  public with sharing class accountMethods {
    public static void updateContactPhones(
    List<Account> priorVersions,
    List<Account> updatedVersions
    ){
      Set<Id> modifiedAccounts_Ids = new Set<Id>();
      for ( Integer i=0;i<updatedVersions.size();i++ ){
        if ( updatedVersions[i].Phone != priorVersions[i].Phone ){
          modifiedAccounts_Ids.add(updatedVersions[i].Id);
```

```
            }
        }
        if ( modifiedAccounts_Ids.size() > 0 ){
            List<Contact> contactQuery = [
            Select Id, Phone, AccountId, Account.Phone
            from Contact
            where AccountId in :modifiedAccounts_Ids
            limit :(
            limits.getLimitQueryRows()-limits.getQueryRows()
            )
            ];
            List<Contact> contactUpdates = new List<Contact>();
            for ( Integer i=0;i<contactQuery.size();i++ ){
                if (
                contactQuery[i].Phone != contactQuery[i].Account.Phone &&
                    contactUpdates.size() < limits.getLimitDMLRows()
                ){
                    contactUpdates.add(contactQuery[i]);
                } else
                if (
                contactQuery[i].Phone != contactQuery[i].Account.Phone &&
                    contactUpdates.size() >= limits.getLimitDMLRows()
                ){
                    Id batchProcessId = Database.ExecuteBatch(new
                        contactBatch());
                }
            }
        }
    }
}
```

Now that we have our class and static method, we can turn back to our trigger and ensure that it calls this method and passes in the appropriate parameters, as shown:

```
trigger accountTrigger on Account (after insert, after update){

    if ( trigger.isAfter && trigger.isUpdate ){
        accountMethods.updateContactPhones(trigger.new, trigger.old);
    }
}
```

You can see from this trigger why we don't think it's necessary to have a separate trigger for each DML operation, let alone two. With such little code inside the actual trigger, it's just more to maintain.

Behind the scenes

If you're paying attention to the **Package Explorer** view in the Force.com IDE, you might have noticed that after creating our class, instead of one new file being created, there were two. The same thing happened after we created our trigger too, as shown in the following screenshot, which shows metadata files exist for each class and trigger:

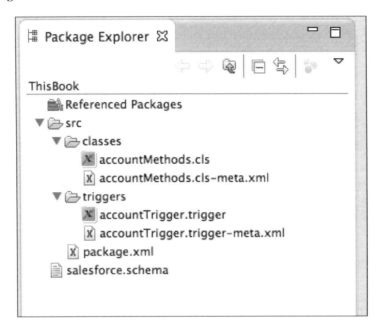

You're not seeing double; these extra files are intentional and serve an important purpose. Remember back in *Chapter 2, Apex Limits*, when we looked at the metadata for our Apex code. These extra files store that metadata. In Apex classes, you can control the API version under which the code executes as well as the versions of any prebuilt packages that you might have installed. For triggers though, you have an added `status` attribute that you can use to turn off your trigger and prevent it from executing. This `status` attribute can be really useful if you need to perform a large data migration and don't want your trigger to execute. This is also the justification to create a trigger for each combination of operations and order of execution. If you have multiple triggers, you can be more selective in turning off just the one you need and reducing the impact on legitimate transactions that need the trigger to execute.

The Pablo Picasso of Apex

In addition to the built-in interfaces we have looked at so far, Apex also includes the ability to create and implement your own interfaces. When you define an interface in Apex, you only supply the methods names and signatures, not the inner logic. This feature allows you to design high-level processes that can be implemented in multiple ways. To define an interface, you replace the word `class` in the definition with the word `interface`. The following code block defines an interface and then later implements it twice:

```
public interface myInterface {

    String compileString();
    Integer calculateNumber();


}


public class budgetClass implements myInterface{
    public String compileString(){
        return 'Our budget is ';
    }
    public Integer calculateNumber(){
        return 1000;
    }
}


public class profitClass implements myInterface{
    public String compileString(){
        return 'Our profit is ';
    }
    public Integer calculateNumber(){
        return 500;
    }
}
```

Interfaces aren't needed on a daily basis, but if you have multiple developers working on a project or multiple processes that are similar, they can be useful. Apex also includes the ability to create virtual classes that you can then extend. The following code is an example of a virtual class:

```
public virtual class profitCalculator{
    public virtual Decimal calculateIncome(){
        return 1000;
    }
```

```
    public virtual Decimal calculateExpenses(){
      return 500;
    }
  }
```

Now that we have defined our virtual class, we can extend it and even override the methods included in it:

```
  public class salesProfitCalculator extends profitCalculator{
    public override Decimal calculateExpenses(){
      return 600;
    }
    public Decimal calculateProfit(){
      Decimal income = calculateIncome();   //1000
      Decimal expenses = calculateExpenses();   //600
      return income - expenses;
    }
  }
```

In the `calculateProfit()` method, the income variable is set to the returned value from the `calculateIncome()` method in our `virtual` class while the expense variable is set from the overridden version of the `calculateExpenses()` method.

If you do not have default logic for your virtual classes, then you can use the `abstract` keyword instead of the `virtual` keyword. Abstract classes do not have any logic defined in their methods, which forces you to write all your code in the classes that extend them.

Summary

This chapter was a doozy and we're moving quickly. You should now have a good understanding of Apex and be able to read the code and understand what it's doing. Now might be a good time to play some more with the Force.com IDE and your Developer Edition. If you're feeling confident, search for some Apex projects that have been uploaded to your favorite public repository. If you find one that involves Visualforce and aren't sure what that is, then keep reading because the next chapter will tell you all about it.

5

Visualforce Development with Apex

Apex on its own is a powerful tool to extend the Salesforce1 Platform. It allows you to define your own database logic and fully customize the behavior of the platform. Sometimes, controlling what happens behind the scenes isn't enough. You might have a complex process that needs to step users through a wizard or need to present data in a format that isn't native to the Salesforce1 Platform, or maybe even make things look like your corporate website. Anytime you need to go beyond custom logic and implement a custom interface, you can turn to Visualforce.

Visualforce is the user interface framework for the Salesforce1 Platform. It supports the use of HTML, JavaScript, CSS, and Flash—all of which enable you to build your own custom web pages. These web pages are stored and hosted by the Salesforce1 Platform and can be exposed to just your internal users, your external community users, or publicly to the world.

But wait, there's more! Also included with Visualforce is a robust markup language. This markup language (which is also referred to as Visualforce) allows you to bind your web pages to data and actions stored on the platform. It also allows you to leverage Apex for code-based objects and actions. Like the rest of the platform, the markup portion of Visualforce is upgraded three times a year with new tags and features.

All of these features mean that Visualforce is very powerful and probably even warrants its own book (subtle hint to our publisher). This chapter will cover a lot of material, so make sure that you have some snacks handy.

s-con, what?

Before the introduction of Visualforce, the Salesforce1 Platform had a feature called s-controls. These were simple files where you could write HTML, CSS, and JavaScript. There was no custom markup language included. In order to make things look like the Force.com GUI, a lot of HTML was required. If you wanted to create just a simple input form for a new Account record, so much HTML code was required that we can't easily show it to you without wasting dozens of pages of this book! The following is just a small, condensed excerpt of what the HTML would look like if you wanted to recreate such a screen from scratch:

```
<div class="bPageTitle"><div class="ptBody"><div class="content">
  <img src="/s.gif" class="pageTitleIcon" title="Account" />
  <h1 class="pageType">
    Account Edit<span class="titleSeparatingColon">:</span>
  </h1>
  <h2 class="pageDescription"> New Account</h2>
  <div class="blank"> </div>
</div>
<div class="links"></div></div><div
  class="ptBreadcrumb"></div></div>
<form action="/001/e" method="post" onsubmit="if
  (window.ffInAlert) { return false; }if (window.sfdcPage
  &amp;&amp; window.sfdcPage.disableSaveButtons) { return
  window.sfdcPage.disableSaveButtons(); }">
<div class="bPageBlock brandSecondaryBrd bEditBlock
  secondaryPalette">
  <div class="pbHeader">
    <table border="0" cellpadding="0" cellspacing="0"><tbody>
      <tr>
      <td class="pbTitle">
      <img src="/s.gif" width="12" height="1" class="minWidth"
        style="margin-right: 0.25em;margin-right: 0.25em;margin-
        right: 0.25em;">
      <h2 class="mainTitle">Account Edit</h2>
      </td>
      <td class="pbButton" id="topButtonRow">
      <input value="Save" class="btn" type="submit">
      <input value="Cancel" class="btn" type="submit">
      </td>
      </tr>
    </tbody></table>
  </div>
  <div class="pbBody">
    <div class="pbSubheader brandTertiaryBgr first
      tertiaryPalette" >
```

```
<span class="pbSubExtra"><span class="requiredLegend
  brandTertiaryFgr"><span class="requiredExampleOuter"><span
  class="requiredExample"> </span></span>
  <span class="requiredMark">*</span>
  <span class="requiredText"> = Required Information</span>
  </span></span>
  <h3>Account Information<span
    class="titleSeparatingColon">:</span> </h3>
</div>
<div class="pbSubsection">
<table class="detailList" border="0" cellpadding="0"
cellspacing="0"><tbody>
  <tr>
    <td class="labelCol requiredInput">
    <label><span class="requiredMark">*</span>Account
    Name</label>
    </td>
    <td class="dataCol col02">
     <div class="requiredInput"><div
       class="requiredBlock"></div>
       <input id="acc2" name="acc2" size="20" type="text">
     </div>
    </td>
    <td class="labelCol">
     <label>Website</label>
    </td>
    <td class="dataCol">
      <span>
      <input id="acc12" name="acc12" size="20" type="text">
      </span>
    </td>
  </tr>
  </tbody></table>
  </div>
</div>
<div class="pbBottomButtons">
  <table border="0" cellpadding="0" cellspacing="0"><tbody>
  <tr>
   <td class="pbTitle"><img src="/s.gif" width="12" height="1"
     class="minWidth" style="margin-right: 0.25em;margin-right:
     0.25em;margin-right: 0.25em;"> </td>
   <td class="pbButtonb" id="bottomButtonRow">
    <input value=" Save " class="btn" title="Save"
      type="submit">
    <input value="Cancel" class="btn" type="submit">
   </td>
  </tr>
```

```
        </tbody></table>
    </div>
    <div class="pbFooter secondaryPalette"><div class="bg">
    </div></div>
  </div>
  </form>
```

We did our best to trim down this HTML to as little as possible. Despite all of our efforts, it still took up more space than we wanted. The really sad part is that all of that code only results in the following screenshot:

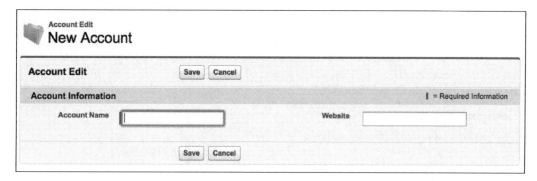

Not only was it time consuming to write all this HTML, but odds were that we wouldn't get it exactly right the first time. Worse still, every time the business requirements changed, we had to go through the exhausting effort of modifying the HTML code. Something had to change in order to provide us relief. That something was the introduction of Visualforce and its markup language.

Your own personal Force.com

The markup tags in Visualforce correspond to various parts of the Force.com GUI. These tags allow you to quickly generate HTML markup without actually writing any HTML. It's really one of the greatest tricks of the Salesforce1 Platform. You can easily create your own custom screens that look just like the built-in ones with less effort than it would take you to create a web page for your corporate website. Take a look at the Visualforce markup that corresponds to the HTML and screenshot we showed you earlier:

```
<apex:page standardController="Account" >
  <apex:sectionHeader title="Account Edit" subtitle="New Account"
    />
  <apex:form>
    <apex:pageBlock title="Account Edit" mode="edit" >
      <apex:pageBlockButtons>
```

```
      <apex:commandButton value="Save" action="{!save}" />
      <apex:commandButton value="Cancel" action="{!cancel}" />
    </apex:pageBlockButtons>
    <apex:pageBlockSection title="Account Information" >
      <apex:inputField value="{!account.Name}" />
      <apex:inputField value="{!account.Website}" />
    </apex:pageBlockSection>
  </apex:pageBlock>
</apex:form>
</apex:page>
```

Impressive! With merely these 15 lines of markup, we can render nearly 100 lines of earlier HTML. Don't believe us, you can try it out yourself.

Creating a Visualforce page

Just like triggers and classes, Visualforce pages can be created and edited using the Force.com IDE. The Force.com GUI also includes a web-based editor to work with Visualforce pages, but as we mentioned earlier, this book focuses on the IDE. To create a new Visualforce page, perform these simple steps:

1. Right-click on your project and navigate to **New | Visualforce Page**. The **Create New Visualforce Page** window appears as shown:

2.   Enter the label and name for your new page in the **Label** and **Name** fields, respectively. For this example, use `myTestPage`.

3.   Select the API version for the page. For this example, keep it at the default value.

4.   Click on **Finish**. A progress bar will appear followed by your new Visualforce page.

 Remember that you always want to create your code in a Sandbox or Developer Edition org, not directly in Production. It is technically possible to edit Visualforce pages in Production, but you're breaking all sorts of best practices when you do.

Similar to other markup languages, every tag in a Visualforce page must be closed. Tags and their corresponding closing tags must also occur in a proper order. The values of tag attributes are enclosed by double quotes; however, single quotes can be used inside the value to denote text values. Every Visualforce page starts with the `<apex:page>` tag and ends with `</apex:page>` as shown:

```
<apex:page>
  <!-- Your content goes here -->
</apex:page>
```

Within the `<apex:page>` tags, you can paste your existing HTML as long as it is properly ordered and closed. The result will be a web page hosted by the Salesforce1 Platform.

Not much to see here

If you are a web developer, then there's a lot you can do with Visualforce pages. Using HTML, CSS, and images, you can create really pretty web pages that educate your users. In the next chapter, we'll show you how to expose these pages publicly. This will allow you to migrate your website from your existing host provider to the Salesforce1 Platform. If you have some programming skills, you can also use JavaScript in your pages to allow for interaction. If you have access to web services, you can use JavaScript to call the web services and make a really powerful application. Check out the following Visualforce page for an example of what you can do:

```
<apex:page>
  <script type="text/javascript">
  function doStuff(){
    var x = document.getElementById("myId");
    console.log(x);
  }
```

```
    </script>
    <img src="http://www.thisbook.com/logo.png" />
    <h1>This is my title</h1>
    <h2>This is my subtitle</h2>
    <p>In a world where books are full of code, there was only one
      that taught you everything you needed to know about Apex!</p>
    <ol>
      <li>My first item</li>
      <li>Etc.</li>
    </ol>
    <span id="myId"></span>
    <iframe src="http://www.thisbook.com/mypage.html" />
    <form action="http://thisbook.com/submit.html" >
      <input type="text" name="yoursecret" />
    </form>
  </apex:page>
```

All of this code is standalone and really has nothing to do with the Salesforce1 Platform other than being hosted by it. However, what really makes Visualforce powerful is its ability to interact with your data, which allows your pages to be more dynamic. Even better, you can write Apex code to control how your pages behave, so instead of relying on client-side JavaScript, your logic can run server side.

Tag, you're it!

Each tag in Visualforce has its own unique set of attributes. Just like for Apex, there is a developer guide for Visualforce that lists all tags, their attributes, and the resulting HTML that they render. **Visualforce Developer's Guide** is available in the HTML and PDF formats at `http://developer.force.com`. The list of tags is too long to list here, and it gets updated three times a year with each major release. We recommend that you familiarize yourself with the entire list, but we'll cover some useful ones to get you started:

- `<apex:page>`: This is the only tag that you must use on every Visualforce page. It allows you to specify the controller and extensions for the page. It also has attributes to control whether the standard header and sidebar are displayed or the page should take on a different Force.com look and feel.

- `<apex:form>`: This tag is required for any page that is going to have input from the user. The best practice is to just have one of the `<apex:form>` tags per page, so it typically comes early in the markup.

- `<apex:pageBlock>`: A page block is the main section of the page when viewing or editing a record in the Force.com GUI.

- `<apex:pageBlockSection>`: A page block section is a section that contains fields in the page block. These sections can have their own titles and are collapsible when viewing a record.

- `<apex:inputField>`: This tag is used for an input for a field when editing a record in the Force.com GUI. This tag will automatically determine the right data type for the field and render it accordingly along with the built-in formatting for that input type.

- `<apex:outputField>`: This tag renders the value of a field as output like you would see when viewing a record in the Force.com GUI. This tag will automatically determine the right data type for the field and render it accordingly.

- `<apex:inputText>`: You can use this tag as an input for any text that might or might not be bound to a specific field on an sObject. This tag renders as an HTML `<input>` tag.

- `<apex:outputText>`: This is a somewhat generic tag that will render any text inside it. It can even render other markup, if you set its escape attribute to FALSE.

- `<apex:selectList>`: This tag renders as an HTML `<select>` tag or what's referred to as a picklist on the Salesforce1 Platform.

- `<apex:selectRadio>`: This tag renders as radio buttons that automatically enforce only one option being selected.

- `<apex:selectCheckboxes>`: This tag renders as a series of checkboxes that allow for multiple selections.

- `<apex:selectOption>`: This tag allows you to set one of the options for either a `selectList`, `selectRadio`, or `selectCheckboxes` component.

- `<apex:selectOptions>`: This tag allows you to set multiple options at once for either a `selectList`, `selectRadio`, or `selectCheckboxes` component. This tag must be bound to a list of `selectOption` objects in your controller or extension.

- `<apex:repeat>`: This tag loops through a list of objects and generates the nested markup for each one.

- `<apex:pageBlockTable>`: This tag generates the markup for a list view or related list table in the Force.com GUI. It is bound to a collection of objects and each row rendered is an item in that collection.

- `<apex:dataTable>`: This tag generates the markup for a standard HTML table. It is bound to a collection of objects and each row rendered is an item in that collection.

- `<apex:column>`: This tag is used in conjunction with tables. It allows you to specify the value of a column's worth of cells in a table.

- `<apex:outputPanel>`: This tag is perhaps the most useful tag. It can render as a `<span>` tag, a `<div>` tag, or just render what's nested inside it without taking on any tag itself.

- `<apex:pageMessages>`:This tag renders any error, information, or confirmation message added by your code or generated by a system validation.

 Visualforce tags are not visible in the HTML-rendered version of your page. This can make it a little harder to troubleshoot, but it means no one else will be able to tell that you wrote your page in Visualforce. You can use HTML comments, such as `<!-- like this -->`, to help mark where your tags are in your Visualforce page.

As the old saying goes, a picture is worth a thousand words. With this in mind, we've put together a Visualforce page that includes most of these tags and labeled each one accordingly. Unfortunately, this type of image is not included in **Visualforce Developer's Guide**, but lucky for you, you're reading this book!

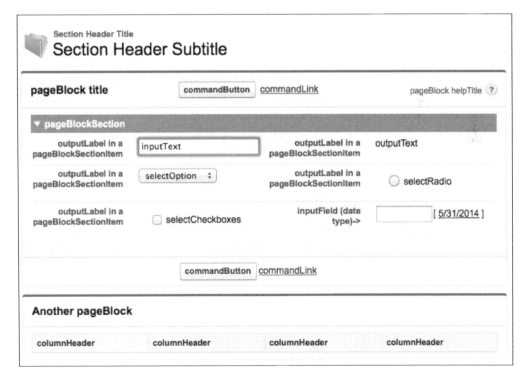

Taking control

In order for your Visualforce pages to be able to interact with your data or code, the pages must have a controller specified. A controller is a class that defines the variables and methods available to the page. There are two types of controllers: custom ones that you create and standard ones that are built in. The Salesforce1 Platform automatically includes a standard controller for every standard sObject built in to the platform. However, the brilliant minds at Salsesforce.com didn't stop there. As soon as you create a new custom sObject, the platform automatically generates a standard controller for that sObject. These standard controllers include the ability to access fields on a record, all related lists on a record, and even fields on related records. They also include the actions behind the standard buttons you would see when viewing or editing a record. As you modify the fields on an sObject, its standard controller is automatically updated too. It's like having a little coding butler!

In order for your page to know which sObject's standard controller to use, you must specify it in the `standardController` attribute in the `<apex:page>` tag, as shown:

```
<apex:page standardController="Account">
  <!-- markup goes here -->
</apex:page>
```

If your standard controller is for a custom sObject that you created, then the API name of the object ends with __c. Even though it's a custom sObject, its controller is provided by the platform, so it's considered to be a standard controller and is specified as shown:

```
<apex:page standardController="My_Custom_Object__c">
  <!-- markup goes here -->
</apex:page>
```

Tags that bind us

Most tags can be bound to either some data or an action. Data bindings are specified using the `value` attribute on a tag and always start with a curly brace followed by an exclamation point and end with a curly brace. Action bindings are specified using the `action` attribute on a tag and follow the same notation. Unlike calling a method though, you do not use parentheses in the `action` attribute. The following code is an example of an action and data bindings in a Visualforce page:

```
<apex:page standardController="account">
<apex:form>
<apex:outputField value="{!account.name}" />
<apex:inputField value="{!account.phone}" />
<apex:commandButton value="Save" action="{!save}" />
```

```
<apex:commandLink value="Cancel" action="{!cancel}" />
</apex:form>
</apex:page>
```

The Salesforce1 Platform already has an easy-to-configure interface. You can create your own custom sObjects, custom fields, validation rules, page layouts, and more. Sometimes though, the standard options are just not enough. Using the features of the standard controller, you can easily modify the look and feel of the Salesforce1 Platform to meet your needs without writing a single line of Apex code. In fact, one of the oldest requests for Salesforce is to change the standard two-column page layout to have three columns, as shown in the following screenshot:

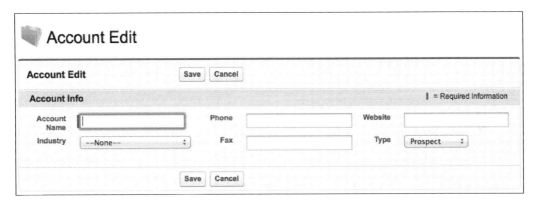

A three-column page sounds like a simple task, and it is. In fact, it's so easy to create one with Visualforce that we're giving you the code for no extra charge:

```
<apex:page standardController="account">
  <apex:sectionHeader title="Account Edit"
     subtitle="{!account.name}" />
<apex:pageMessages />
<apex:form>
  <apex:pageBlock title="Account Edit" mode="edit" >
    <apex:pageBlockButtons>
      <apex:commandButton value="Save" action="{!save}" />
      <apex:commandButton value="Cancel" action="{!cancel}" />
    </apex:pageBlockButtons>
    <apex:pageBlockSection title="Account Info" columns="3" >
      <apex:inputField value="{!account.name}" />
      <apex:inputField value="{!account.phone}" />
      <apex:inputField value="{!account.website}" />

      <apex:inputField value="{!account.industry}" />
      <apex:inputField value="{!account.fax}" />
```

```
          <apex:inputField value="{!account.type}" />
          <!-- keep adding more fields -->
        </apex:pageBlockSection>
      </apex:pageBlock>
    </apex:form>
  </apex:page>
```

As you can see, creating a three-column page is as easy as using the `columns` attribute in a `pageBlockSection` tag. In fact, you can put any integer you want in there, so go ahead and create a 10-column page if you want. Don't worry about what all those tags and attributes mean just yet; we'll go over all of them in this chapter.

Paging the doctor variable

The standard controllers are perfect for simple pages that just need to display data differently. Often though, you need to do more than just display data differently. You might need greater control over the data or logic for your page. When that's the case, you might choose to write your own custom controller instead of using the standard ones provided. Believe it or not, you already know how to write a custom controller. A custom controller is really just an Apex class. We refer to it as a controller because it controls the page. In fact, the only way to be sure that a class is a controller is to find a page that lists it as its controller. Otherwise, it's just a class with methods and variables.

 We discussed classes in *Chapter 4, Triggers and Classes*, so if you skipped that chapter, now is a good time to go back and read it. Be sure to pay attention to the steps on how to create a new class, as you'll need that now.

In order for an Apex class to function as a controller for a Visualforce page, the variables and methods in the class need to use the correct syntax. The variables in the class are made accessible to the page through the use of getter and setter methods. A getter method is a nonstatic method that has no input parameters and returns an object. Visualforce pages use getter methods to get objects from your custom controller. A setter method is a nonstatic method that has only one input parameter and does not return anything. Visualforce pages use setter methods to set the value of an object in your custom controller. Let's take a look at some getter and setter methods:

```
//First declare your variable
Account myAccount;

//Here is the getter
public Account getMyAccount(){
```

```
//We don't want to return a null value
if ( myAccount == null ){
  myAccount = new Account();
}
return myAccount;
}


//Here is the setter
public void setMyAccount(Account a){
myAccount = a;
}
```

Pretty neat, right? Just by naming our method `getX` or `setX` and using the right signature, they are automatically accessible by our Visualforce page. This just gets better; our getter and setter are using a whole record and our page has access to all of the fields on that record. We can even use a collection of records and have access to all of the records in the collection and all of their fields. In fact, your getters and setters can work with any object and your Visualforce page automatically has access to all of the instance attributes and action methods on that object.

Getters and setters seem simple, but the previous example really seems like a lot of code to just allow our Visualforce page to work with a single object. This is why Apex also includes a shortcut for getters and setters called properties. A property combines the instance of our variable with the getter and setter methods and greatly reduces the amount of code you need to write. Take a look at the property equivalent to the previous code block:

```
//Declare your property and you're done
Account myAccount {get;set;}
```

Yes, we are serious that one line of code replaces the variable and the getter and setter methods. It really doesn't get more efficient than that! Now, if you've been paying attention, you will see a flaw in our property. If our `myAccount` variable is null, our Visualforce page can get a nasty error. Our getter took care of that possibility, but our property does not. There are two options to get around this. Let's look at the first option:

```
//Declare your property with logic and you're done
Account myAccount {
  get{
    if ( myAccount == null ){
      myAccount = new Account();
    }
  }
  set;
}
```

In this property, we expanded the getter to include our logic. This combines the getter method with the property concept. Although perfectly legitimate, the second option is actually the most common one, and this is to set the value of your attributes in your class' constructor, as shown in the following lines of code:

```
public class myCustomController{

  //Here's our property
  Account myAccount {get;set;}

  //Here's our constructor
  public myCustomController(){
    myAccount = new Account();
  }
}
```

The key to this code block is in knowing that constructors are called prior to getters. This allows us to execute our code before the Visualforce page communicates with our controller. This pattern of using properties and setting their initial state in the constructor is very common and uses a lot less code. In fact, most classes used with Visualforce have a whole list of properties at the top of the class.

Actions speak louder than methods

Data bindings allow our pages to work with data and other objects defined in our controller. Action bindings allow our pages to execute a block of code in our controller. Just as a controller is a class, an action is just a method. In order for our page to be able to call a method, it must be an instance method, not have any input parameters, and must return a `PageReference` object or nothing at all (void).

A `PageReference` object is basically an object that represents a URL. It can be any URL you want, but typically it's a URL on the Salesforce1 Platform. When redirecting a user to another place on the platform, it's a best practice to use standard functionality to determine the correct URL rather than hardcoding it in. This ensures that if the directory structure should change in the future, your page will continue working. If you must hardcode the URL, then definitely use a relative URL. Remember that we write our code in a Sandbox environment. The subdomain of Sandbox URLs will differ from that of Production, so if you don't use a relative URL, you're going to have code that works in one environment but not the other. See the following examples on how to generate your `PageReference` objects:

```
//Create a pageReference to a URL outside of the platform
pageReference outside = new PageReference('http://thisbook.com');

//Create a pageReference using the built-in page class and the name of
your Visualforce page
```

```
pageReference visualForcePage = page.MyPage;

//Create a relative URL to a screen on the platform
pageReference relative = new PageReference('/001');

//Create a pageReference using the apexPages class (preferred)
pageReference standardView =
  new apexPages.standardController( new Account() ).view();
```

Just because your page is calling an action doesn't necessarily mean that you want the user to be redirected to another URL. In this case, your action can return null or you can use `void` as the output of the method instead of `pageReference`. This allows you to build pages with multiple steps that a user can interact with to perform complex processes. These actions can be called through the use of the following Visualforce tags:

- `<apex:commandButton>`: This tag renders as a clickable button that calls an action in your controller.
- `<apex:commandLink>`: This tag renders as a clickable hyperlink that calls an action in your controller.
- `<apex:actionSupport>`: This tag adds the ability to call an action to its parent tag. The action is called based on a JavaScript event such as `onchange` or `onclick`.
- `<apex:actionPoller>`: When this tag is used on a Visualforce page, the page will periodically call your action method over and over until certain criteria are met.
- `<apex:actionFunction>`: This tag renders as a JavaScript function that you can call from elsewhere in the page. When called via JavaScript, it will call your action method in your controller.

Let's take a look at what an action method looks like inside our class:

```
public class myCustomController{

public PageReference save(){
  insert myAccount;
  return new apexPages.standardController(myAccount).view();
}

public void cancel(){
  //don't return anything
}

}
```

Now that we have defined our methods to be used as actions, we can use the `action` tags with them, as shown in the following lines of code:

```
<!-- a standard hyperlink that calls our action -->
<apex:commandLink value="Cancel" action="{!cancel}" />

<!-- an input button that calls our action -->
<apex:commandButton value="Save" action="{!save}" />

<!-- a Javascript event added to an image -->
<apex:image value="http://www.thisbook.com/save.png" >
  <apex:actionSupport event="onclick" action='{!save}" />
</apex:image>

<!-- a Javascript function that can be called from elsewhere -->
<apex:actionFunction name="jsSave" action="{!save}" />
<script type="text/javascript" >
function doSave(){
  jsSave();
}
</script>

<!-- a poller that will keep executing each interval -->
<apex:actionPoller action="{!cancel}" interval="60" />
```

As you can see, there are a lot of options on how to use actions. Actions are what make our pages more than just simple input and output. They allow us to build dynamic interfaces that simplify complex processes. The more actions on a page, the more powerful it becomes.

Ajax your actions

If you're playing around with your Developer Edition while reading, you might have already tested out an action or two on your Visualforce page. If the page is simple, you probably didn't notice that calling an action re-rendered the entire page. However, if your page was complex with a lot of content, you would definitely notice it and probably be a little annoyed.

Well, this is the 21st century, so of course, the Salesforce1 Platform supports Ajax. You don't have to re-render the entire page every time anyone clicks a button or selects a value. In order to make your actions leverage Ajax, you have to use the `reRender` attribute on your `action` tag. The `reRender` attribute can contain one or more IDs of other Visualforce tags that you want to be re-rendered when the action is invoked. If you don't use the `reRender` attribute, then the entire page will be re-rendered. If you specify an ID that doesn't exist, then nothing will be re-rendered.

Let's assume that our business requirements state that the account name should not be changed after the record is saved. Of course, we can prevent this from occurring using Apex code or even declarative features. However, you don't want to even make it look as if a user can change the name, because they'll just complain when it doesn't work. Look at the following code block to see how we can use the reRender attribute to change a portion of the page when an action is called:

```
<apex:page standardController="account">
  <apex:sectionHeader title="Account Edit" />
  <apex:pageMessages id="pageMessages />
  <apex:form id="theForm" >
    <apex:pageBlock title="Account Edit" mode="edit" >
      <apex:pageBlockButtons>
        <apex:commandButton value="Save" action="{!save}"
          reRender="pageMessages, theForm" />
        <apex:commandButton value="Cancel" action="{!cancel}" />
      </apex:pageBlockButtons>
      <apex:pageBlockSection title="Account Info" columns="3" >
        <apex:inputField
        required="true"
        value="{!account.name}"
        rendered="{!account.id == null}"
        />
        <apex:outputField
        value="{!account.name}"
        rendered="{!account.id != null}"
        />
        <!-- keep adding more fields -->
      </apex:pageBlockSection>
    </apex:pageBlock>
  </apex:form>
</apex:page>
```

In this code block, we added an outputField tag to display the account name as text. Using the rendered attribute, we ensure that the outputField tag is only displayed after the record has been saved and thus has an ID. The rendered attribute is also used to ensure that the inputField tag is only displayed before the record has been saved and thus does not have an ID. This is a common pattern in Visualforce for those of us that do not like to create two different pages to edit and view a record. Used in conjunction with the reRender attribute on the <apex:commandButton> tag, it allows us to dynamically change just a portion of the page rather than the whole thing. The best practice is to re-render only a small portion of the page. However, you can only re-render tags that are already displayed. This sometimes means that you have to add an <apex:outputPanel> tag that will always be rendered around the tags that are dynamic.

> Visualforce can be a little vexing when it comes to
> re-rendering a page. It's a best practice to always include the
> ID of your `<apex:pageMessages>` tag when re-rendering a
> portion of the page. This will ensure that any error that occurs
> as a result of the invoked action will be displayed on the
> screen. Otherwise, the user cannot tell why the button they
> are clicking does not seem to work.

Communication is key

If you're very comfortable with programming methods, you might be scratching
your head a little right now. It's easy to understand how to call a method in your
controller from a page, but it seems to be impossible to pass parameters to that
method. Well, relax; you are correct. It is impossible to pass parameters into an action
method. Fear not though, because your methods still have ways of knowing the
values of your page variables. The key again is to understand the order of operation
for Visualforce. Let's review what happens the very first time you go to a page:

1. The controller's default constructor is called, which allows you to set
    your variables.
2. Setters are executed.
3. Getters are executed.

As we discussed earlier, your constructor sets the values of your variables.
Technically, your page can next call your setters, but usually the first time you go to
the page, there's nothing for it to set. Next, your getters are called, which allows your
page to know the values of the objects it needs to display.

Once you're able to view a page, you can fill out a form and then click a button to call
an action method. Now pay attention to what happens when you click this button:

1. Setters are executed.
2. An action method is executed.
3. Getters are executed.

Is it starting to make sense yet? Your page passes values to your controller via the
setters. The setters set the values of the variables in your class. Your method then
references these variables to perform some logic and updates other variables. Finally,
the getters are executed, passing the values of the variables back to the page. For
logic-focused programmers, it's not always intuitive, but once you understand it, it's
easy to make it work.

Param face

In addition to the variables in your class, you can also use URL parameters to pass values to your controller. One of the standard classes built into Apex is the `ApexPages` class. This class has a method called `currentPage()`, which can be used to get the `PageReference` object for the current page. As we discussed earlier, a `PageReference` object is basically just a URL, and a URL can have parameters and values in it. Your controller can get a map of parameters from the URL and use the values of these parameters to affect how your page should behave.

Typically, this pattern is used in the constructor for pages with a custom controller. System administrators can configure custom buttons on standard screens that redirect a user to a Visualforce page and pass in various parameters. Depending on where the button is located, the parameters and/or their values can differ. Your code gathers the parameters and determines what it needs to do. This usually looks something like this:

```
public class myCustomController{

  //Our property
  public String myId {get;set;}

  //Constructor
  public myCustomController(){
    if (
    apexPages.currentPage().getParameters().containsKey('id') ){
      myId = apexPages.currentPage().getParameters().get('id');
    }
  }
}
```

It might look complex, but this code actually makes a lot of sense. The `apexPages` class has a `currentPage()` method that returns a `PageReference` object. A `PageReference` object has a `getParameters()` method that returns a map, `<String,String>`, of the parameters in the URL. Maps have a `containsKey()` method that determines whether a parameter with the specified key exists. Maps also have a `get()` method that gets the corresponding value for the specified key and voilà!

Parameters can also be used when a user is interacting with a page they're already on. You can update the parameters in the current page using the `<apex:param>` tag nested inside an action tag. This technique is often used to debug pages that just don't seem to work properly. Take a look at the following markup that has a nested `<apex:param>` tag:

```
<!-- an input button that calls our action with some params -->
<apex:commandButton value="Save" action="{!save}" >
  <apex:param name="idParam" value="0123456789" />
```

```
        <apex:param name="nameParam" value="John Doe" />
    </apex:commandButton>
```

When the previous button is clicked, our `save()` method can get the value of the `myId` parameter as follows:

```
//Save action
public PageReference save(){
  String myId =
  apexPages.currentPage().getParameters().get('idParam);
  String myName =
  apexPages.currentPage().getParameters().get('nameParam);
  //Do something with these strings, like setting them as the    values
  //of some variables
}
```

As we've mentioned in the comments in the previous code block, these parameter values are typically set as the value of variables in our class. It only takes one line of code to do this, but there's an even easier way. The `<apex:param>` tag includes an `assignTo` attribute that allows you to automatically set the value of a property or pass the value to a setter in your controller, as shown:

```
<!-- an input button that calls our action with some params -->
<apex:commandButton value="Save" action="{!save}" >
    <apex:param name="idParam" value="0123456789"
    assignTo="{!myId}" />
    <apex:param name="nameParam" value="John Doe"
    assignTo="{!myName}" />
</apex:commandButton>
```

Now we don't even need to manually check the parameters in the page; they're automatically set for us to the appropriate variables.

Put your hands together

As we saw earlier, standard controllers include action methods for all the standard buttons, such as **Save** and **Cancel**. Custom controllers don't include any of those methods or attributes and have to be written from scratch. That's why our previous example includes both `save()` and `cancel()` methods; most of the input pages need both. Let's put our property, constructor, and action methods together into a complete class. Before we do though, we're going to make a few more changes; see if you can spot them:

```
public class myCustomController{

    //Our property
```

```
public Account myAccount {get;set;}

//Constructor
public myCustomController(){
  myAccount = new Account();
  if (
  apexPages.currentPage().getParameters().containsKey('id') ){
    try {
      Id accountId =
      apexPages.currentPage().getParameters().get('id');
      myAccount = [
      select Fax, Id, Industry, Name, Phone, Type, Website
      from Account
      where Id =:accountId
      limit 1
      ];
    } catch (exception e) { }
  }
}

//Save action
public PageReference save(){
  upsert myAccount;
  //Redirect them to view the new record
  return new apexPages.standardController(myAccount).view();
}

//Cancel action
public PageReference cancel(){
  //Send them back to the Accounts tab
  return new PageReference('/001/o');
}

}
```

We'll look at the markup for our page in just a little bit. Before we do, let's examine our controller. Like before, we have our property and its value set by our constructor. This time though, we have an `if` statement that examines the URL of the current page and checks to see whether an `id` parameter exists. This is an extremely useful technique to pass parameters into a page to alter its behavior. In this case, if an Account ID is passed in, we query for the record and use it instead of a new one. As we used a `try-catch` block, we don't need to worry about ensuring that the parameter value is a valid Account ID or the record actually exists.

You probably spotted that change; it was a big one. Did you spot the other difference? If you didn't, go back and look. Instead of performing an `insert` operation, we performed an `upsert` operation. An `upsert` operation is a special DML operation that will check to see whether the record you are operating upon has an ID. If it does, it performs an update; if it doesn't, it performs an `insert` operation. This will allow our page to work on both new records and existing records.

Now, let's look at our updated markup that uses the property in our custom controller instead of the standard controller:

```
<apex:page controller="myCustomController">
  <apex:sectionHeader title="Account Edit"
    subtitle="{!myAccount.name}" />
  <apex:pageMessages id="pageMessages" />
  <apex:form>
    <apex:pageBlock title="Account Edit" mode="edit" >
      <apex:pageBlockButtons>
        <apex:commandButton value="Save" action="{!save}" />
        <apex:commandButton value="Cancel" action="{!cancel}" />
      </apex:pageBlockButtons>
      <apex:pageBlockSection title="Account Info" columns="3" >
        <apex:inputField value="{!myAccount.name}" />
        <apex:inputField value="{!myAccount.phone}" />
        <apex:inputField value="{!myAccount.website}" />

        <apex:inputField value="{!myAccount.industry}" />
        <apex:inputField value="{!myAccount.fax}" />
        <apex:inputField value="{!myAccount.type}" />
        <!-- keep adding more fields -->
      </apex:pageBlockSection>
    </apex:pageBlock>
  </apex:form>
</apex:page>
```

As you can see, there's not much of a difference. So in this case, it really wasn't worth writing all that code in our controller, because we could have just used the standard controller instead.

Extending control

There are times where it might make more sense to use a custom controller, for example, if the page is not tied to a specific type of sObject. However, there are also times where the page is tied to a specific type of sObject and the standard controller makes more sense, but you just need one extra bit of data or functionality. Unfortunately, pages can only use either a standard controller or a custom controller, but not both.

Don't worry though, there's a simple solution. While you cannot use both a standard controller and custom controller, you can extend either of them with a controller extension. As you probably guessed, an extension is just an Apex class that follows certain syntax. Extensions really do allow you to have the best of both worlds. You can use the built-in functionality and only write code for what's not included. Your pages can actually use multiple extensions; this allows you to write reusable functionality that can be used across multiple pages.

Let's say that in addition to the standard `save()` and `cancel()` actions, we need a new custom action called `genericPhone()`. We can write an extension for the standard controller that will allow our page to call this action, shown as follows:

```
public class myExtension{

  Account myAccount {get;set;}

  //Constructor
  public myExtension(apexPages.standardController controller){
    myAccount = (Account)controller.getRecord();
  }

  public PageReference genericPhone(){
    if ( string.isBlank(myAccount.phone) ){
      myAccount.phone = '(818) 555-1212';
    }
   return null;
  }
}
```

In this code block, notice how the constructor for an extension differs from that of a controller. In order for the extension to extend a controller, it must have a constructor that has that controller as its input. In this case, we are extending a standard controller. We can then use the `getRecord()` method on the standard controller to set the value of our variable. Although the page was written for an Account record, the `getRecord()` method returns a generic sObject, so we have to cast it as an Account.

We mentioned that you can reuse the code in your extension across multiple pages. If you wanted to extend pages for the same sObject, the previous code will work fine. However, if you wanted to extend pages for different sObjects, you'd have to make a few modifications, as shown:

```
public class myExtension{

  sObject myRecord {get;set;}

  //Constructor
```

```
      public myExtension(apexPages.standardController controller){
         myRecord = controller.getRecord();
      }

      public void genericPhone(){
         //These 3 sObjects have a field named 'phone'
         if (
         myRecord instanceof Account ||
         myRecord instanceof Contact ||
         myRecord instanceof Lead
         ){
            if ( string.isBlank(myRecord.get('phone')) ){
               myRecord.put('phone','(818) 555-1212');
            }
         }
      }
   }
}
```

Now our `genericPhone()` method can be used on pages that use the standard controller for Accounts, Contacts, or Leads. But wait, what about a page that uses a custom controller? We can extend custom controllers too. In order to do so, you have to define a constructor that has the custom controller class as its input, as shown:

```
public class myExtension{

   sObject myRecord {get;set;}

   //Constructor to Extend a Standard Controller
   public myExtension(apexPages.standardController controller){
      myRecord = controller.getRecord();
   }

   //Constructor to Extend a Custom Controller that has a
   //Class name of myCustomController
   public myExtension(myCustomController controller){
      myRecord = controller.myAccount;
   }

   public void genericPhone(){
      //These 3 sObjects have a field named 'phone'
      if (
      myRecord instanceof Account ||
      myRecord instanceof Contact ||
      myRecord instanceof Lead
      ){
```

```
        if ( string.isBlank(myRecord.get('phone')) ){
          myRecord.put('phone','(818) 555-1212');
        }
      }
    }
  }
}
```

Extending custom controllers is a little more work because you have to write a constructor for each one. This makes the process a little less dynamic, but it's still better than rewriting the same method over and over in different classes. Now that we have our extension complete, let's take a look at the markup for a Visualforce page that uses the standard controller and our extension, shown as follows:

```
<apex:page standardController="account" extensions="myExtension" >
<!—note the extensions attribute above -->
  <apex:sectionHeader title="Account Edit"
    subtitle="{!account.name}" />
  <apex:pageMessages />
  <apex:form>
    <apex:pageBlock title="Account Edit" mode="edit" >
      <apex:pageBlockButtons>
        <apex:commandButton value="Save" action="{!save}" />
        <!-- add a new button to call our genericPhone() method --
          >
        <apex:commandButton value="Generic Phone"
          action="{!genericPhone}" />
        <apex:commandButton value="Cancel" action="{!cancel}" />
      </apex:pageBlockButtons>
      <apex:pageBlockSection title="Account Info" columns="3" >
        <apex:inputField value="{!account.name}" />
        <apex:inputField value="{!account.phone}" />
        <apex:inputField value="{!account.website}" />

        <apex:inputField value="{!account.industry}" />
        <apex:inputField value="{!account.fax}" />
        <apex:inputField value="{!account.type}" />
        <!-- keep adding more fields -->
      </apex:pageBlockSection>
    </apex:pageBlock>
  </apex:form>
</apex:page>
```

The `extensions` attribute allows us to reference the variables and methods in one or more controller extension classes. When using multiple extensions, the platform will start looking for the attribute or method in the first extension and then continue through the other extensions in the order last followed by the controller. This allows you to use the same names in multiple classes but still have some control over which one is used.

More internal goodies

Besides standard controllers, there are a lot of other built-in functionalities in the Salesforce1 Platform that you can leverage from your Visualforce pages without code. Most of these items are configurable from the GUI by a nonprogrammer. Just like we said earlier, if you don't have to write code to accomplish something, then don't. So, pay attention because this will save you time later.

Global variables

We've seen a lot of controllers that query for the current user's name. It's a nice touch to add a name to the screen and make it look personalized. It's also a total waste of time because you can access that information without even performing a query. As we mentioned in *Chapter 2, Apex Limits*, fewer queries is a good thing. The way you access it is by binding to a global variable. The platform includes a whole list of global variables that are cached and available to you without having to perform a query. These global variables are not only used in Visualforce, but also in declarative features such as formula fields, workflow rules, and validation rules. The following list presents some of the global variables; for the full list, check out **Visualforce Developer's Guide** available at http://www.salesforce.com/us/developer/docs/pages/:

- `$User`: This global variable gives you access to the values in fields on the user record of the person viewing your page.

- `$Profile`: This variable controls what a user can and can't do; sometimes, you need to know that in order to control how your page should behave.

- `$UserRole`: This variable determines where a person is in the corporate hierarchy. This too can help you determine whether to display certain fields or buttons based on the seniority of the user.

- `$ObjectType`: This global variable gives you access to the metadata about an sObject and its fields. You can use this to determine whether a user has access to an sObject or a field or what the appropriate label is for a field or sObject.

- `$CurrentPage`: Rather than writing Apex code to check for a parameter in the URL, you can use this global variable to do it and adjust your markup accordingly.

- $Action: If you ever need to call an action in a standard controller that your page is not using, you can use this global variable to do so.

- $Label: Labels allow you to create a library of text strings managed by administrators. We'll discuss labels later in this chapter.

- $Resource: Resources are files uploaded to the Salesforce1 Platform that can be inserted into your pages. We'll discuss resources later in this chapter.

Functions galore

You've probably heard of Microsoft Excel; who hasn't? A lot of the functions in Excel are also included in the Salesforce1 Platform. These functions can't be used in Apex but they can be used in Visualforce. Why would you ever write code to add two values together when your markup can do it for you? Besides the basic math operations, Visualforce includes dozens of other functions to operate on strings, dates, datetimes, and of course, numbers. They're all listed in **Visualforce Developer's Guide**, but here are some of our favorites:

- IF(): This is the most useful function. It operates like a ternary operator and accepts three parameters: the condition you are evaluating, the value if the condition is true, and the value if the condition is false.

- CASE(): There's no case method in Apex, but there is one in Visualforce! The first parameter is the expression you are checking. This parameter is followed by pairs of possible values and results. The last parameter is the result should no previous values be found.

- SUBSTITUTE(): This function allows you to replace text inside your data binding expression.

- FIND(): This function will find the first instance of text in a string.

- TODAY(): This function returns today's date.

- NOW(): This function returns the current date and time.

- DAY(): This is a function to extract the day from a date.

- MONTH(): This is a function to extract the month from a date.

- YEAR(): This is a function to extract the year from a date.

- TEXT(): This function converts a nonstring value to a string value.

- VALUE(): This function converts a string to a number value.

- URLFOR(): Use this function to get the URL out of a page reference.

- REGEX(): This function allows you to use a regular expression in Visualforce. This is much more efficient than a bunch of IF() statements.

You can use these functions inside your binding expressions, as shown:

```
<apex:outputText value="{!'Copyright '&TEXT(YEAR(TODAY()))}" />

<apex:outputText value="{!IF(5+5==10,'Math works','Oh no!')}" />

<apex:outputText value="{!CASE(
MONTH(TODAY()),
1,'Jan',
2,'Feb',
3,'Mar',
4,'Apr',
5,'May',
6,'Jun',
7,'Jul',
8,'Aug',
9,'Sep',
10,'Oct',
11,'Nov',
12,'Dec',
'Error'
}" />

<!-- This will output "Good Bye Mr. Bond" -->
<apex:outputText value="{SUBSTITUTE('Hello Mr. Bond','Hello','Good
   Bye')}" />
```

As you can see, it's fairly easy to use functions in Visualforce, and hopefully, they already look somewhat familiar to you. Each function is well described in **Visualforce Developer's Guide**, so before you embark on writing any Apex, always double-check the guide to see whether you can use a function instead.

Static cling

Web pages can have a lot of moving parts. The average site is much more than just plain HTML. There are **Cascading Style Sheets (CSS)** to define the look and feel, image files, JavaScript, and other elements to control and define the appearance and behavior of your page. In order to incorporate all these things into a Visualforce page, you'll need a place to store them. You can host them on an external web server, but that makes maintaining things more cumbersome. Why not host these files in the same place where you host your Visualforce pages, on the Salesforce1 Platform?

Static resources are files uploaded to the Salesforce1 Platform that can be used directly from Visualforce. Unlike Visualforce and Apex, they're uploaded and managed by system administrators from the setup console. The average end users can't access them directly, so they're typically changed less often than other files. The great news is that you don't need to write code to query for them, so they don't count toward our query limits. To create a new static resource, perform the following steps:

1. Click on the **Setup** link at the top of the Force.com GUI.

2. Navigate to **Developer | Static Resources**.

3. Click on the **New** button. The **New Static Resource** page appears.

4. Enter a unique name without spaces or special characters in the **Name** field. This is the name that you will use to refer to the static resource in your markup.

5. In the **Description** field, enter a useful description to let others know what this static resource is for.

6. Use the file picker to select the file from your computer.

7. Set the **Cache Control** field to **Public**, as shown in the following screenshot:

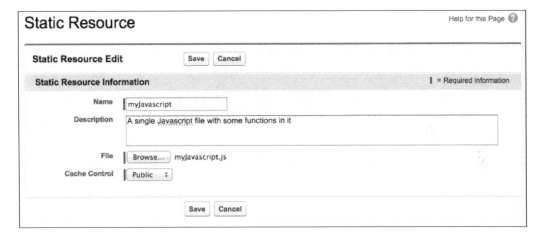

8. Click on the **Save** button.

Now that we've uploaded our static resource, we can reference it in Visualforce. Depending on what type of file you uploaded, you will use the appropriate Visualforce tag. The data binding for that tag will use the `$Resource` global variable along with the name of your static resource. The following demonstrates how to reference different resources:

```
//Reference a Javascript file uploaded as a Static Resource
<apex:includeScript value="{!$Resource.myJavascript}" />

//Reference an image file uploaded as a Static Resource
<apex:image value="{!$Resource.myImage}" />

//Reference a CSS file uploaded as a Static Resource
<apex:stylesheet value="{!$Resource.myCss}" />
```

In this code block, we referred to three different files uploaded as static resources. If you have worked a lot with CSS, you know that your styles often reference image files. This can be extremely difficult to do with static resources if you are uploading your CSS file and images separately. Fortunately, static resources support ZIP files, so you can upload an entire directory structure with CSS that refers to your images using relative URLs. In order to access these files, you have to use the `URLFOR()` function in conjunction with the `$Resource` global variable as shown:

```
//Reference a Javascript file inside our zip file Static Resource
//named webAssets
<apex:includeScript
value="{!URLFOR($Resource.webAssets, 'js/myJavascript')}" />

//Reference an Image file inside our zip file Static Resource
<apex:image
value="{!URLFOR($Resource.webAssets, 'images/myImage')}" />

//Reference a CSS file inside our zip file Static Resource
<apex:stylesheet
value="{!URLFOR($Resource.webAssets, 'css/myCss')}" />
```

As you can imagine, static resources make it very easy to migrate existing web pages to the Salesforce1 Platform. Even better, your graphic designers and web developers don't need to master Visualforce or Apex to still do their jobs. Once a static resource has been created, you can upload new versions of it without having to rename them. Your pages will continue to point to the same static resource record even though the file uploaded has changed. Just be sure to maintain the same folder structure; otherwise, your images, CSS, or JavaScript won't be loaded on the page.

Dynamic pages

Minds tend to change, so business requirements do too. If you hardcode text in your pages, it's likely that you'll be asked to revise that text at some point in the future. While this is great for your job security, it's not that great for your sanity. We'd much rather spend our time working on solving complex problems than tweaking text over and over. We hope you feel the same way, so we're now going to cover the ways in which you can make your pages more dynamic and even allow your business users or system administrators to modify how their pages are rendered.

Creating a custom label

The simplest way to introduce dynamic text into your Visualforce pages is through the use of labels. Labels are snippets of text that are managed from inside the setup console. This allows your system administrators to control the verbiage of text that is changed often without the need to modify your actual markup. The platform even includes a translation workbench, so your labels can be translated into other languages and used by users around the world. Perform the following steps to create a new custom label:

1. Click on the **Setup** link at the top of the Force.com GUI. The setup console page appears.
2. Navigate to **Create | Custom Labels**.
3. Click on the **New Custom Label** button. The **New Custom Label** page appears.
4. Enter a user-friendly name in the **Short Description** field.
5. Enter a unique name in the **Name** field.
6. Enter any categories that describe this label in the **Categories** field.

7. In the **Value** field, enter the text to be displayed when the custom label is referenced, as shown in the following screenshot:

8. Click on the **Save** button.

Once your label has been created, you can reference it in your Visualforce pages just like any other data binding, as shown:

```
<apex:page>
//Reference a Label
Here's our slogan:<br/>
<i><apex:outputText value="{!$LABEL.Our_Slogan}" /></i>
</apex:page>
```

Just like with static resources, you can delegate the management of labels to system administrators. Let them deal with the business users and their latest change of mind. Your page will work regardless of how they want to spell things.

Creating a custom setting object

The day might come when you have conflicting requirements from your users and it seems like everyone wants a page to behave differently. You can push back and say it's not possible or you can create multiple versions of the page and hope they go to the right one. If you're clever though, you can leverage a custom setting to allow users to set their preference and have your page use this preference to determine the appropriate behavior. Not only will you make everyone happy, but if anyone changes their mind later, they can just change their setting without you even lifting a finger.

You can create a new custom setting as follows:

1. Click on the **Setup** link at the top of the Force.com GUI. The setup console page appears.

2. Navigate to **Develop | Custom Settings**. The **Custom Settings** page appears.

3. Click on the **New** button.

4. Fill in the **Label** field with the name of your setting. For now, just use `personalSetting`.

5. Fill in the **Object Name** field the same as the **Label** field but without any spaces. For now, just use `personalSetting`.

6. Select **Setting Type** from the list given. For now, leave it on **Hierarchy**.

7. Select the **Visibility** field. For now, leave it on **Protected**.

8. Enter some helpful text in the **Description** field to let others know what this setting is for.

9. Click on **Save**. Your new custom setting object is displayed, as shown in the following screenshot:

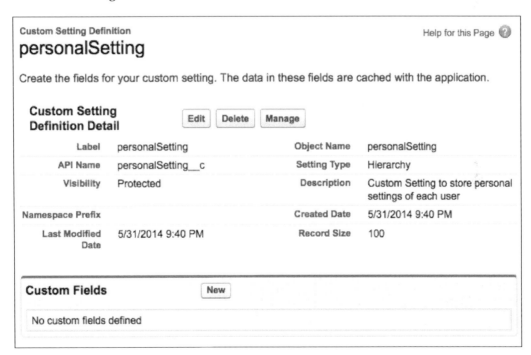

In these steps, we created a **Hierarchy** setting. A **Hierarchy** setting behaves like a personal setting unique to each user. When a user does not already have a setting record, their setting will default to that of their assigned profile. If this profile does not already have a setting record, then it will default to that of the entire org, which you (or a system administrator) can set ahead of time.

Just like with a regular custom object, once you have created your custom setting, you need to create custom fields on it. There are fewer field types for custom settings than normal sObjects. There are no picklists, long text fields, rich text fields, formula fields, or anything else that has an extra layer of complexity to it. The reason for these limitations is to ensure that custom settings are easy for the platform to cache and ensure that you use them for the appropriate purposes.

The main downside to using a custom setting is that users cannot access them through the Force.com GUI unless they are a system administrator. This means that you have to create a Visualforce page and controller to enable your users to modify their settings. In exchange for all these limitations, custom settings are cached and can be accessed without executing a query (one of our favorite things to avoid). Once again, the platform automatically takes care of things for you. When you create a custom setting, a new class is generated that has built-in methods to get your setting data. There's also a global variable called $Setup that automatically gains access to the **Hierarchy** type settings, so you don't even need to write any Apex code to access the data.

Let's assume that after creating our custom setting, we then created a custom field called `Favorite Color`. We can then reference the value in the field for the user viewing the page using the $Setup global variable as follows:

```
<apex:page>
//Reference a Label
My Favorite Color is
<apex:outputText
value="{!$Setup.personalSetting__c.Favorite_Color__c}" />
</apex:page>
```

Global variables are used in pages. If you want to get the value of the `Favorite Color` field into your custom controller, you use the automatically generated class for the custom setting and its `getInstance()` method as follows:

```
//Get the setting based on the current user
personalSetting__c thisUsersSetting =
  personalSetting__c.getInstance(userInfo.getUserId());
//Now get the value in the field
String favoriteColor = thisUsersSetting.Favorite_Color__c;
//NO QUERIES HERE!
```

The Salesforce1 Platform also includes a different type of custom setting called a **List** setting. These settings have the same limitations as **Hierarchy** ones, but are not tied to a specific user. Instead, they behave just like a normal table that stores data. They're not accessible via Visualforce, but they are still accessible via Apex without performing a query.

Regardless of the custom setting type, you can perform queries against them if you want to. You can also use our DML operations against them. So, they can be programmatically set rather than through the user interface.

Data-driven pages

Although a lot of websites out there are still based on static HTML, the majority of them have a database as part of their backend. There's no reason why you can't use the Salesforce1 Platform's database as the backend to store the markup for your web pages. In fact, this is the technique we have used time and time again for our customers. We still often leverage labels and settings, but the meat of the page is just stored as a string on a record in the database.

This technique allows you to take advantage of all the easy-to-use declarative functionalities built in to the Salesforce1 Platform along with the robust functionality of Apex and Visualforce. We start by creating a new custom object called `Webpage`. On this object, we then create a long text area field that can store up to 32,768 characters. This field will be used to store the HTML that will be rendered by our Visualforce page.

Typically, we also create fields to control the status of the page, the date/time that it should be published or expired, and so on. From here, you can interact with the custom objects and records just like you would with any other sObject. You can assign ownership of them to various employees, create an approval process for publishing, and even run reports on them.

Your Visualforce page can then use the `<apex:outputText>` tag to render the HTML code in the long text area field. In order to make this work, you have to use the `escape` attribute. This attribute defaults to TRUE, which means any markup inside it will be escaped and rendered as text. However, if you set it to FALSE, then the markup inside it will not be escaped and will be rendered as HTML instead! Take a look at the following sample page:

```
<apex:page standardController="Webpage__c" >
  <!-- various css -->
  <!-- maybe some Javascript -->
<apex:outputText
```

```
value="{!webpage__c.custom_long_text_area_field__c}"
escape="false"
/>
</apex:page>
```

As you can see from this markup, it really is easy. Best of all, it allows your business users to control the markup of a page without ever having to talk to you.

Visualforce components

Once you have mastered the use of Visualforce pages, you will have probably written many useful snippets of markup that you use over and over. While it's easy to just copy and paste these snippets, you can be more efficient and take advantage of Visualforce components. Components are stored snippets of Visualforce markup that you can reference multiple times in a single page or across multiple pages.

You can create a Visualforce component in the Force.com IDE as follows:

1. Right-click on your project and navigate to **New | Visualforce Component**. The **Create New Visualforce Component** window appears, as shown in the following screenshot:

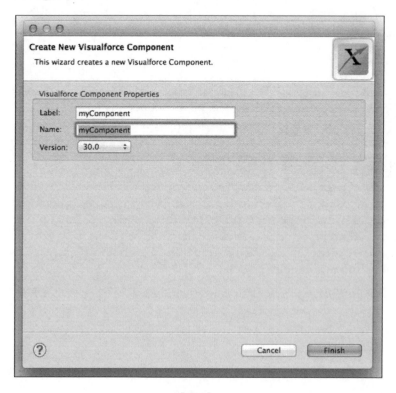

2. Enter the label and name for your new component. For this example, use `myComponent`.

3. Select the API version for the page. For this example, keep it at the default value.

4. Click on **Finish**. A progress bar will appear followed by your new Visualforce component.

Just like pages, components can include HTML, CSS, JavaScript, and Visualforce tags. They also support a special Visualforce tag called `<apex:attribute>`. Attributes allow you to define variables in the component. These variables can then be used to alter the way a specific instance of the component looks or behaves. Take a look at the attribute in the following sample component:

```
<apex:component>
  <apex:attribute
  name="bgcolor"
  description="Background Color"
  type="String"
  default="Red"
  />
  <apex:attribute
  name="color"
  description="Font Color"
  type="String"
  default="Black"
  />

  <table bgcolor="{!bgcolor}" width="100%">
    <tr>
      <td style="color: {!color}" >
      This table has a {!bgcolor} background and {!color} font
      </td>
    </tr>
  </table>
</apex:component>
```

As you can see in the previous code block, the first `<apex:attribute>` tag defines a variable that is used to set the background color of the table. The second `<apex:attribute>` tag defines a variable that is used to set the font color of the text in the table cell. In the previous examples, this variable is a string; however, it can be other data types, including an sObject, a collection, or even a custom class you wrote.

Components are used inside Visualforce pages using a different notation than standard tags. When you create a component, the platform automatically creates a new tag for you that starts with `c:` followed by the name of your component. So, to use our sample component, we will use the `<c:myComponent>` tag, as shown in the following Visualforce page:

```
<apex:page showHeader="false" sidebar="false" >
  <c:myComponent /> //Use the default bgcolor
  <c:myComponent bgcolor="Orange" />
  <c:myComponent bgcolor="Yellow" />
  <c:myComponent bgcolor="Green" color="Yellow" />
  <c:myComponent bgcolor="Blue" color="White" />
</apex:page>
```

Although little markup exists in the page, when rendered, the entire markup from the component is displayed five times. This allows you to easily change all instances of that markup by just modifying the one component instead of hunting down every place you pasted your snippet. Take a look at the following figure to see what the resulting page looks like, which shows a single component used five times in a page:

This table has a Red background and Black font.
This table has a Orange background and Black font.
This table has a Yellow background and Black font.
This table has a Green background and Yellow font.
This table has a Blue background and White font.

Your component library

Although we don't spend much time writing comments in our code in this book, it's definitely a best practice to do so. This is especially true for Visualforce components because they are designed for reusability. If you and your colleagues don't want to reinvent the wheel, then you need to provide descriptive information about your components. Fortunately, there's a built-in Description attribute in components just for this purpose. You can access this Description attribute on the metadata of the component. In case you don't remember from *Chapter 1, Apex Assumptions and Comparisons*, the metadata for a file is accessed in the IDE via the **Metadata** tab at the bottom of the editor, as shown in the following screenshot:

Once you've provided a useful description for all of your components, you and your fellow developers can browse through the list of components from inside the Force.com GUI, as follows:

1. Click on the **Setup** link at the top of the Force.com GUI.

2. Navigate to **Developer | Components**. The **Visualforce Components** page is displayed, as shown in the following screenshot:

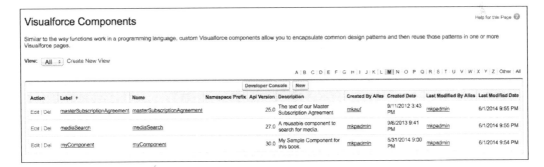

Controlling components

Components are not just for static markup. A component can have its own controller that enables users to interact with it. This is useful for web functions that occur on multiple screens, such as a search bar that only searches through records of the sObject in the standard controller. It's also useful for web functions that occur multiple times on a single page. A great example is uploading files. Normal behavior on the Salesforce1 Platform is to upload one file at a time. Most people are okay with this, but sometimes when you're uploading a long list of files, you might forget which ones you've already done. You could just use a Visualforce page with a bunch of `<apex:inputFile>` tags on it, but wouldn't it be so much cooler to perfect your upload user interface in a component and then reuse that component multiple times on the same page? Let's start by creating an Apex class named `fileUploaderComponentController`:

```
public with sharing class fileUploaderComponentController {

  public Attachment file {get;set;}

  public fileUploaderComponentController(){
    file = new Attachment();
  }

  public PageReference upload(){
    insert file;
    //we need to set the body to null to avoid the viewstate limit
    file.body = null;
    return null;
  }
}
```

Our controller is pretty simple. It has a property for the file that we are going to upload. In this case, we are uploading it as an `Attachment` object, but we can also upload files as a Document, ContentVersion, or Chatter FeedItem. It also has a default constructor to initialize our `Attachment` file (we don't want to get a `nullPointerException`). Finally, it has an `upload()` method that can be called as an action that inserts the file. This method also nulls out the body of the file after insertion. This step is necessary to avoid our view state limit. If you remember from *Chapter 2, Apex Limits*, in Visualforce, the view state is the state of all variables on the page. Most files are well over the limit, so it's necessary to null out their bodies after your DML operation.

Now that we have our component's controller, let's create a new Visualforce component called `fileUploader`:

```
<apex:component controller="fileUploaderComponentController"
  allowDML="true" >
  <apex:attribute
name="parentId"
assignTo="{!file.ParentId}"
type="Id"
description="Parent Record Id"
/>
  <apex:form>
    <apex:pageBlock mode="edit" >
      <apex:pageBlockSection>
        <apex:pageBlockSectionItem rendered="{!file.Id==null}">
          <apex:outputLabel value="File" />
          <apex:inputFile
          value="{!file.body}"
          fileName="{!file.Name}"
          />
        </apex:pageBlockSectionItem>
        <apex:pageBlockSectionItem rendered="{!file.Id==null}">
          <apex:commandButton
          value="Upload"
          action="{!upload}"
          />
        </apex:pageBlockSectionItem>
        <apex:pageBlockSectionItem rendered="{!file.Id!=null}" >
          <apex:outputLabel value="You just uploaded" />
          <apex:outputText value="{!file.Name}" />
        </apex:pageBlockSectionItem>
      </apex:pageBlockSection>
    </apex:pageBlock>
    <apex:pageMessages />
  </apex:form>
</apex:component>
```

Our `fileUploader` component has the `allowDML` attribute set to `true`. DML operations cannot normally occur in the controllers of a Visualforce component. To get around this, you must set the `allowDML` attribute to `true`. Note how our `<apex:attribute>` tag assigns its value to the `ParentId` field on the `Attachment` record. The `ParentId` field determines which record the attachments should be saved on. Later in the markup, we use the `rendered` attribute to ensure that the file picker and the `Upload` button are only displayed prior to the upload occurring. We also use the `rendered` attribute to display an output of the filename after the upload has occurred. This type of pattern provides a feedback system to the user so that they can be more confident that the upload occurred and remind them of the filename.

We now need to create the Visualforce page that will reference our component. Let's call the page `fileUploader`, and for now, let's assume we want our page to be used on Account records:

```
<apex:page standardController="account" >
  <apex:sectionHeader
  title="Upload Multiple Attachments"
  subtitle="{!account.Name}"
  />
  <c:fileUploader parentId="{!account.Id}" />
  <c:fileUploader parentId="{!account.Id}" />
  <c:fileUploader parentId="{!account.Id}" />
  <c:fileUploader parentId="{!account.Id}" />
  <c:fileUploader parentId="{!account.Id}" />
</apex:page>
```

We've kept our page pretty simple for now. It's using the Account sObject standard controller and has our component hardcoded five times. We pass in the ID of the Account record into the `parentId` attribute of our component. Our component then assigns this ID to `ParentId` of the file in our controller. Not bad, huh? Take a look at what the resulting page looks like:

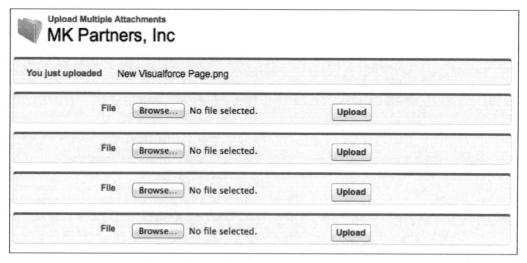

Uploading multiple attachments to an account using Visualforce

This looks pretty good. We can now create a custom button on the Account sObject that redirects the user to this page. Before we do that though, we want to turn it up a notch! Let's add some additional functionality to our Visualforce page. First, it needs a button to go back to the Account record we came from; otherwise, you'd never leave this screen. Next, let's add a functionality that allows the user to dynamically add more instances of our component to the page. Finally, let's really go crazy and make this page use a custom controller so that it isn't dependent on any one sObject's standard controller. In order to do all this, we'll need to create a new Apex class called `fileUploadController` that will be used as the controller for our page:

```
public with sharing class fileUploaderController {

    //Define a list of integers to loop through on our page
    public List<Integer> integerList {get;set;}

    public fileUploaderController (){
      //Get the id parameter from the URL
      Id parentId =
        apexPages.currentPage().getParameters().get('id');

      //initialize our integerList to avoid a nullPointerException
      integerList = new List<Integer>{1,2,3};
    }

    public void addInteger(){
      //add an additional item to our list
      integerList.add(integerList.size()+1);
    }

    public PageReference cancel(){
      //redirect the user to the view page for the record using
      //a relative URL
      return new PageReference('/'+parentId).setRedirect(true);
    }
  }
```

That's not much code for all of the changes we discussed. There are still a few more changes that we need to make to our page's markup though, so let's modify our `fileUploader` page to be as follows:

```
<apex:page controller="fileUploaderController" >
  <apex:sectionHeader
  title="Upload Multiple Attachments"
  />
  <apex:pageMessages />
  <apex:form>
    <apex:pageBlock>
```

```
        <apex:pageBlockButtons location="top" >
        <apex:commandButton
          action="{!addInteger}"
          value="Upload another file"
        />
        <apex:commandButton
          action="{!cancel}"
          value="Go Back"
          />
        </apex:pageBlockButtons>
      </apex:pageBlock>
    </apex:form>
    <apex:repeat value="{!integerList}" var="i" >
    <c:fileUploader parentId="{!parentId}" />
    </apex:repeat>
  </apex:page>
```

As you can see, our page has changed somewhat. We are no longer using a standard controller. Instead of hardcoding five instances of our component, we use the `<apex:repeat>` tag to loop through the list of integers in our controller. By the way, it didn't have to be integers; it could have been strings or any other object for that matter. For each integer in the list, we display our component. Every time a user clicks the button that calls the `addInteger()` method, our list increases in size and an additional component is displayed.

Before we can view the page, we need to create a custom button on the Account sObject that will redirect us to our `fileUploader` page and pass in the `id` parameter. Here are the steps to do this:

1. Click on the **Setup** link at the top of the Force.com GUI.

2. Navigate to **Customize | Accounts | Buttons, Links, and Actions**.

3. Click on the **New** button. The **Buttons, Links, and Actions for Account** page appears.

4. Click on the **New Button or Link** button. The **New Button or Link** page appears.

5. In the **Label** field, enter `Upload Multiple Attachments`. The **Name** field is automatically populated for you.

6. Select the **Detail Page Button** option for the **Display Type** radio buttons.

7. Select **Display** in existing window without a sidebar or header in the **Behavior** dropdown.

8. Enter the following in the content text area input:

    `"/apex/fileUploader?id="{!Account.Id}`

9. Click on the **Save** button. Your new button details are displayed, as shown in the following screenshot:

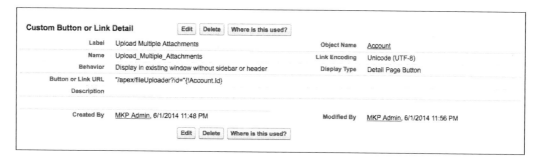

Now that we've created the button, there's one last step we need to take, and that's adding the button to our **Account** page layout:

1. Click on the **Setup** link at the top of the Force.com GUI.

2. Navigate to **Customize | Accounts | Page Layouts**.

3. Click on the **Edit** link to the left of your Account Layout. If you have more than one, you will need to do this on all of them.

4. In the **Field Chooser** box at the top, select the **Buttons** option.

5. Drag the **Upload Multiple Attachments** button from the box to the **Custom Buttons** section of the Account detail.

6. Click on the **Save** button.

7. Finally, you can see the fruits of our labor. Go to an Account record on the **Accounts** tab and click on the **Upload Multiple Attachments** button. You should see a screen that looks just like the following screenshot:

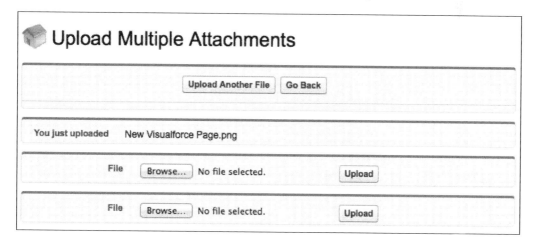

Wow! once again, we have provided you with fully functional code at no extra charge. This book is really the gift that keeps on giving. Be sure to order extra copies for your friends!

Summary

Well, you've made a lot of progress. Not only can you write code to control how the database behaves, but you can create beautiful-looking pages too. You're an Apex rock star and nothing is going to hold you back. It's time to show your skills to the world, and the next chapter is going to show you how to go global!

6

Exposing Force.com
to the World

We've seen in previous chapters how powerful, and easy to use, Visualforce and Apex are internally on the Salesforce1 Platform. Now it's time to take things one step further, kicking our game up a notch, and leveraging the collective power of the Internet.

This chapter will cover the different ways that Force.com is available outside the internal Force.com environment and revisit our discussion of limits as pertinent to implementing them. We'll also list common mistakes and pitfalls to save you from some frustration as well as from the pros and cons of each method, so that you can make an informed decision. After all, we want you to play safe online, and preferably not talk to strangers – unless they have yummy candy.

There's also a bonus goodie we'll cover once we have our web services set up and we'll even show you how to communicate from Force.com with other services, which will come in handy in subsequent chapters as well as for connecting to other things we'll work on throughout this chapter.

Three ways to skin a cat

The Salesforce1 Platform provides several ways to expose yourself online, but none of them include taking off your clothes, so keep your pants on – we're talking about code here. Although the Salesforce1 Platform provides a data API as well as a metadata API (which are out of the scope of what this title covers), you can easily create your own web services and public-facing functional pages using Visualforce and Apex, and we'll show you how!

Seeing is believing

This section is going to focus on exposing a public-facing page on the Salesforce1 Platform via Force.com sites. We're going to use two pages from *Chapter 5, Visualforce Development with Apex*, one with the component for colors (`componentExample`) and the other for modifying an Account (the 3 column example), which we've named `account3Column` for simplicity. There are a few steps to enable sites and configure them properly, so pay attention, and try not to skip ahead as later sections depend on this setup.

The following steps are required to enable Force.com sites for a Salesforce instance:

1. Click on the **Setup** link at the top-right of the Force.com GUI.

2. Under the **Build** section, navigate to **Develop | Sites**.

3. If you don't see a prompt to set up the site's domain name, as shown in the following screenshot, skip to step 7:

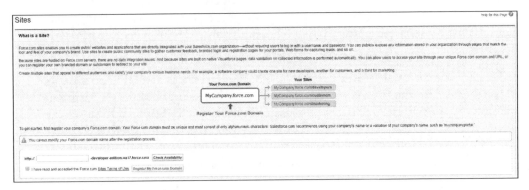

4. Enter in a domain name and click on **Check Availability**.

 If the domain exists, you will have to choose a different one. These domains must be unique across all of the Salesforce1 Platform. You may also not use reserved or trademarked words such as Apex.

5. Accept the terms and click on **Register My Force.com Domain**.

6. Click on **OK** to confirm that you cannot change your domain once set.

7. Click on **New** and fill in **Site Label**; **Site Name** will be auto-filled.

8. Check the **Active** checkbox (this enables the site).

9. Set **Active Site Home Page** to our `componentExample` page.

10. Click on **Save**.

Awesome! We now have a public site hosted on the Salesforce1 Platform. We used `PACKTLearningA` (because Apex is not allowed) and so the URL for our developer org site is `packtlearninga-developer-edition.na17.force.com`. Next step? Configure access so that our Force.com org allows our visitors to see what we want them to!

Access to everything on Salesforce1 revolves around profiles (as well as permission settings and other security settings, but these are also covered in this book). Chances are you are using the system administrator profile, which inherently grants you all the access you need. When we created the site, a new site guest user profile was created along with it and now we need to grant access as needed. The profile will typically be named after the site, so in this case it is called the `LearningApex` profile.

This profile is a little special, however, because you can't get to it via **Manage Users | Profiles** like every other profile type. To get to the site user profile specific to your site (you can have multiple sites in a single instance of Salesforce), perform the following steps:

1. Click on the **Setup** link at the top-right of the Force.com GUI.
2. Under the **Build** section, navigate to **Develop | Sites**.
3. Click on the site you are interested in under the **Site Label** column.

 This page shows us important information about the site, its configuration, status, and some statistics.

4. Click on the **Public Access Settings** button.

On this page you can configure all the access our guest user will need. For starters, they will need access to our `componentExample` and `account3Column` pages. To add these pages to the profile, perform the following steps:

1. It is assumed that you are already on the profile page, if not follow the previous steps 1-4.
2. Scroll down to **Enabled Visualforce Page Access** and click on **Edit**.
3. Find what you would like to add in the left column (**Available Visualforce Pages**) and use the **Add** button (right arrow) to move it to the right-hand side (**Enabled Visualforce Pages**).
4. Click on **Save** to enable your selection and return to the profile.

Notice that because we set our `componentExample` page as **Active Site Home Page**, it was automatically added to the Visualforce pages enabled for **Site Guest User Profile**.

 If your profile management screen looks different, it is likely that your organization is using **Enhanced User Profile Interface**. In this situation, Apex class and Visualforce page permissions would be found under the **Apps** section, along with object and field security settings.

Our visitors can now view both our `componentExample` page as well as the `account3Column` page. However, they would not be able to create new Accounts using our `account3Column` page because we never granted them access to the `Account` object, or the fields they need. Assuming you are still on the profile page, perform the following steps:

1. Scroll to the top and click on **Edit**.

2. Scroll down to **Standard Object Permissions**. **Custom Object Permissions**, if any, would appear below this section.

3. Click on **Create** next to **Accounts** and click on **Save**.

 Granting **Create** permission, auto-adds the **Read** permission, saving a click.

4. Now you are back at the profile page, scroll down to **Field-Level Security**.

5. Click on **View** next to **Account**.

6. Click on **Edit**.

7. Make sure all fields we need are **Visible** and not **Read Only**, which are as follows:

   ° **Name**

   ° **Phone**

   ° **Website**

   ° **Industry**

   ° **Fax**

   ° **Type**

8. Click on **Save** and then **Back to Profile**.

Now that we have set up all of our permissions, navigating to `packtlearninga-developer-edition.na17.force.com` will present us with **Active Site Home Page** and our `componentExample` page. If we want to visit our `account3Column` page, we can navigate to that specific page by going to `packtlearninga-developer-edition.na17.force.com/account3Column`. We could also add a link to this page on our `componentExample` page using the relative link `<apex:outputlink value="/account3Column">New Account</apex:outputlink>` for ease of access.

 You can also use valid HTML markup for your link `<a href="/account3Column">New Account</a>`.

Let's try our new page out. Navigate to `packtlearninga-developer-edition.na17.force.com/account3Column` and let's make a new Account called testing site. Click on **Save** after filling in the only required field, **Account Name**.

What happened?

Well, the Account was saved, but because we are using the standard controller for Accounts, the **Save** button takes us back to the view page for that Account, and the guest user doesn't have access to that. That's why we got an unauthorized access error page. There are many workarounds, but suffice it to say that when exposing things via Force.com sites, you must custom develop all display and input pages; you can only rely on the standard controller to pull in the ID automatically for you from the URL.

The best solution would be to use a custom controller or extension as discussed in *Chapter 5, Visualforce Development with Apex*. In your custom controller/extension, you could determine whether the current user is the guest user, and if so, call a different `save` method using the `rendered` attribute on the `<apex:commandbutton>` tag in your Visualforce page. Here is a quick extension to do just that:

```
public with sharing class accountExtension {

    //Holder variable for our Account
    public Account thisAccount {get;set;}

    //Boolean true if this is a Guest User, false otherwise
    public boolean isGuestUser {
      get{ //Defines the return value of the Getter
        return 'Guest'.equalsIgnoreCase( UserInfo.getUserType() );}

    }
```

```
        //Constructor which extends the Account Standard Controller
        public accountExtension(Apexpages.StandardController sCon) {
        //Retrieve our Account from the standard controller
    thisAccount = (Account)sCon.getRecord();
    }

    //Our custom save method
    public PageReference customSave(){
        upsert thisAccount; //Upsert Account
        //Display a confirmation message, styled like Force.com
        ApexPages.addMessage(
          new ApexPages.message(
            ApexPages.Severity.Confirm,
            'Account Saved Successfully'));
        return ApexPages.currentPage();
    }
}
```

 The ApexPages.Severity enumerator defines the styling of our message. CONFIRM is green schemed with a checkmark, ERROR is red with an X, and INFO is blue with an i symbol.

Ok, that's our extension (remember to add it to **Enabled Apex Class Access** on the site guest user profile). Now we have to make some changes on our Visualforce page, the changes are highlighted:

```
<apex:page standardController="account"
  extensions="accountExtension">
  <apex:sectionHeader title="Account Edit"
    subtitle="{!account.name}" />
  <!-- pageMessages will show our messages!-->
  <apex:pageMessages />
  <apex:form>
    <apex:pageBlock title="Account Edit" mode="edit" >
      <apex:pageBlockButtons>
        <!--Standard Save for non-guests-->
        <apex:commandButton value="Save"
          action="{!save}"
          rendered="{!NOT(isGuestUser)}"/>

        <!--Custom save method shown if Guest user-->
        <apex:commandButton value="Save"
          action="{!customSave}"
          rendered="{!isGuestUser}"/>

        <!-- Standard Cancel not shown for Guest-->
```

```
            <apex:commandButton value="Cancel"
              action="{!cancel}"
              rendered="{!NOT(isGuestUser)}"/>

    <!--Custom Cancel will take Guests back to componentExample-->
            <apex:commandButton value="Cancel"
              action="/componentExample"
              rendered="{!isGuestUser}"
              immediate="true"/>
        <!-- Immediate allows us to ignore required fields-->
        </apex:pageBlockButtons>
        <apex:pageBlockSection title="Account Info" columns="3" >
            <apex:inputField value="{!thisAccount.name}" />
            <apex:inputField value="{!thisAccount.phone}" />
            <apex:inputField value="{!thisAccount.website}" />
            <apex:inputField value="{!thisAccount.industry}" />
            <apex:inputField value="{!thisAccount.fax}" />
            <apex:inputField value="{!thisAccount.type}" />
        </apex:pageBlockSection>
      </apex:pageBlock>
    </apex:form>
</apex:page>
```

We now have a fully functioning page that makes some accommodations for our guest users. A message displays confirming the success of the save and remains on the page showing guests the new Account, while internal users are still sent to the default internal view page as shown in the following screenshot:

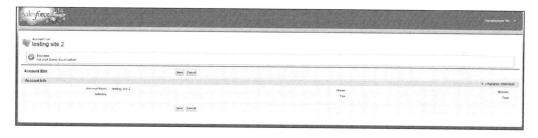

Let's make the user experience slightly better. Since guest users cannot edit Accounts (recall we were only able to give them **Read** and **Create** permissions), we should hide the **Save** button once saved, and **Cancel** should read **Exit**. Change the following two lines:

```
<!-- Once a record is Inserted in Force.com, it gains an Id, so that
will be our check-->
<apex:commandButton value="Save" action="{!customSave}"
rendered="{!isGuestUser && thisAccount.id != null}"/>
```

```
<!-- Conditionally change the display label on the button with
  same check-->
<apex:commandButton
value="{!IF(thisAccount.id==null,'Cancel','Exit'}"
action="/componentExample" rendered="{!isGuestUser}"
  immediate="true"/>
```

 If we take a look at this Account from within Salesforce, you'll notice that the record was created by the site guest user and also last modified by that user rather than one of our internal users.

Well there you have it, how to expose your Force.com customization via public-facing pages hosted on Force.com sites. What will you do with it next? Get creative, just remember to set permissions.

 When exposing pages to the public, it's rare that you will want the Salesforce branding, header, and sidebar on your pages; remember to turn these off using the following attributes:

showHeader="false" and sidebar="false".

Keep in mind this also takes away some of the standard stylesheets, so your pages may look different!

At your service

We now know how to expose Visualforce pages, which typically includes some custom Apex code as well (controllers/extensions), but the interaction is still rooted in a graphical user interface. What if we want to allow an external application to interact with our Force.com data in a way we can control? That's where custom web services come in. Currently, this can either be a REST or SOAP XML-based web service. Let's take a look at each, and then compare them side by side and explore a few nuances.

Let's REST

Arguably, the easiest web service to set up on Force.com is REST-based. Once you have a public site enabled (see the previous section), creating a public REST web service is a simple matter of creating a global class, setting the endpoint, and configuring permissions. Here is what a simple public GET REST web service to retrieve an Account we created earlier looks like:

```
//The first line must define this class as REST
//The urlMapping parameter defines the endpoint
```

```
@RestResource(urlMapping='/learnRest_Endpoint/*')

//the class must be global
global class learnREST {

  //Define GET behavior
  @HttpGet
  global static void response(){
    //Retrieve url parameters
    string acctId = RestContext.request.params.get('aid');

    //in case URI format was used /learnRest_Endpoint/aid
    acctId = RestContext.requestURI.substringAfterLast('/');
    string aName = RestContext.request.params.get('aName');

    //Query for Account record where the id is a match
    //Alternately find account where name is a match
    Account a = [select id, name, phone, industry, website,
    fax, type
    from Account
    where
    id = :acctId
    or
    name = :aName];

    //Use standard JSON methods to convert Account sObject //into
      JSON representation
    string responseValue = JSON.serialize(a);

    //Set return type
    RestContext.response.addHeader('Content-Type',
      'application/json');

    //Set value of return
    //For all return types other than text, should be blob
    RestContext.response.responseBody =
      Blob.valueOf(responsevalue);

    //Set the response code of the response
    //HTTP Response codes
    RestContext.response.statusCode = 200;
  }
}
```

When returning an sObject, or list of sObjects, from a REST web service method hosted through Force.com sites (as opposed to direct API), it is automatically returned as XML; JSON is the default return type for non-Force.com exposed REST services. The previous example, using a void return type, demonstrates how to manually set the response type and body in the event you wish to return a custom class or other JSON constructed object as your response.

Recall from earlier discussions that our site URL was `packtlearninga-developer-edition.na17.force.com`. To connect to our new REST web service, we use HTTPS and we would append `/services/apexrest/[name of mapping]`. This brings our new URL to look like `https://packtlearninga-developer-edition.na17.force.com/services/apexrest/learnRest_Endpoint`. Note that you can also expose your REST web service without using a Force.com site using `https://instance.salesforce.com/services/apexrest/[name of mapping]` and passing in a session ID. In order to retrieve your session ID, you would have to first create a connected app, and perform the OAuth flow, more on these later, but for now keep in mind that you do not have to expose a REST service through a Force.com site and are able to leverage existing authentication procedures to secure your service.

Based on our logic in the `@HttpGet` method, we can either pass in an ID or name as URL parameters to the service to retrieve an Account that matches. To verify our REST service is working, perform the following steps:

1. Open your favorite browser.
2. Go to `https://packtlearninga-developer-edition.na17.force.com/services/apexrest/learnRest_Endpoint?aName=testing%20site%202`.

We named our second test Account as testing site 2. URL parameters must be encoded, which makes it `testing%20site%202`.

Did you get a forbidden error? We did too. Can you think of what we forgot to do? Remember permissions on the site guest user profile! We need to revisit the profile and add our `learnREST` class to the enabled Apex classes like we did earlier for our custom extension. Here's a quick reminder how:

1. Navigate to **Setup | Develop | Sites**.
2. Select the appropriate site.
3. Click on **Public Access Settings**.

4. Scroll down to **Enabled Apex Class Access** and click on **Edit**.

5. Move `learnRest` from left to right and click on **Save**.

Let's try that again.

That's better, we received a JSON object representation of the Account we queried for, with the fields we queried for, along with some other standard data such as the sObject type as well as a data API link (for use in interacting with the record via the data API). See the following:

```
{
  "attributes": {
    "type": "Account",
    "url": "\/services\/data\/v30.0\
      /sobjects\/Account\/001o0000007zh9rAAA"
  },
  "Name": "testing site 2",
  "Phone": "(654) 654-6544",
  "Website": "website.com",
  "Type": "Prospect",
  "Fax": "(235) 235-2356",
  "Id": "001o0000007zh9rAAA",
  "Industry": "Agriculture"
}
```

The full range of HTTP method functional annotations that Apex REST provides you with are:

- `@HttpGet`: This is typically reserved for retrieval
- `@HttpDelete`: This is typically reserved for deletion
- `@HttpPost`: This is typically reserved for creation
- `@HttpPush`: This is typically reserved for augmenting data (or update)
- `@HttpPatch`: This is typically reserved for updating

Each of these HTTP methods can only be used once per class/mapping endpoint.

The `@HttpGet` and `@HttpDelete` methods both appear like a GET operation, in that they have no body in the request and receive input from URL parameters or through URI construction. The remaining methods appear like a POST, in that they can receive input via URI constructs or URL parameters, but also include a transmitted body with instructions/information/or data for processing.

Keep in mind that HTTP Patch is new and not all HTTP libraries include it. If you are using a library that does not include the HTTP Patch method, you can specify it via a URL parameter as follows:

? _HttpMethod=PATCH

We've taken a look at how to use a GET method ? with REST to accomplish something, now let's take a look at POST. POST methods can automatically decode JSON data into input parameters for your function, and can also access the RestContext request and response properties for retrieving URL parameters and configuring the response. Let's take a look at how we can update an Account by including attributes in the body, but also including a new name in the URL parameters in our updated learnRest class:

```
//The first line must define this class as REST
//The urlMapping parameter defines the endpoint
@RestResource(urlMapping='/learnRest_Endpoint/*')

//the class must be global
global class learnREST {

  //Define GET behavior
  @HttpGet
  global static void response(){
    //commented out, see earlier version for GET
  }

  //Define POST behavior
  @HttpPost
  global static void posting(Account acct){

//Retrieve URL parameters
    string aName = RestContext.request.params.get('aName');
    try{
      //Set new name if supplied
      if (string.isNotBlank(aName)) acct.name = aName;

//Upsert Account
    upsert acct;

//Success
    RestContext.response.statusCode = 200;
    RestContext.response.responseBody = blob.valueof('Success');
    }
```

```
    catch(Exception e){

//Error
      RestContext.response.statusCode = 400;
      RestContext.response.responseBody =
      blob.valueOf(e.getLineNumber()+' | Error: '+e.getMessage());
    }
  }
}
```

Our `@HttpPost` method has been configured to accept a JSON Account object in the POST body and an URL parameter `aName` for the new name of the Account.

If you use Chrome, the easiest way to test our new `@HttpPost` method is to use the REST Console extension (`https://chrome.google.com/webstore/detail/rest-console/cokgbflfommojglbmbpenpphppikmonn`). You can use any other method of *POSTing* to test if you don't use Chrome. Here are the steps to test using the REST Console extension:

1. Set **Request URI** to your endpoint (including the URL parameter):

   ```
   https://packtlearninga-developer-edition.na17.force.com/services/
   apexrest/learnRest_Endpoint
      ?aName=newName
   ```

2. Set **Request Method** to POST.

3. Set **Content-Type** to `'application/json'`.

4. Set **RAW Body** to the following:

   ```
   {
     "acct": {
       "Name": "testing site 2",
       "Phone": "(654) 654-6544",
       "Website": "website.com",
       "Type": "Prospect",
       "Fax": "(235) 235-2356",
       "Id": "001o0000007zh9rAAA",
       "Industry": "Agriculture"
     }
   }
   ```

   Note that the JSON object is defined as `acct`, which is the same name as the Account type parameter for our method, for automatic decoding.

5. Click on **Send**.

If all is well, you should see **Success** in the **Response** section of the page, which is what we configured our service to return. If you go back and look at the Account in Salesforce now, your changes should be reflected (we only changed the Account name, but you can modify any of the attributes and resubmit to see it changing; just remember to use a valid Account ID). Please note that although you would typically not pass both a payload as well as parameter values in a RESTful approach, the previous example serves to demonstrate just how flexible you can make your service be.

In the previous methods, both the `RestContext.Response` and `RestContext.Request` properties of `RestContext` were used, and they are pivotal to REST functionality. They are simple and straightforward classes with a fair amount of power, the major properties are:

- `RestContext.Request.Headers`: This represents a map of request headers

- `RestContext.Request.httpMethod`: This represents which HTTP method was used

- `RestContext.Request.params`: This represents a map of URL parameters

- `RestContext.Request.remoteAddress`: This represents an IP of the requesting client

- `RestContext.Request.requestBody`: This represents a body of the request as blob

- `RestContext.Response.responseBody`: This represents a body of the response as blob

- `RestContext.Response.headers`: This represents a map of headers of the response

- `RestContext.Response.StatusCode`: This represents the status code of the response

The more you can make these `RestContext` properties work for you, the more you can make your REST logic handle complex operations. It is important to keep in mind exactly what you are permitting users to do. In this case, we are allowing anyone (public) to read as well as write to our database. Sometimes this is desirable, but security must be taken into account whenever you expose a public service. You can limit the amount of data that can be viewed using the `with sharing` keyword as well as explicit exclusion of data in your methods, by requiring custom-generated API keys or using authentication procedures and session IDs.

Getting SOAP

Where the REST services are pretty quick and painless to implement and use, SOAP is a stickler and much more finicky in who can connect and what it can accept. For starters, all requests must be made with HTTP POSTs. Let's look at some differences that make our classes available as SOAP web services:

```
//Web service methods must be contained in global classes
global class learnSOAP {

  //Define method
  static string updateAccountName(id acctId, string newName){
    // Do something here
  }
}
```

Our declaration here exposes the `updateAccountName()` method globally, but that's still internal and it's not a web service yet! With some minor changes, we can make our code attain its full potential as a full-blown web service, as shown:

```
global class learnSOAP {

  //Define web service method using 'webservice' keyword
  webservice static string updateAccountName(id acctId, string
    newName){

    //String to hold return message
    string resultMessage;

    try{
      //Instantiate a new Account with existing Id
      Account a = new Account(id=acctid);

        //Set account name
        a.name = newName;
        update a; // perform DML
        resultMessage = 'Success'; //set success
    }
    catch(Exception e){
      //Catch exception and gather information
      resultMessage = e.getLineNumber()+ ' | ';
      resultMessage += 'Error: '+e.getMessage();
    }
    return resultMessage; //return
  }
}
```

Now that there is a web service method in our global class, **Web Services Description Language** (**WSDL**) has automatically been generated for it, and is available for download and distribution from the GUI.

To find this, perform the following steps:

1. Click on the **Setup** link at the top of the Force.com GUI.

2. Under the **Build** section, navigate to **Develop | Apex Classes**. You should see the following screen:

			Developer Console	
Action	**Name** ↑	**Namespace Prefix**	**Api Version**	**Status**
Edit | Del | Security	learnREST		30.0	Active
Edit | Del | WSDL | Security	learnSOAP		30.0	Active

3. Right-click on the **WSDL** link and click on **Save As** to generate the WSDL file and download.

 Some browsers open the WSDL file as an XML file in the browser. This method allows you to download it without worrying about that.

This WSDL file acts as your de facto documentation of your web service. Granted, it's not very human readable, but those you share it with may have a way to consume it in order to generate a class for them to use to interact with your web service.

Recall that it was mentioned earlier that in order to use a SOAP web service on the Salesforce1 Platform, you have to first log in with a valid user (with API permissions) and retrieve the session ID. In order to do so, you need to use the Enterprise web services endpoint for Force.com to call the standard `login()` method. To find this file and provide it to others, perform the following steps:

1. Click on the **Setup** link at the top-right of the Force.com GUI.

2. Under the **Build** section, navigate to **Develop | API**.

3. Locate **Enterprise WSDL heading**.

4. Right-click and select **Save As** on **Generate Enterprise WSDL**.

If there are installed packages in your organization, this method will not work as the **Generate Enterprise WSDL** link, which will take you to a page to select which version of those packages you wish to include, with a button to generate WSDL. If your browser opens WSDL files as XML documents in the browser, the only way around this is to then copy and paste the entire contents of the next screen into a text editor and save the file with a `.wsdl` extension. You will want to omit the `This XML file does not appear to have any style information associated with it. The document tree is shown below.` line and start with the `<!--`.

Since all we need from this WSDL file is the `login` method for our purposes, we've extracted it for you here. The following is the RAW XML you'll need to post (replacing the username and password with your own):

```
<soapenv:Envelope
  xmlns:soapenv="http://schemas.xmlsoap.org/soap/envelope/"
  xmlns:urn="urn:enterprise.soap.sforce.com">
  <soapenv:Body>
    <urn:login>
      <urn:username>YOUR USERNAME</urn:username>
      <urn:password>YOUR PASSWORD</urn:password>
    </urn:login>
  </soapenv:Body>
</soapenv:Envelope>
```

Taking this body, you will POST it to the Enterprise SOAP service endpoint, `https://login.salesforce.com/services/Soap/c/32.0`.

Note 32.0. You've seen it numerous times by now. It's the version of the API you are trying to use. Keeping in mind that Salesforce guarantees backwards compatibility, it's not an issue for something like the `login()` method. However, if you want to use new functionality that was not available in a previous release, you must use the first API version it was available in or higher.

The response will contain important information for you as well as more information that is not needed for our current discussion, so we've trimmed it out, and highlighted the two most important pieces of information:

```
<soapenv:Envelope xmlns:soapenv="http://schemas.xmlsoap.org/soap/
envelope/" xmlns="urn:enterprise.soap.sforce.com" xmlns:xsi="http://
www.w3.org/2001/XMLSchema-instance">
  <soapenv:Body>
```

```
      <loginResponse>
        <result>
          <passwordExpired>false</passwordExpired>
            <sandbox>false</sandbox>
            <serverUrl>https://na17.salesforce.com/
            services/Soap/c/30.0/00Do0000000aSGl</serverUrl>
            <sessionId>00Do0000000aSGl!ARcAQCVCdN0hrr.
            9keK1aGsJaKo9KKOZ_O4QDOd4clgLscC.
            mP8e6J2GoxeqeLPCstlbAaTFDXOp9OQdAe47FR86pR7n6Ldu
            </sessionId>
            <userId>005o0000000jjdIAAQ</userId>
          <userInfo>
            <organizationId>00Do0000000aSGl</organizationId>
            <profileId>00eo0000000ujCTAAY</profileId>
            <sessionSecondsValid>7200</sessionSecondsValid>
            <userEmail>test@test.com</userEmail>
            <userFullName>First Last</userFullName>
            <userId>005o0000000jjdIAAQ</userId>
            <userName>test@test.com</userName>
            <userType>Standard</userType>
            <userUiSkin>Theme3</userUiSkin>
          </userInfo>
        </result>
      </loginResponse>
    </soapenv:Body>
  </soapenv:Envelope>
```

The most important piece of information in the response at this stage of our discussion is serverUrl, sessionId, and how long sessionId will be valid for in seconds (sessionSecondsValid), but it also provides you with organizationId, userId, profileId, userType, and other information about the user and organization that can help you construct better logic as your web services get more involved.

Now that we have serverUrl and sessionId, we can call any web service method we have exposed across the instance of Salesforce. serverUrl denotes which Force. com server your organization's instance of Salesforce is hosted on. To use our web service methods, we have to connect to the correct server. Here is the RAW XML to utilize our updateAccountName web service method:

```
<soapenv:Envelope xmlns:soapenv="http://schemas.xmlsoap.org/soap/
envelope/" xmlns:lear="http://soap.sforce.com/schemas/class/
learnSOAP">
  <soapenv:Header>
    <lear:SessionHeader>
      <lear:sessionId>YOUR SESSION ID</lear:sessionId>
    </lear:SessionHeader>
```

```
      </soapenv:Header>
      <soapenv:Body>
        <lear:updateAccountName>
          <lear:acctId>THE ACCOUNT ID</lear:acctId>
          <lear:newName>THE NEW NAME</lear:newName>
        </lear:updateAccountName>
      </soapenv:Body>
    </soapenv:Envelope>
```

Taking this body, you will POST it to the SOAP endpoint for the server instance you are on. If you look at serverUrl retrieved in the login() method response, you can pull out the server instance, it's the bit before salesforce.com. In this case, na17, and add in the SOAP services bit similar to how the REST service endpoint is constructed https://na17.salesforce.com/services/Soap/class/learnSOAP.

 Notice the long jumble of characters at the trailing end of serverUrl that is organizationId (also provided on its own in the login() response).

The response this time around is fairly short, consisting of only what we have included in it, which is a simple string of Success, as follows:

```
<soapenv:Envelope
  xmlns:soapenv="http://schemas.xmlsoap.org/soap/envelope/"
  xmlns="http://soap.sforce.com/schemas/class/learnSOAP">
  <soapenv:Body>
    <updateAccountNameResponse>
    <result>Success</result>
    </updateAccountNameResponse>
  </soapenv:Body>
</soapenv:Envelope>
```

If we had forgotten to include the Account ID in our request, we would have caught the exception and modified our response to look like the following code:

```
<soapenv:Envelope
  xmlns:soapenv="http://schemas.xmlsoap.org/soap/envelope/"
  xmlns="http://soap.sforce.com/schemas/class/learnSOAP">
  <soapenv:Body>
    <updateAccountNameResponse>
      <result>11 | Error: Invalid id value for this SObject
      type:</result>
    </updateAccountNameResponse>
  </soapenv:Body>
</soapenv:Envelope>
```

Our response message includes the line on which the error occurred as well as the exact error message that was returned by the system; in this case, attempting to assign a blank value as an ID of an Account.

 We added in a condition for passing in a blank value for name so that would not have generated an error.

You're probably very anxious to test your new web service now? Right, of course, you are! Our tool of choice for SOAP tests is an application called SOAP UI, www.soapui.org. You don't need the pro version, just the plain online regular will do. Once you have it downloaded and installed, perform the following steps:

1. Navigate to **File | New soapUI Project**.

2. Give your project a name, such as `Apex SOAP test`.

3. For **Initial WSDL/WADL**, navigate to the Enterprise WSDL file we downloaded before.

4. Leave the **Create Requests** checkbox checked (or check whether it's unchecked).

5. Once the project is created, right-click on the project in the project explorer left sidebar.

6. Select **Add WSDL** and select the WSDL file for our `learnSOAP` Apex class.

7. Under the `SoapBinding` node, find the `login` method.

8. Expand it to find the sample request and open it.

9. Replace this request with ours or modify as needed.

10. Click on the green arrow to send the request and receive your session ID.

11. Copy your session ID.

12. Collapse `SoapBinding` and expand `learnSoapBinding`.

 If you named your class differently, `learnSoapBinding` will not be its name.

13. Expand `updateAccountName` for the sample request.

14. Repeat the process of sending a request to receive response.

SOAPUI Request action panel with green send arrow:

That's it for SOAP! Time to get your hands dirty with some elbow grease and let your imagination run wild with the possibilities; just don't forget the SOAP when you clean up.

JavaScript buttons jubilee

A neat side effect of the SOAP web service methods we just wrote is that they are now accessible via JavaScript thanks to the AJAX toolkit. What this means to you is that if you have a very simple operation to perform, where going to the edit page is a nuance and a Visualforce page is overkill, you can create an OnClick JavaScript button. The following snippet is your template:

```
//Required Import Statements
{!REQUIRESCRIPT("/soap/ajax/32.0/connection.js")}
{!REQUIRESCRIPT("/soap/ajax/32.0/apex.js")}

//Call your method, replace variables as needed
sforce.apex.execute("CLASS NAME", "METHOD NAME",{PARAM :
  '{!VALUE}' });

//Refresh the page to show updates to current record
location.reload(true);
```

> If you are not actually modifying data on the current view page, you can omit the location reload. Refreshing the page is only required so that any data updates your web service method does to the current record you are viewing are visible once the process completes.

Here are the steps to create an OnClick JavaScript button:

1. Click on the **Setup** link at the top of the Force.com GUI.
2. Navigate to **Customize | Account | Buttons, Links, and Actions**.
3. Fill in **Label** and **Name** (the label is what will show as button text).
4. Select **Detail Page Button**.
5. For **Behavior**, select **Execute JavaScript**.
6. **Content Source** should be set to **OnClick JavaScript**.
7. Paste the JavaScript code into the edit area and you are done!

Using this template and our `updateAccountName()` web service method, the following code would execute the method, updating the Account name to `JavaScript is cool`, and refresh the page so it is visible:

```
//Required Import Statements
{!REQUIRESCRIPT("/soap/ajax/32.0/connection.js")}
{!REQUIRESCRIPT("/soap/ajax/32.0/apex.js")}

//Call your method, replace variables as needed
var result = sforce.apex.execute("learnSOAP",
  "updateAccountName",{acctId : '{!Account.Id}', newName :
  'JavaScript is cool' });

//Recall our web service method returns a success/error string.
if (result == 'Success'){
  //Refresh the page to show updates
  location.reload(true);
}
else {alert(result); }//show errors
```

You can also use JavaScript prompts to collect information to pass to the method in the first place! Also, if you make your result response more elaborate, for example, a JSON object, you can also do more complex logic in your JavaScript function based on the response.

Your completed button (and layout) should look something like this:

Account Detail Edit Delete Include Offline Update Name to JS is cool

Account Owner   Michael Wicherski [Change]

Account Name   Burlington Textiles Corp of America. [View Hierarchy]

Account name before clicking button

By clicking the button, we get the following result:

Account Detail Edit Delete Include Offline Update Name to JS is cool

Account Owner   Michael Wicherski [Change]

Account Name   JavaScript is cool [View Hierarchy]

You'll have to add the button to **Page Layout** in order to actually see and click it (navigate to **Setup** | **Customize** | **Account** | **Page Layouts**).

For your consideration

When deciding on which technology to use to interact with other systems, there are several aspects to keep in mind. What are our limitations, what are the other system's limitations, do we need authentication, should our data be XML or JSON? and so on.

If you are creating users that will only be interacting with your web services and APIs, you can mark this on their profile as API-only to protect the rest of your organization. Also, unless you specify IP range whitelists for your users' profiles, a security token will be required in order to authenticate the user and retrieve a valid session ID for use. A security token is a unique string that is generated on request from a user's personal settings and is tied to the password, meaning that it is reset when the user changes their password.

Pros and cons

As with everything else in life, there are pros and cons to every decision we make. We're going to choose to use a table for these, as follows:

	Force.com site	REST	SOAP
Return type	Page	Can be custom defined	XML only
Accessibility	Public via sites, private with authenticated user (community/portal)	Public, via sites, private with authenticated user	Private, requires login
Platform limitations	Site page views, view state limits	Site page views and API requests	API requests
Ease of writing	Easy like HTML	Loosely typed	Strongly typed
Flexibility	Extreme	At most 5 distinct branches based on `Http` method per class	No technical limit to methods per class
Error handling	What you add in	Limited	Strong
Graphical interface	Yes	No	No

Limits

Public REST web services (which also consume API requests) and Force.com sites share a site page view limit. Since limits change, don't take this number to be final, but the current limit for Enterprise edition instances is 500,000 page views per month, while Unlimited/Performance editions start with 1,000,000 page views per month. Additional page views can be purchased if needed. For a public REST web service, a view is counted as a single request made to the service. If you perform a GET 5 times, that counts as 5 views (and 5 API requests). Visualforce pages are a bit more complex to account for, but there is a whole knowledge base article about it available from Salesforce at `https://help.salesforce.com/HTViewHelpDoc?id=sites_limits.htm`. This link may change, but searching for `Force.com Sites Limits` will bring it up on your search engine of choice.

Private REST and SOAP services, on the other hand, count against an organization's API request limit and do not influence site page views. There is a static number that the cap starts at for these per organization and is increased with each additional user license, and additional increases can be purchased as well. There is a standard report for monitoring API usage under **Administrative Reports**, and a package of reports related to site view statistics available on AppExchange called **Force.com Sites Usage Reporting**.

Pitfalls and gotchas

We've all been there when learning a new platform or language, anything new really. We sit and beat our heads against the wall trying to figure out why something isn't working as intended; after all, we followed the instructions to the last letter! Well, fear not! We've got your back; the following is a compiled list of the most common mistakes first timers and veterans alike make, which cause happy hour at the local watering hole to be so appealing.

Profile permissions

Our colleagues have a rule of thumb: if you can't find the error in your code in 15 minutes, that's not where the problem is. If you're having trouble getting any of the previous code to work, but it compiles, check and make sure your permissions are set up correctly! Things to look for include:

- Figure out which profile the user experiencing an issue is assigned. If this is for a public REST service, this would be the site public access settings for the specific site domain being used. For private REST services, the profile for the authenticated user should be checked.
- Is the **Visualforce page / Apex** class enabled for the profile?

- Are objects exposed with the necessary CRUD permissions, such as:
  - ◦ Create
  - ◦ Read
  - ◦ Update
  - ◦ Delete

- Are the fields you are interested in visible? If trying to edit, are they set to read only?
- Is the API enabled under administrative privileges (if applicable)?
- Are there any other restrictions such as IP ranges and so on?

There are some screenshots for visual cues on where to find some of these, which are as follows:

API Enabled has been checked

 Keep in mind that this permission is not applicable for some profile types.

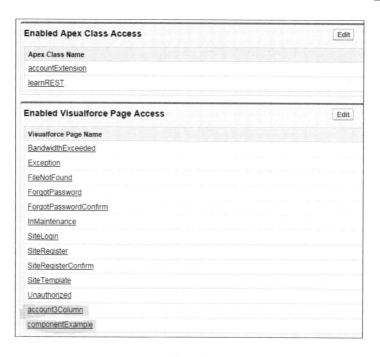

Code happens

Beginner and veteran alike, we all make mistakes from time to time. The hardest mistakes to spot are when our code compiles but encounters either a runtime exception or behaves differently than what we are convinced should be happening. Some things to look out for in this category include:

1. Visibility is hard to get wrong, the compiler will typically catch these, unless….

2. Sometimes we'll declare instance variables in a method with the same name as a class variable (reused variables), and so the values are not what we expect them to be if we set visibility incorrectly and the compiler doesn't catch these.

   ° Typos in our URL mapping or method definitions.

   ° Overloaded methods (different parameters) are not in sync from a recent update to one, but not all variations.

   ° Overly generic `try-catch` blocks, where everything is wrapped into a giant generic exception `try-catch` and you have not accounted for all possible errors so your `try-catch` feedback message is not accurate as to what the real issue is.

   ° Missing characters/typos in any kind of dynamic query/binding. Admit it, you've done the comma hunt at some point too.

My turn!

Up to this point, we have been looking at how to allow other systems and external guests to interact with our data and customization on the Salesforce1 Platform. Now, it's our turn to talk to other systems! Introducing Callouts. These are `HttpRequests` that allow Force.com to perform programmatic requests over the Internet to available web service APIs such as Google Maps, Google Calendar (we'll show you how in *Chapter 7, Use Case – Integration with Google Calendar*), payment processors (we'll show you how in *Chapter 8, Creating a Property Management Application*), and others. Plus, as an added benefit, we'll show you how to connect back to the web services that we just worked on together, and test them right from within the same instance of Salesforce. Let's get started!

Permissions again...

You'd think we could just talk to anyone we wanted, but Salesforce expects you to play the parenting role yet again. Just like you have to configure profiles for accessing data in Salesforce, you must configure **Remote Site Settings** in order to communicate with external services. For the purposes of our testing of the web services we just worked on, let's add your current instance of Salesforce. If you look at the URL, you will see a server prefix before the `salesforce.com`. You will need this prefix, and it should look like na## or cs##, where na## means you are on a production (or developer) server instance and cs## means you are on a sandbox server instance. Follow the leader now:

1. Click on the **Setup** link at the top of the Force.com GUI.

2. Under the **Administer** section, click on **Security Controls**.

3. Click on **Remote Site Settings**.

4. Now click on **New Remote Site**.

5. **Remote Site Name** is your internal label for the site (no spaces, please). **Remote Site Url** will be the endpoint.

6. Make sure the **Active** checkbox is checked.

7. Finally, click on **Save**.

In our case, the endpoint would be `https://packtlearninga-developer-edition.na17.force.com`.

Let's get loud

Let's get loud, turn the music up, and let's do it! Ahem. Let's pretend that never happened and take a look at what a Force.com callout looks like in Apex. It consists of three different `Http` classes interacting: `Http`, `HttpRequest`, and `HttpResponse`. What's that look like? Take a look:

```
//The Http Object, facilitates communication
Http ht = new Http();

//Http Request Object, what we will send
HttpRequest req = new HttpRequest();

//Http Method we will use for sending
//Options here are POST, GET, etc.
req.setMethod(string method);

//Milliseconds to wait for response, max 120000)
```

```
req.setTimeout(integer milliseconds);

//Set body as string, if not blob
req.setBody(string body);

//Set body as blob, if not string
req.setBodyAsBlob(blob body);
//Set endpoint, where are we sending request
req.setEndpoint(String endpoint);

//Repeat for all headers
//Be careful with this one, some services are
   //very picky and will not accept your request
   //without headers like Content-Length
   //or Content-Type
req.setHeader(String key, String value);

//Http Response Object, houses the response
HttpResponse res = new HttpResponse();

//Set the response to result of sending request
res = ht.send(req);

//Outputs response status code to console
system.debug(res.getStatusCode());

//Outputs all response header keys to console
system.debug(res.getHeaderKeys());

//Use to output specific header key to console
system.debug(res.getHeader(string key));

//Output the body of response to console
system.debug(res.getBody());
```

That's a complete run down of the Apex callout process. There are a few more attributes you can set on the request, but they're extremely specific and rarely used, so we won't go into them here. They are available in the Force.com documentation.

Well RESTed

Let's begin by testing out our REST GET method. We've created a new class, but this is technically optional, you can continue adding to an existing one if you prefer. The code is as follows:

```
public with sharing class callouts {

   public static string callRest_GET(){
      Http ht = new Http();
      HttpRequest req = new HttpRequest();
      req.setMethod('GET');
      req.setTimeout(120000);
      //No body for GET
      //req.setBody();
      //req.setBodyAsBlob(blob body);
      req.setEndpoint('https://packtlearninga-developer-
         edition.na17.force.com/services/apexrest/learnRest_Endpoint
         ?aName=testing%20site%202');
      //We don't need any special headers
      //req.setHeader(String key, String value);
      HttpResponse res = new HttpResponse();
      res = ht.send(req);
      system.debug(res.getStatusCode());
      system.debug(res.getHeaderKeys());
      system.debug(res.getHeader('Content-Type'));
      system.debug(res.getBody());
      return res.getBody();
   }
}
```

One new thing we have to cover is how to actually run methods on demand. We've covered how they get called by triggers in *Chapter 4, Triggers and Classes*, and we've seen them used by controllers in *Chapter 5, Visualforce Development with Apex*, and then by web services in this chapter; but what if you want to just run one, right here, right now? That's where Developer Console comes into play or the Execute Anonymous view of Eclipse. We'll show you both.

Console my Force.com developer

The Force.com Developer Console is a browser-based developer tool that can perform many administrative/debugging tasks on the fly, and it is continually being upgraded to become more useful/easier to use. To access the Developer Console's Execute Anonymous feature, perform the following steps:

1. Click on your name at the top of the Force.com GUI and select **Developer Console**.

 If you don't see this option, make sure your profile has the Author Apex permission.

2. Under **Debug**, select **Open Execute Anonymous Window**.

3. Let's call our `callREST_GET()` method from the callouts class, as shown:

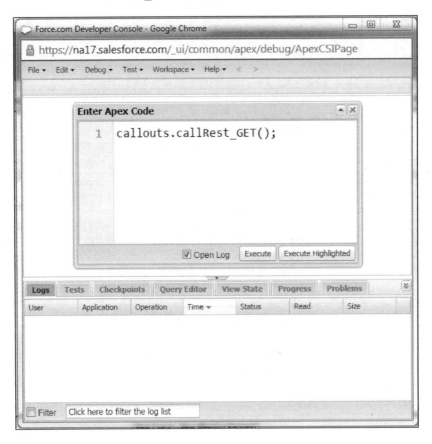

4. Check the **Open Log** and click on **Execute**.

The corresponding log that opens will include the trace of everything that has happened. This includes the construction of the request, displaying the endpoint a request is being sent to, the response status code, the header key map, the response body itself, as per the standard, and our added debug statements. The debug log also contains information about resources consumed by the executed thread, which includes a rundown of how it compares to current limits. That's the Developer Console; we'll cover Eclipse while testing our SOAP methods. Before we put a wrap on the REST services callout testing, here is how to perform POST to our service:

```
public with sharing class callouts {

    public static string callRest_GET(){
      //shown earlier
    }

    public static string callRest_POST(){
      string body = '
      {
        "acct": {
            "Name": "testing site 2",
            "Phone": "(654) 654-6544",
            "Website": "website.com",
            "Type": "Prospect",
            "Fax": "(235) 235-2356",
            "Id": "001o0000007zh9rAAA",
            "Industry": "Agriculture"
        }
      }';
      Http ht = new Http();
      HttpRequest req = new HttpRequest();
      req.setMethod('GET');
      req.setTimeout(120000);
      req.setBody(body);
      //Using string not blob for body
      //req.setBodyAsBlob(blob body);
      req.setEndpoint('https://packtlearninga-developer-
      edition.na17.force.com/services/apexrest/learnRest_
      Endpoint?aName=testing%20site%202');
      req.setHeader('Content-Type', 'application/json');
      HttpResponse res = new HttpResponse();
      res = ht.send(req);
      system.debug(res.getStatusCode());
      system.debug(res.getHeaderKeys());
      system.debug(res.getHeader('Content-Type'));
      system.debug(res.getBody());
      return res.getBody();
    }
}
```

Be sure to include the `Content-Type` header as a rule of thumb for POST callouts.

We can also test our REST service by setting up a **Connected App** and connecting via the default web service endpoint (aka without using Force.com sites) at `https://instance.salesforce.com/services/apexrest/[url mapping]`. What is a Connected App? A Connected App is an external application that the user wants to grant access to. You've been exposed to this idea when you use Facebook to log into any number of different services, you log into Facebook and grant permission to the service (external app) to act on your behalf; but you never provide your Facebook login information to that app. In order to configure a Connected App in Salesforce, navigate to **Setup | Create | Apps** and under the last section, **Connected Apps**, select the **New** button. There is a whole process for configuring your app for authentication, depending on your needs, and is documented in a step-by-step fashion in the API REST developer documentation from Salesforce, found at `http://www.salesforce.com/us/developer/docs/api_rest/`. In *Chapter 7, Use Case – Integration with Google Calendar*, we will review how to perform an OAuth exchange, which will allow you to utilize your new Connected App. Keep in mind that if you are authenticating as specific users, their profiles must have your web service class added to their enabled Apex classes on their profile.

Squeaky clean

Time for SOAP. Now remember how we had to log in and get `sessionId`? Well, since you're already logged in, you can get `sessionId` from the `UserInfo` global variable. We've updated the callouts class once again to now include the SOAP `updateAccountName` callout. Remember to update the following code snippet with the correct ID and desired `newName` parameters:

```
public with sharing class callouts {

  public static string callRest_GET(){
    //shown earlier
  }

  public static string callRest_POST(){
    //shown earlier
  }

  public static string callSOAP_updateAccountName(){
    string body = '
      <soapenv:Envelope
      xmlns:soapenv="http://schemas.xmlsoap.org/soap/envelope/"
      xmlns:lear="http://soap.sforce.com/schemas/class/learnSOAP">
        <soapenv:Header>
```

```
              <lear:SessionHeader>
                <lear:sessionId>'+userInfo.getSessionId()+'
                </lear:sessionId>
              </lear:SessionHeader>
          </soapenv:Header>
          <soapenv:Body>
            <lear:updateAccountName>
                <lear:acctId>THE ACCOUNT ID</lear:acctId>
                <lear:newName>THE NEW NAME</lear:newName>
            </lear:updateAccountName>
          </soapenv:Body>
        </soapenv:Envelope>
      ';
      Http ht = new Http();
      HttpRequest req = new HttpRequest();
      req.setMethod('GET');
      req.setTimeout(120000);
      req.setBody(body);
      //Using string not blob for body
      //req.setBodyAsBlob(blob body);
      req.setEndpoint('https://na17.salesforce.com
        /services/Soap/class/learnSOAP');

      req.setHeader('Content-Type', 'text/xml');
      req.setHeader('Content-Length',
      string.valueof(body.length()));
    req.setHeader('SOAPAction','http://schemas.xmlsoap.org
      /soap/envelope/');
      HttpResponse res = new HttpResponse();
      res = ht.send(req);
      system.debug(res.getStatusCode());
      system.debug(res.getHeaderKeys());
      system.debug(res.getHeader('Content-Type'));
      system.debug(res.getBody());
      return res.getBody();
  }
}
```

Even though the SOAPAction header technically doesn't do anything anymore, it is required by SOAP 1.1 and should be included regardless. Note that Content-Type and Content-Length have also been included.

Anonymous Eclipse

To use the Execute Anonymous feature of Eclipse, the assumption here is that you already have your Force.com project imported into Eclipse (we've used it a few times in earlier chapters; if not, refer to *Chapter 1, Apex Assumptions and Comparisons*, for step-by-step instructions). In Eclipse, open the Execute Anonymous view by performing the following steps:

1. Navigate to **Window** | **Show View** | **Execute Anonymous**.

2. Verify that you have the correct **Active Project** selected (if you have multiple).

3. Type in `callouts.callSOAP_updateAccountName();`.

4. Click on **Execute Anonymous**. You should see something similar to the following screenshot:

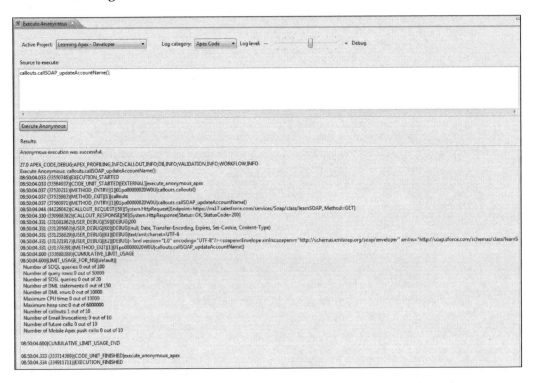

You get the same information as in Developer Console, including the request and response as well as a rundown of limits. The request is cut off on the far right in the previous screenshot, but I can vouch for it being a success value from our method.

Now that you've seen both ways to execute anonymous code, it's up to you to decide whether you prefer Eclipse or Developer Console. From experience and day-to-day code wrestling, we prefer the Eclipse version, since the code is being written in Eclipse, it's easier to run anonymous code blocks there than logging into the UI and launching a browser-based debugging tool; but to each his own. With this in mind, the Force.com IDE has recently been released as open source, and a plugin for Sublime Text called Maven's Mate has surfaced as a result. It is yet another alternative for those interested in checking it out (it also has an Execute Anonymous functionality to add to the list of options).

Summary

That's all folks! Whew! Well that's a ton of information in a comparatively small amount of space. A word of caution/forewarning to the bold ones out there; it's difficult enough getting an application running alone in a language you are just learning. When you throw in an external service to the mix, be it them calling you or you calling them, the difficulty rises exponentially and it's easy to get frustrated/discouraged when things don't work as you expect them to.

Patience is key to learn something well, and even if you were able to run through this entire chapter successfully on the first go, we encourage you to go back and really understand what is going on and try to write your own classes/methods before moving on. The next chapters will build on the ideas explored in this chapter more in depth and moving forward with a shaky understanding that will just leave you confused and annoyed.

The next chapter will explore the interactions with external services that originate from within Salesforce (this chapter discussed how to handle requests originating externally). We'll illustrate the capability by creating a sync process with the Google Calendar API.

7
Use Case – Integration with Google Calendar

Use case, how detestable the term is. Remember all those awful papers you had to write in school for use cases of someone selling widgets in candy land? Thankfully, this is a book about code, and code is always useful, and always has a use case; even the Hello World application has a practical application! (Say that five times fast, I dare you.)

For this use case chapter, our goal is to really show you how to do something very useful that comprises of more than just a couple lines of code. We'll be focusing on the steps to get things done, and start moving at a slightly faster pace, after all, you should know how to get to **Setup** by now. This chapter will have many moving parts, as we are building a full-blown app and not just writing standalone controllers, extensions, methods, pages, or triggers; though we will be using all of them in turn.

Since this chapter involves using an external system, we want to highlight the importance of **Terms of Service (ToS)** of the other system. We all know that most of us skim this pile of mumbo jumbo before accepting; however, when you are building an application that will, at its core, be relying on the service, you should take care to not violate any stipulations in the provider's ToS or all your hard work will be for naught. Typically, the most important things to look for are presented in easy to see places, but you should take note of the following important factors:

- Is there a rate limit? (how often can you hit the service?)
- Is there a hit limit? (how many times can you hit the service?)
- If there is a hit/rate limit, are these limits per user? (per license/API key?)
- Is there a fee for going over the limit?
- Is there an upfront fee?

- Are there any explicit prohibitions? (some web services explicitly prohibit you from programmatically logging in/retrieving their data)

- Does every user of the service have to register, or can you register and include the credentials as part of your app for everyone to use?

All of these are very important. At the best, you can get locked out of the service for a period of time (rate/hit exceeding). At the worst, you can have your account disabled or incur large fees; made worse if you are breaking copyright/intellectual property laws by programmatically accessing data you are expressly forbidden from doing so in the ToS.

Now that I've scared you a bit and have your attention, let's briefly go over the authentication methods. There are many services out there, some requiring authentication and others that do not. The following are the most common ways in which current web service providers authenticate their users:

- **No authentication**: Anyone can use it (like our REST service in *Chapter 6, Exposing Force.com to the World*).

- **No authentication but rate/hit limit by IP address**: Anyone can use this, but please don't abuse it.

- **API key authentication**: Just pass your API key (unique) along with your request, so we know who you are (can also be rate/hit limited). This can also just be a random access code that changes.

- **Basic authentication**: Encrypt your username and password and pass it along with your request (can also be rate/hit limited).

- **Session ID**: Authenticate and get a session ID in the response, which expires after a period of time (we saw this with our SOAP example in *Chapter 6, Exposing Force.com to the World*).

- **OAuth**: A more complex method of logging in, authorizing an application, and ultimately receiving a unique token to be used along with your requests. This is the method that we will be using in this chapter.

OAuth is probably the most common way of providing a secure connection over the web. Most of your favorite services use it; Google, Facebook, and Twitter to name a few. If you've ever seen the option to log in with your Google Account option for a non-Google service, you know what we're talking about and have unknowingly used OAuth.

Gimme an O!

The OAuth protocol uses a process known as **handshake** to facilitate its authentication flow. Basically, you request access, the server verifies the user's identity, the user grants access, and the server allows you to make requests. The real flow is more like this:

Fake step 1:

- Redirect user to the authentication provider's request URI endpoint along with parameters of your request, including scope and redirect URI (where the response should be sent)

- User logs in and grants access to your app after reviewing the permissions you have requested

- Server verifies the user's identity and provides a request token to the redirect endpoint you specified

Fake step 2:

- You take the request token from the response and pass it back to the server, this time to the authentication endpoint

- The server exchanges this for an access token and a refresh token

Fake step 3:

- You make your requests with the access token

> If your access token has expired, you can pass the access token along with a refresh token back to the authentication endpoint to receive a new access token and corresponding refresh token.

(Fake steps because they aren't real *industry standard* steps, just groupings I made up that match the steps you have to programmatically do.)

We'll go over the specific process of requesting a Google authentication token from Force.com later in this chapter, but if you want to be a smarty pants by then, here is the URL for the specification, `https://developers.google.com/google-apps/calendar/auth`.

Googol

If spellcheck had been around in 1997 or rather, if Stanford students knew how to use it, the face of today's Internet would be much different. Where would we all be without Google? Probably using Googol.... In any case, Google, a word play on googol, provides a number of services to the Internet world, one of which is a free Account that comes with a calendar app; one that is very widely used.

For the remainder of this chapter, we're going to dive into the depths of Google's app locker and pillage for treasure that is widely available to everyone, but only if we know where to look. We'll cover how to create a new app, enable the required services, enable authentication via OAuth (OAuth 2.0 specifically), and then how to code the Force.com side of things to connect to, and use our new app.

We're going to make the assumption that you have a Google Account already. If not, head on over to `https://accounts.google.com` and sell your soul for an account; just kidding, it's free! Once you take care of all the administrative hoopla of registering, keep reading!

Hello, I'm new

Go ahead and visit `https://cloud.google.com` after signing in to access the basement of Google's developments and secrets. Click on **Go to my Console** or skip this and go straight to this link `https://console.developers.google.com/project`.

If this is your first Google App, you'll see a big blue button in the middle of the screen saying **Create Project**. If you already have Google Apps, then you should see a list of them, with the same **Create Project** button at the top-left of your screen, as shown in the following screenshot:

After clicking on the **Create Project** button, you will see a prompt requesting a project name and acceptance of ToS. You can name the project anything you like; **Project Id** is irrelevant for all intents and purposes, but you can cycle through them if you are picky.

Ooo shiny!

It's hard to believe just how many shiny goodies Google provides for free; looking at the list of available APIs is enough to make one's head spin. To see this list, click on **APIs** under the **APIs & auth** section of the sidebar (refer to the next image). Google already enables some APIs for you by default, as shown in the following screenshot, and it's up to you whether to leave them on or disable them (makes no difference for our purposes):

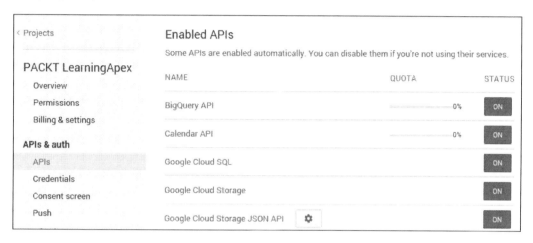

We do need, the however, Google Calendar API to be enabled. Scroll through the list until you find **Calendar API**, and click on the gray **OFF** button. This will prompt a pop up for acceptance of terms specific to the Calendar API.

Needle in a haystack

With the monolithic size of Google, it's all fine and dandy that we have our own little app out there, but how in the heck do we find it so that we can connect to it? We'll need a client ID. A client ID is a unique identifier, which is paired with a client secret to uniquely identify an app with a specified set of configuration settings.

This part is so important; you get a picture to make sure you get it right! In the sidebar of your Google Cloud console, under **APIs & auth**, select **Credentials** and then click on **Create new Client ID**. Configure it in the following way:

1. **APPLICATION TYPE**: This refers to the type of app you are building, methods of connecting and authenticating differentiate these. Select **Web Application**, this is what our app is. We won't get into the other types now.

2. **AUTHORIZED JAVASCRIPT ORIGINS**: This is the domain where authorization/API requests will be coming from.

All of our requests will be coming from Salesforce. You should enter the server subdomain (or custom domain if your instance uses the My Domain feature) your organization is located on. Our developer org is located at `na17.salesforce.com` so our origin is `https://na17.salesforce.com`.

3. **AUTHORIZED REDIRECT URI**: This is where Google should be allowed to send responses to. This is typically passed as a parameter in your authorization request.

   We will be creating a custom "Visualforce" page later to handle our authorization requests called googleAuthorization. Add the following two links (keeping your server instance in mind):

   `https://na17.salesforce.com/apex/googleAuthorization`
   `https://c.na17.visual.force.com/apex/googleAuthorization`

4. Click on **Create Client ID**.

> Note that if you are using a Sandbox instance, your server instances will be `csXX.salesforce.com` and `c.csXX.visual.force.com` where XX is the number.

Here's the promised image to give you a quick recap. Please be careful with this step, nothing will work if this is done wrong.

One more thing that throws people for a loop, listen up! You will be banging your head on the desk if you don't. Right under the **Credentials** link, under **APIs & auth**, click on **Consent Screen**. Select an e-mail address from the drop-down menu and give your app a product name, and click on **Save** at the bottom, as shown in the following screenshot. Now give it a few minutes to propagate, simply reading on should do the trick time wise.

Forget me not

Being able to log in to Google is great. But do you really want to do that for every event, every time? Didn't think so. Let's fire up that clicking finger and do some administrative overhauls in the UI. First stop, Users. Perform the following steps:

1. Click on the **Setup** link at the top-right of the Force.com GUI.

2. Under the **Customize** section, click on **Users** (these are not in alphabetical order).

3. Click on **Fields**.

4. In the **User Custom Fields** section, click on the **New** button.

5. Create two **Text** fields, 255 characters in length, and one **Email**, as follows:

   Google Email (e-mail)

   Google Access Token (text)

   Google Refresh Token (text)

You might be asking yourself, why a Google **Email** field? Why not just use the user's e-mail? It's a valid question, but experience has shown that people may wish to use a different e-mail account for their Salesforce login than Google, and this facilitates both approaches. But wait! Isn't OAuth supposed to mitigate the need to store the user's login (also known as e-mail)? Yes, but the primary Google calendar is referenced through the user's e-mail (and ironically, login), so we need it. We could technically retrieve this from Google once we have access, but that involves another permission scope. Stop asking good questions and follow along! Here is what it should all look like once done:

User Custom Fields		New	Field Dependencies	
Action	Field Label	API Name		Data Type
Edit | Del	Google Access Token	Google_Access_Token__c		Text(255)
Edit | Del	Google Email	Google_Email__c		Email
Edit | Del	Google Refresh Token	Google_Refresh_Token__c		Text(255)

Now that we have somewhere to store our authentication information (without storing the user's password mind you!), we can make use of the access type feature of our Google oAuth credentials. We can specify this scope parameter to be offline. This will allow us to continue interacting with Google on the user's behalf without requiring them to log in every time.

Ready for some code? The subsequent sections will quench your thirst!

I'm late, very, very late!

If you're anything like me, your life is driven by your calendar; and if you are one of those people who actually enjoy an Amish way of life (why are you reading this book?), then you might have customers/colleagues who rely on their calendars to know when to walk their dog, thankfully, I don't have one!

For all of these reasons and more, we're sure, we're now going to go over how to send your Salesforce created calendar events through to Google calendar. There are different ways to do this (are you noticing a pattern with Force.com yet?), and we'll cover the more popular options.

First, we are going to need a way to match up our Google calendar events with our Salesforce events. Some more clicking is in store for us. Proceed with the following steps:

1. Click on the **Setup** link at the top-right of the Force.com GUI.

2. Under the **Customize** section, click on **Activities**.

3. Then click on **Activity Custom Fields**.
4. Create a new **Text** field and **Google Id**, marked as **External ID**.

Storing this ID will allow us to update and delete the event after pushing it to Google, should we wish to do so. The fact that this is **External ID** will also allow us to update and/or delete the Salesforce version of an event without knowing its Salesforce ID based on messages from Google. Unfortunately, retrieving and parsing event data from Google is beyond the scope of our discussion—after all, we want to challenge you to go out and use what you have learned to do; new, fun, and exciting things rather than just spoon feed it to you.

Now that our administrative clicking around is done, we can get to keyboard mashing and toss aside the mouse (ok, might still need it... maybe). For those curious cats in all of us, here's the link to Google's documentation for the Calendar API https://developers.google.com/google-apps/calendar/?csw=1.

O, Auth me mighty Google!

First things first, we need to be able to talk to Google. Remember that **googleAuthorization** page we mentioned earlier? Let's make it! (Refer to *Chapter 5, Visualforce Development with Apex*, if you forgot how, or skipped). Short version: right-click on **Project** in Eclipse and navigate to **New | Visualforce Page** and name it accordingly. While we're at it, let's make the corresponding controller, googleAuthorization_Controller (navigate to **New | Apex Class** for this).

Let's start with our code for the controller. We're going to need a holder variable for the Google e-mail that we are authenticating and a button to initiate the process. Now, remember how we talked about using a different e-mail than the user e-mail? Although that is a potential use case, if it's not we should just prepopulate this with the user info anyway. Ok, so here is our powerful little page, packed full of little goodies! (Don't worry about the giant regular expression, you can get that from the code files for this chapter.):

```
<apex:page controller="googleAuthorization_Controller"
    showHeader="true"
    sidebar="true"
    id="thePage">
    <apex:sectionHeader title="Google Authorization"
        subtitle="Calendar"/>

<!--give everything an id-->
    <apex:form id="theForm">
<!-- The pageblock mode only controls styling-->
```

```
      <apex:pageblock mode="edit" id="block"
        title="Authorize the following calendar:">
<!-- Setting columns to 1, allows the button to appear below the
field-->
        <apex:pageblocksection id="sec" columns="1">
<!-- This inputtext binds to our email variable, displays placeholder
text when the field is empty, has an id, and verifies validity of the
input after keyup-->
          <apex:inputtext value="{!googleEmail}"
            html-placeholder="Google Email"
            label="Google Email:"
            id="email"
            onkeyup="verifyEmail(false);"/>
<!-- We're using a pageblocksectionitem strictly for the sake of
organizing our elements in the section nicely-->
          <apex:pageblocksectionitem>
<!-- This requires an empty label-->
            <apex:outputlabel/>
<!-- Our commandbutton is action packed, verifying if the email is
valid before communicating with the server; if our JavaScript function
returns false, the onclick of the commandbutton will also return false
- causing it to interrupt the request client-side-->
            <apex:commandbutton
                value="Authenticate"
action="{!requestAuthorization}"
onclick="if(!verifyEmail(true)){
                return false;}"/>
          </apex:pageblocksectionitem>
        </apex:pageblocksection>
      </apex:pageblock>
    </apex:form>
<!--Some JavaScript for validation / looks-->
  <script>
//this function verifies our email
    function verifyEmail(pop){
//retrieve element by id
//(this is why we gave everything an id!)
      var ele = document.getElementById(
          'thePage:theForm:block:sec:email');
      //if nothing is typed in
      if (!ele.value){
        return showError(ele,pop);;
      }
      else{ //otherwise, is the value valid
        //regular Expression to validate email
        var regExp =
          /^(([^<>()[\]\\.,;:\s@\"]+(\.[^<>()[\]\\.,;:\s@\"]+)*)
```

```
      |(\".+\"))@((\[[0-9]{1,3}\.[0-9]{1,3}\.[0-9]{1,3}\.[0-
      9]{1,3}\])|(([a-zA-Z\-0-9]+\.)+[a-zA-Z]{2,}))$/;
    //use regexp to test validity
    var valid = regExp.test(ele.value);
    //invalid, react!
    if (!valid) showError(ele,pop);
    else clearError(ele); //clears error look
    return valid; //returns result
    }
  }
  //our reaction to invalid inputs
  //the pop boolean dictates if we should show the popup
  //which we only want to do when the user submits!
  //remember we are checking as the user types too!
  function showError(e, pop){
    //set some styling on the input
    e.style.border = '2pt solid DarkRed';
    e.style.color = 'DarkRed';
    e.style.background = '#FFB2B2';
    if (pop) //display the popup message
      alert('Please enter valid email address.');
    return false;
  }
  //remove error styling on input as you type
  function clearError(e){
    e.style.border = 'none';
    e.style.color = '#000';
    e.style.background = '#FFF';
  }
  </script>
</apex:page>
```

The associated custom controller (for now) is:

```
public with sharing class googleAuthorization_Controller {

  //our email variable
  public string googleEmail {get;set;}

  //constructor
  public googleAuthorization_Controller() {
    //preset user's email
    googleEmail = userInfo.getUserEmail();
  }

  //what our command button will do
  public pagereference requestAuthorization(){
```

```
        Pagereference p;
        //be patient, coming soon
        //call googleCalendar_API.loginRequestPage();
        return p;
    }
  }
```

Whoa! JavaScript? Yep, believe it or not, you can use JavaScript to its fullest, including libraries such as jQuery with Visualforce. We typically use it for form validation and user *flashiness* experience rather than the controller/extensions. There is strong support for both camps, with valid points, but JavaScript is the clear winner in terms of speed as everything is done client side rather than the entire contents of the form element being transmitted back to the server, processed, and then sent back for display.

So what does this page do so far? It pulls in the current user's e-mail, allows them to change it if that is not the calendar they wish to authenticate, validates that the e-mail provided is valid, and provides a button for us to click to authenticate. You'll notice in the controller that there is a placeholder method call to googleCalendar_API.loginRequestPage(). Why a holder? Well, we haven't made the class yet silly! Let's get on with that.

Make the class (again, right-click on **Apex Class** under **New**) and add in the method as follows:

```
public with sharing class googleCalendar_API {
//client id from app creation
static String GOOGLE_API_CLIENT_ID =
'INSERT HERE';

   //client secret from app creation
   static String GOOGLE_API_CLIENT_SECRET =
'INSERT HERE';

   //necessary access scope from calendar documentation
   static String GOOGLE_CALENDAR_SCOPE =
'https://www.googleapis.com/auth/calendar';

   //our authorization page - make sure to change to yours!
   static String SF_AUTH_PAGE =
   'https://c.na17.visual.force.com/apex/googleAuthorization';

// our request method, takes in our authorized redirect URI //(recall
from setting up the Google App)
   public static PageReference loginRequestPage
     (String redirectURI, String state){
```

```
//set the endpoint for authorization requests per
//Google documentation
  PageReference p =
  new PageReference
  ('https://accounts.google.com/o/oauth2/auth');

//add in all necessary parameters
//Determines if the Google Authorization Server returns an
authorization code (code), or an opaque access token (token)
  p.getParameters().put('response_type','code');

//our client id
  p.getParameters().put('client_id',GOOGLE_API_CLIENT_ID);

  //our authorized redirect uri
  p.getParameters().put('redirect_uri',redirectURI);

//this forces our user to accept the app permissions //every time they
visit this url
  p.getParameters().put('approval_prompt','force');

  //which permissions are we requesting?
  p.getParameters().put('scope',GOOGLE_CALENDAR_SCOPE);

//This optional parameter is used for anything you want //Google to
return in its reply so you can use it.
  p.getParameters().put('state',state);

//this will allow us to log in without the user's //involvment
  p.getParameters().put('access_type','offline');
  return p;
  }
}
```

Make sure to replace the static variables such as client ID with what you retrieved earlier during Google app creation, otherwise it won't work! Also, make sure to update your Visualforce page location to one that you authorized during app creation. Then go and update your controller method:

```
//command button for request action
  public pagereference requestAuthorization(){
    return googleCalendar_API.loginRequestPage(
      googleCalendar_API.SF_AUTH_PAGE,
      googleEmail);
  }
```

We're now calling our API class method to construct the request URL and navigating straight to it! Let's go test our page out. How do we get to it again? Right, let's make a tab for simplicity's sake:

1. Navigate to **Setup | Create | Tabs**.
2. Click on **New** under **Visualforce Tabs**.
3. Select **googleAuthorization** from the drop-down menu of **Visualforce Pages**.
4. Name the tab something that makes sense.
5. Select a tab style; I'm partial to the **Compass** and **Chalkboard** styles.
6. Click on **Next**, select one or many profiles that should have access.
7. Play with these settings or just click on **Save**.

Depending on how much stuff you have, it should resemble the following:

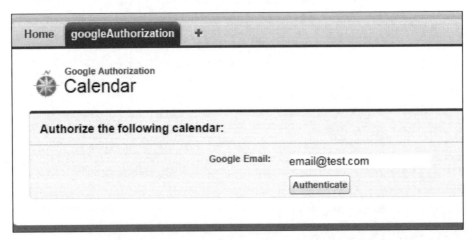

Great! Play with it; try erasing the e-mail, entering in invalid e-mails, and so on. See our JavaScript in action; or, since we know you're anxious, verify your Google e-mail and hit **Authenticate**. You should get the Google login screen. Go ahead and log in, and be greeted with the following screenshot:

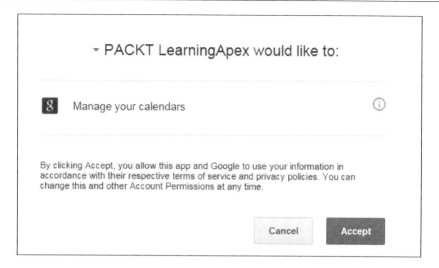

You'll see that we are requesting permission to access the calendar for the specified user. Once you, or they, accept it, Google will send a response token to our authentication page, and we have more work to do. If you accept, you'll notice you're back where we started… looks the same! Tilt your head up a bit (or just your eyeballs), and look at the URL. You'll notice the `state` parameter we passed, as well as a `code` parameter. We need to do something with those. We're going to take you down the rabbit hole of dynamic Visualforce so hang on to your hat.

We're going to use a feature of Visualforce pages that allows you to call a controller or extension method `onload` and the `action` attribute. In the method we call, we will determine whether or not there is a `code` parameter in the URL, and if so, do something with it. Otherwise, we are going to leave it well enough alone, and it'll be like we never changed anything.

 Although you cannot perform DML operations in the constructor of a controller or extension, you can perform DML in the action (`onload`) method of a page.

If we have a `code` parameter, we need to grab it, and immediately do the callout to Google's authentication server to exchange our request token for our access token. Hop to it while it's hot! Let's tackle the API class first (it's grown a bit):

```
public with sharing class googleCalendar_API {
  static String GOOGLE_API_CLIENT_ID = 'INSERT HERE';
  static String GOOGLE_API_CLIENT_SECRET = 'INSERT HERE';
  static String GOOGLE_CALENDAR_SCOPE =
    'https://www.googleapis.com/auth/calendar';
```

```
static String SF_AUTH_PAGE =
  'https://c.na17.visual.force.com/apex/googleAuthorization';

public static PageReference loginRequestPage(String redirectURI,
String state){
  //no change
}

//obtain our access token
//pass in the user, request token (code), redirect to authpage
public static User obtainAccessToken(User u, String code,
String redirectURL){
//any url you want, we are using this as a shortcut to //URL encode
our parameters
  PageReference p = new
  PageReference('http://www.replace.com');
    p.getParameters().put('client_id',GOOGLE_API_CLIENT_ID);
    p.getParameters().put('client_secret',
    GOOGLE_API_CLIENT_SECRET);
    //no scope this time
    p.getParameters().put('scope','');
    p.getParameters().put('redirect_uri',redirectURL);

//declaring we want an access token
    p.getParameters().put('grant_type',
    'authorization_code');
    //adding in our valid request token
    p.getParameters().put('code',code);
    //retrieve the constructed, URL encoded url
    String body = p.getURL();
    //grab only the parameters
    body = body.subStringAfter('?');
    //use our callGoogle method to POST our body
    httpResponse googleAuth =
    callGoogle('https://accounts.google.com/o/oauth2/token',
    'POST',body);
    //handle success
    if ( googleAuth.getStatusCode() == 200 ){
      //updates user with tokens
      u = parseGoogleAuth(googleAuth.getBody(), u);
    }
    //handle failure
    else u.Google_Access_Token__c ='error';
    return u;
}
```

```
    //parses response from Google authentication
//into the user fields
  public static User parseGoogleAuth(String body, User u){
    //the response is JSON, use a parser
    jsonParser parser = json.createParser(body);
    while ( parser.nextToken() != null ){
      if ( parser.getCurrentToken() == JSONToken.FIELD_NAME &&
      parser.getText() != null && parser.getText() ==
      'access_token' ){
        parser.nextToken();
        //assign access token
        u.Google_Access_Token__c = parser.getText();
      } else
      if ( parser.getCurrentToken() == JSONToken.FIELD_NAME &&
      parser.getText() != null && parser.getText() ==
      'refresh_token' ){
        parser.nextToken();
        //assign refresh token
        u.Google_Refresh_Token__c = parser.getText();
      }
    }
    return u;
  }


  //generic callout method to Google
  public static httpResponse callGoogle(String endpoint,
  String method, String body){
    HttpRequest req = new HttpRequest();
    req.setEndpoint(endpoint);
    req.setMethod(method);
    req.setCompressed(false);
    req.setHeader('User-Agent','learnApex API');
    req.setHeader('Encoding','iso-8859-1');
    req.setHeader('Content-Type', 'application/x-www-form-
    urlencoded');
    req.setTimeout(120000);//max timeout
    if( body != null ){ //should be null if a GET
      req.setBody(body);
      req.setHeader('Content-length',
      string.valueOf(body.length()));
    }
    HttpResponse res = new http().send(req);
    return res;
  }
}
```

Oof! What a whopper. Before we go further, we need to add Google as an approved remote site for us to perform callouts. Quick refresher: navigate to **Setup | Security Controls | Remote Site Settings | New Remote Site | Remote Site Name** — your pick (how about `Google Auth`, clever, we know), and add `https://accounts.google.com` as **Remote Site URL**.

Now we need that `onload` method in our controller:

```
public with sharing class googleAuthorization_Controller {
  public string googleEmail {get;set;}
  //to store our code for dynamic rendering
  public string code {get;set;}
  //to store our user record
  public User u {get;set;}
  public googleAuthorization_Controller() {
    googleEmail = userInfo.getUserEmail();
  }

  //page action
  public pagereference doOnLoad(){
    //retrieve current page
    Pagereference p = ApexPages.currentPage();
    //does it have a code as parameter?
    code = p.getParameters().get('code');
    //no? then stop
    if (string.isBlank(code)) return null;
    //it had one! get the state, aka email we passed
    //note you don't want to use googleEmail here
    //since we came back to the page, it reloaded and
    //the controller was reinstantiated, overriding our
    //input with the user's email
    string passedEmail = p.getParameters().get('state');

    //query for the user, with token fields so we can modify
    u = [select id, Google_Access_Token__c,
    Google_Refresh_Token__c from User where id =
    :userInfo.getUserId()];

    //call our api method to get tokens parsed into user
    u = googleCalendar_API.obtainAccessToken(u, code,
    googleCalendar_API.SF_AUTH_PAGE);

    //if we had no error
    if (u.Google_Access_Token__c != 'error'){
      //set the google email
```

```
      u.google_email__c = passedEmail;
      //update the user and display success message
      update u;
      ApexPages.addMessage(new
        ApexPages.message(ApexPages.severity.confirm,'Authorized
        Successfully!'));
    }
    else{
      //had an error? well then let us know <sadface>
      ApexPages.addMessage(new
        ApexPages.message(ApexPages.severity.error,'Authorization
        Error.'));
    }
    //stay here, not going anywhere!
    return null;
  }

  public pagereference requestAuthorization(){
    return googleCalendar_API.loginRequestPage(
      googleCalendar_API.SF_AUTH_PAGE,
      googleEmail);
  }
}
```

Last but not least, our Visualforce page update, shown as follows:

```
<apex:page controller="googleAuthorization_Controller"
  showHeader="true"
  sidebar="true"
  id="thePage"
  action="{!doOnload}">
  <!-- action =onload!-->
  <apex:sectionHeader title="Google Authorization"
      subtitle="Calendar"/>
      <!--display this block only if we have a code-->
  <apex:pageblock title="Authorization Status"
    rendered="{!NOT(ISBLANK(code))}">
    <apex:pageblocksection columns="1">
      <apex:pagemessages/>
      <apex:outputfield value="{!u.google_email__c}"/>
      <apex:outputfield value="{!u.google_access_token__c}"/>
      <apex:outputfield value="{!u.google_refresh_token__c}"/>
    </apex:pageblocksection>
  </apex:pageblock>
```

```
<!-- display this form only if we don't have a code-->
<apex:form id="theForm" rendered="{!ISBLANK(code)}">
  <!--no change in form-->
</apex:form>
<script>
  //no change in script
</script>
</apex:page>
```

Remember all those cool functions you learned in *Chapter 5, Visualforce Development with Apex*? Yeah, we used NOT() and ISBLANK() to dynamically control what our page displayed. Note the <apex:pagemessages/> tag as well, this gets populated with our corresponding styled messages from the controller for success/failure.

Shall we? Let's! Hop on back to our tab, refresh the page if you were already there, punch in an e-mail, click on the authorize button, log in to Google if you have to (bathroom break?), accept the permissions, take a deep breath, and bam! You should see a green confirmation message as follows:

If you don't see the preceding screenshot, check to make sure you have set up your Google app properly, including redirect, origins, consent screen settings, and that the Calendar API is enabled. Then check your remote site settings in Salesforce, check your field-level security for the Google fields you created on the user, and lastly double check every line of code if you typed it manually. (Try using the provided files.) You can play with this page to make it more user friendly, for example, we have no buttons for the users to click on now to take them to their home page, or to their calendar or www.addictinggames.com.

Manual labour

Regardless of how amazing automations are, it's always good to have a backup plan in case they fail, for whatever reason, which typically involves some form of manual process. Therefore, we're first going to take a look at how to manually push events into Google calendar through the use of a custom button on the calendar event itself. This will have the added benefit of ensuring that our code works before we try to automate it or make it process more data at a time. We're going to lay down tons of coded groundwork here for use later in bulk processing, so don't go cross-eyed on me now!

We need a few new things in our `googleCalendar_API` class; I'm going to break them out one by one and then throw everything together at the end. First, we're going to use a wrapper class of primitives to describe our events. This class will allow us, through the constructor, to take in a Salesforce Event record and convert it into a set of strings with all the proper formatting and "time zone" conversions, and so on, which Google expects from us. The code is as follows:

```
public class calloutWrapper{
  public String body {get;set;}
  public String endpoint {get;set;}
  public String googleCalendarEmail {get;set;}
  public String googleEventId {get;set;}
  public String method {get;set;}
  public String ownerName {get;set;}
  public Id salesforceEventId {get;set;}
  public Id salesforceOwnerId {get;set;}
  //the constructor will allow us to automatically build wrapper
  public calloutWrapper(Event e){
    salesforceEventId = e.Id;
    if ( string.isNotBlank(e.Google_Id__c) ){
      googleEventId = e.Google_Id__c;
    }
    //call body build method
    body = compileBodyFromEvent(e);
  }
}
```

The following is our method to construct the message body from an event; our body building method, sans gym membership, and as per the Google Calendar API documentation for event structure:

```
public static String compileBodyFromEvent(Event e){
  //we're building a JSON body manually!
  String body = '{'+cr+' "end": {'+cr;
  if (e.isalldayevent){
```

```
          body += ' "date": "'+ e.StartDateTime.formatgmt('yyyy-MM-dd')
            +'"'+cr;
       }
       else {
          body += ' "dateTime": "'+
            convertDateTimeToString(e.EndDateTime) +'"'+cr;
       }
       body += ' },'+cr+' "start": {'+cr;
       if (e.isalldayevent){
          body += ' "date": "'+ e.StartDateTime.formatgmt('yyyy-MM-dd')
            +'"'+cr;
       }
       else{
          body += ' "dateTime": "'+
            convertDateTimeToString(e.StartDateTime) +'"'+cr;
          }
          body += ' },'+cr;
          if ( string.isNotBlank(e.Subject) ){
            body += ' "summary": "'+ e.Subject +'",'+cr;
          }
          if ( string.isNotBlank(e.Description) ){
            body += ' "description": "'+
              e.Description.replace('\n','\\n').replace('\r','\\r')
              +'",'+cr;
          }
          if ( string.isNotBlank( e.Location ) ){
            body += ' "location": "'+ e.Location +'",'+cr;
          }
//we've been blindly adding returns
          body = body.subStringBeforeLast(',');
          body += '}'+cr;
          return body;
       }
```

You'll notice that we used a `convertDateTimeToString()` method, here it is:

```
   public static String convertDateTimeToString(DateTime dt){
     //retrieve the user's timezone and calculate offset
     Integer x = tz.getOffset(dt)/3600000;
     String z = '';
     if ( x > 0 ) z += '+';
     else z += '-';
     //if less than 9, prepend a 0, since 2 digit expected
     if ( x > 9 || x < -9 ) z += math.abs(x);
     else z += '0'+math.abs(x);
```

```
   z += ':00';
   //return string formatted datetime+timezone offset
   return dt.format('yyyy-MM-dd\'T\'HH:mm:ss'+z);
}
```

Now we have a wrapper class that can contain our events ready for Google! Note that we have been using a `cr` reference in the previous methods. This is our carriage return holder, which we have defined as a class-level variable; we've also updated `userMap` too:

```
Static string cr = '\r\n';
static map<id,User> userMap = new map<id,User>([select id,
   name, google_Email__c, Google_Access_Token__c,
   Google_Refresh_Token__c from User where isActive=true]);
```

Once you add these changes to your class, you should be able to compile. Now it's time for the next big concept. You already know that Salesforce has its limits on the number of callouts per thread and so on. Google also has some limits of its own. For example, you can only process events for one Google user at a time. We know we are manually adding in one event right now, but the logic is similar for constructing a request for bulk. We are going to go over the bulk mode now, and you can just mentally ignore the `for` loops and lists until we need them. We're going to group our events by the Salesforce `ownerId` (which happens to coincide with which Salesforce Calendar event is on; user IDs are the calendar IDs):

```
public static map<String, list<calloutWrapper>>
wrapEventsByOwner(List<Event> eventList, boolean deleting){
   //while we're at it, we'll convert to our wrapper
   map<String, list<calloutWrapper>> ownerMap = new
     map<String, list<calloutWrapper>>();
   //you can ignore the for loop, or follow along
   for ( Event e : eventList ){
     //Google requires all events to have a start and end
     //if our Salesforce event is incomplete, we can't use it
     if (   e.StartDateTime != null &&
       e.EndDateTime != null ){
//new callout wrapper
       calloutWrapper w = new calloutWrapper(e);
       //set the method; if this event has a Google
       //id, then we want to update (PATCH) rather
       //than insert (POST); if deleting, we want
       //to delete
       w.Method =
         (string.isnotBlank(w.googleEventId))?
         ((deleting)?'DELETE':'PATCH'):
         'POST';
```

```
            //if owner already has events, add to list
            if ( ownerMap.containsKey(e.OwnerId))
              ownerMap.get(e.OwnerId).add(w);
            //otherwise new list for owner
            else ownerMap.put(e.OwnerId, new
            list<calloutWrapper>{w});
        }
    }
    return ownerMap;
}
```

We're almost done! Really! We just need to process the wrapped lists now:

```
public static void processEventList(  list<Event> eventList,
boolean deleting){
  //generate a map of all events by ownerid
  //we'll need this because Google only
//lets us work with 1 user at a time
  map<String, list<calloutWrapper>> eventsByOwnerId =
  wrapEventsByOwner(eventlist);

  //list to collect events for update; new Google events will
  //have ids for us to store.
  List<Event> eventUpdates = new List<Event>();

  //for every owner
  for (string userId : eventsByOwnerId.keyset()){
    //refresh user Google Credentials, and store in userMap
    userMap.put(userid,refreshToken(usermap.get(userid)));

    //send the request in one fel swoop
    //we have a method (shown after this) to construct
    //the actual HttpRequest we need
    httpResponse res = new
    http().send(buildRequest(userMap.get(userid),
    eventsByOwnerId.get(userid)));
    //retrieve response body for work
    String resBody = res.getBody();
    //debug the response; in case something goes wrong
    system.debug(resbody);
    //what's the boundary Google is using?
    String googBoundary =
      resBody.subStringBefore('Content-Type:');
    //use that boundary to split the response
    List<String> parts = resBody.split(googBoundary);
```

```
//for every split part of the response by boundary
for ( String p : parts ){
  //if this is an event response
  if ( p.contains('Content-ID: <response-') ){
//add event to list for update with its Google Id
     Event e = new Event(Id =
     p.subStringBetween(
     'Content-ID: <response-','>'));
     e.Google_Id__c =
        p.subStringBetween('"id": "','"');
        eventUpdates.add(e);
  }
}
//as long as we aren't deleting
if (!eventUpdates.isEmpty() && !deleting)
update eventUpdates;
}
}
```

And now! The final piece of the puzzle! Building HttpRequest:

```
public static HttpRequest buildRequest(User u,
  list<calloutWrapper> eventList){
httpRequest req = new httpRequest();
  //boundary to be used to denote individual events in our batch
  //this can be anything, since this is a use case, foobar :)
  String boundary = '_____batch_foobarbaz';
  //let Google know what our boundary is
  req.setHeader('Content-Type','multipart/mixed;
  boundary='+boundary);
  //add the access token as our authentication
  //note the space after Bearer
  req.setHeader('Authorization','Bearer '
    +u.Google_Access_Token__c);
  req.setMethod('POST');
  //we're sending a batch request, so we have a special endpoint
  req.setEndpoint('https://www.googleapis.com/batch');
  //max timeout
  req.setTimeout(120000);
  //construct our body
  String reqBody = '';
  //for every wrapped event
  for ( calloutWrapper e : eventList ){
    //start every event with a boundary
    reqBody += '--'+boundary+cr;
    //define type
    reqBody += 'Content-Type: application/http'+cr;
```

```
        //identify with our Salesforce id
        reqBody +='Content-ID: <'+e.salesforceEventId+'>'+cr+cr;
        //what are we doing to this event? insert,update,delete?
        //aka post,patch,delete
        reqBody += e.Method+' ';
        //identify the calendar, by email address
        reqBody +=   '/calendar/v3/calendars/'+
        encodingUtil.urlEncode(
        u.google_email__c,'UTF-8');
//add in the path for events on calendars
        reqBody += '/events';
        //need an id to delete / update
        if ( string.isNotBlank(e.GoogleEventId) &&
        (e.Method == 'PATCH' || e.Method == 'DELETE')){
            reqBody += '/'+e.googleEventId;
        }
        reqBody += cr+
'Content-Type: application/json;charset=UTF-8'+cr;
        //delete requests don't need these
        if ( e.method != 'DELETE' ){
           reqBody += 'Content-Length: '+e.Body.length()+cr;
           reqBody += cr;
           reqBody += e.Body;
        }
        reqBody += cr;
    }
    //close off our batch request with a boundary
    reqBody += '--'+boundary+'--';
    // for debugging, let's see what we've got
    system.debug(reqBody);
    //set the body
    req.setBody(reqBody);
    //be good and set required length header
    req.setHeader(
'Content-Length',string.valueOf(reqBody.length()));
    return req;
}
```

 Since we are using batch mode to potentially send multiple events to Google, Google has a special endpoint that needs to be added as a remote site, `https://www.googleapis.com/batch`, just like the accounts one before. This endpoint is different if you are processing single events and can be found in the Google Calendar API documentation if needed.

Woo-hoo! We've done it! Congratulations! Why should you be so happy you ask? Because we are now *armed to the teeth* to start spamming a Google calendar. Don't believe us? Open up Execute Anonymous (Eclipse or Developer Console, refer to *Chapter 6, Exposing Force.com to the World*) and run this (make sure to replace the highlighted ID with the ID of an event that you own, or any other whose Google calendar you can see, and if they have authenticated through our app. If you don't have a Salesforce event handy, go stick one on your Salesforce calendar, we'll wait (make sure to set start and end dates/times!):

```
googleCalendar_API.processEventList([Select Subject,
    StartDateTime, OwnerId, Location, IsAllDayEvent, Id,
    EndDateTime, DurationInMinutes, Description, ActivityDateTime,
    ActivityDate, google_id__c From Event where id =
    '00Uo0000001JVWT'], false);
```

The `false` value in our snippet is for that `deleting` Boolean, just in case you were wondering; we also have to query for all the fields we use in our methods. Did the event appear on your Google calendar? Awesome. If not, follow the troubleshooting tips we've been discussing, as well as those from *Chapter 6, Exposing Force.com to the World*.

Ok, now about that button—super simple. All you have to do is proceed with the following steps:

1. Flip our `googleCalendar_API` class to global.

2. Make a `webservice` method like in *Chapter 6, Exposing Force.com to the World*.

3. Create a corresponding custom `onClick` JavaScript button on the event object.

4. Pass in the Event ID as a parameter to the `webservice` method from the button.

5. For the body of your method, use the previous snippet and just swap the hardcoded ID with the passed in variable one. Don't forget to add a button to the page layout!

Here's the `webservice` method:

```
webservice static void pushEvent(id eventid){
    googleCalendar_API.processEventList([Select Subject,
    StartDateTime, OwnerId, Location, IsAllDayEvent, Id,
    EndDateTime, DurationInMinutes, Description, ActivityDateTime,
    ActivityDate, google_id__c From Event where id = :eventid],
    false);
}
```

Here is the JavaScript button:

```
//Required Import Statements
{!REQUIRESCRIPT("/soap/ajax/32.0/connection.js")}
{!REQUIRESCRIPT("/soap/ajax/32.0/apex.js")}
//Call your method, replace variables as needed
var result = sforce.apex.execute("googleCalendar_API", " pushEvent
   ",{eventid : '{!Event.Id}'});
```

Done! Now, obviously we don't want to be syncing every single event manually! Let's take a look at some automation.

Let me google that for you

The **let me Google that for you** website, `http://lmgtfy.com`, is a great website to use when your friends ask you a silly question, which no one could possibly know the answer to, and you have to Google it; but we digress. You would think that if you're busy enough, you need a calendar to control the minutiae of your life, then you could afford a personal assistant to enter in all your calendar entries for you. However, we all know that isn't really the case, and since you are already paying for a Salesforce1 Platform license, why not let Force.com be your personal assistant?

We've already demonstrated that triggers are excellent at automating tasks when a database operation is performed—in this case, insertion, update, or deletion of a calendar event. With a fairly simple trigger, we can push our calendar events to Google's calendar when they are acted upon through DML. Let's take a look. Please refer to *Chapter 4, Triggers and Classes*, for more information regarding triggers, and why the following is being split into a trigger and class if that's confusing to you for any reason. Here's the trigger:

```
trigger event_Trigger on Event (after insert, after update,
   after delete) {

   //joint after insert/update methods
//are typically referred to as upsert
   if (trigger.isAfter &&
   (trigger.isInsert || trigger.isUpdate))
   event_Methods.afterUpsert(trigger.new);

   //after delete triggers only have old collections
//refer to chapter 4
   if (trigger.isAfter && trigger.isDelete)
   event_Methods.afterDelete(trigger.old);
}
```

Here's our class:

```
public with sharing class event_Methods {
  public static void afterUpsert(list<Event> newlist){
    googleCalendar_API.processEventList(newlist), false);
  }
}
```

Simple right? But alas, it is not. The `processEventList` method results in callouts being performed. You can't do that in a trigger. I would recommend you to review *Chapter 4, Triggers and Classes* again and fix the problem like this:

```
public with sharing class event_Methods {

//note the deletion Boolean for the different operations
  public static void afterUpsert(list<Event> newlist){
    processLater(JSON.serialize(newlist), false);
  }

  public static void afterDelete(list<Event> oldlist){
    processLater(JSON.serialize(oldlist), true);
  }


  //the @future annotation allows us to get around the Trigger
  //limitation of no callouts by performing the task /  //
asynchronously
@Future(callout=true)
  public static void processLater(string serializedEvents,
  boolean deleting){
    list<Event> eventsList =
      (list<Event>)JSON.deserialize(serializedEvents,
      list<Event>.class);
    googleCalendar_API.processEventList(eventsList, deleting);
  }
}
```

You might be wondering, why did we just serialize the list into a JSON string and then deserialized it right back again? Well, the `@future` methods can only take in primitive parameters, again, back to *Chapter 4, Triggers and Classes*! Try it out. Make a new event and watch it *automagically* appear on your Google calendar. Ok, now update it. Oops? Another new event was created, but the old one is still there. What gives? Well, remember that we are updating our events with the new Google IDs. Essentially, we are inserting, Google IDs, which is calling our @future method. The @future method updates the event, which causes us to call another `@future`. I'm shaking my finger right now; can't do that. If you look at the debug logs, you'll see a nasty error about it. Fortunately, it's really easy to get around it; just add a check to see if you are already in an `@future` method. The `system.isFuture()` method will return the Boolean you need, and you can update your methods as shown (remember to do it to the delete too):

```
if (!system.isFuture())
    processLater(JSON.serialize(newlist), false);
```

That's it. If you have a very small organization, in which single users do not edit large amounts of events in one action, you're done. This includes something like data loading events in—this would not work with the current setup.

Not so fast

Triggers with the `@future` methods are all well and good, but remember that there is a limit to how many callouts you can do per thread, as well as how many future methods you can schedule at a time. Due to the simplicity of the Salesforce1 Platform, many starting developers forget about all the limits and design apps that do not scale well at all. This could potentially be one of those times.

Let's crunch some numbers. With our current configuration, we are doing two callouts per owner of events (token refresh and actual callout). This means we are limited to events changing for five owners in a single `@future` method (10 callouts per `@future` method currently allowed) and would have to take care to group them in such a way that our current code does not do this. Moreover, you are currently limited to 10 `@future` calls per thread, so if we uniquely split owners apart, we could at most handle 50 owners. But wait! There's more! Google has a limit of 50 requests per batch request, which means we could at most handle 250 event updates per DML thread. Ouch! If someone ever did a data load or sync with a different calendar (we're looking at you Outlook users), we would be in trouble. Custom code that creates/updates/deletes events could also be bad news. Nasty exceptions would abound and we'd have partially synced data, eww!

Now granted, we are probably talking about less likely instances than common place occurrences, but as developers striving for excellent quality, we can't just roll over and deploy code that can't scale!

So what do we do? Are we completely out of luck? No way! This is where batches come to the rescue. As you can recall from *Chapter 3, More and Later*, batches allow us to chunk our data up and are very commonly used to bypass limits due to volume of data. So order some pizza and grab a cold one, we're not even close to being done yet.

Wow, a section with all text, no pictures, and no code – we'll make up for it, we promise!

My, aren't we busy?

Chances are you don't need to have your calendars sync instantly or maybe you do? You'll have the option to set the batch as close to instant as possible shortly. First, let's take a look at what in the heck it is that we are planning on doing.

Long story short, we want the ability to bulk process calendar events that have been created, updated, or deleted with a certain frequency. We are worried that we will start hitting limits, and are trying to make our code scalable. So we are turning to batches, which is what these buggers are for! The logic is going to be—find me all events, since our last sync, that have been created/changed and push them. Then find me all the events that have been deleted since our last delete, and get rid of them in Google. Ok. We're going to need somewhere to store our last sync and last delete times.

Custom settings

These are probably some of the most useful and powerful tools available to us developers when we want to give the end user control over something that would typically be hardcoded, or something that simply doesn't belong in a user table, especially if we don't want to query for just one row! They are similar to **Custom Labels** described in *Chapter 5, Visualforce Development with Apex*, in that they are ever-present and available and can be modified through the UI. Let's create our custom setting to hold our sync times. Proceed with the following steps:

1. Click on **Setup**, you know how to get here right?
2. Under the **Build** section, navigate to **Develop | Custom Settings**.
3. Click on **New**.
4. Give it a label and an API name (object name), for example, `GoogleCalendar`.
5. Change **Setting type** to **List** (hierarchy is a beast left alone for now).
6. **Visibility**, we tend to set this to public in case we ever toss it into a managed package, but either works for us.
7. Enter description only if you're feeling talkative.
8. Now click on **Save**.
9. On this page, click on **New** in the **Custom Fields** section.

10. Make a new **DateTime** field called `LastSync`.

11. To complete the steps, click on **Save and New**.

12. Make a new **DateTime** field called `LastDelete`.

13. Save this and click on **Manage** at the top of the next page.

14. Now, create a new **DateTime** field, call it `BatchSync` and save it.

Picking up where we left off

Clicking is exhausting isn't it? Now that we can store our `LastSync` and `LastDelete` values, let's tackle the batch class:

```
//recall from chapter 4 how to instantiate a batch
//Database.AllowsCallouts is necessary for us to perform callouts
//during the batch, and Database.Batchable is the batch interface
global class batch_GoogleCalendar_Sync implements
Database.Batchable<sObject>, Database.AllowsCallouts{
   //class variables for use during processing
   global final string queryString;
   global final boolean deleting;
   global final dateTime lastSync;
   global final dateTime lastDelete;

   //constructor taking in our infamous deletion boolean
   global batch_GoogleCalendar_Sync(boolean del) {
     //retrieve our custom setting for last sync/delete times
     GoogleCalendar__c gcBatchSync =
     GoogleCalendar__c.getInstance('BatchSync');
     lastSync = gcBatchSync.lastSync__c;
     lastDelete = gcBatchSync.lastDelete__c;

     //if there has never been a sync/deletion set a
     //time long, long ago, in a galaxy far, far away
     if (lastSync==null) lastSync =
     dateTime.newinstance(1970,1,1);
     if (lastDelete==null) lastDelete =
     dateTime.newinstance(1970,1,1);

//just copying our constructor instance variable to //class level
     deleting = del;

     //construct the query string to include necessary fields
     //this is the same as our execute anonymous
     if (string.isBlank(queryString)){
```

```
    string temp = 'Select   Subject, StartDateTime,
    OwnerId, Location, IsAllDayEvent, Id, EndDateTime,
    DurationInMinutes, Description, ActivityDateTime,
    ActivityDate, google_id__c From Event';
  //if deleting is true, our query is different        //we have to
add the isDeleted attribute
    if (deleting){
      temp += ' where lastModifiedDate >
      :lastDelete AND isDeleted = true';
      //and the query ALL ROWS flag
//which enables us to query deleted records in the //Recycle Bin; if
they have been removed from the
//Recycle Bin, we can't query them anymore
      temp += ' ALL ROWS';
    }
    //if not deleting, just get modified date
    else temp += ' where lastModifiedDate >
    :lastSync';

    //this will become clearer in chapter 9
    if (test.isRunningTest()) temp += ' limit 1';

    //assign the query string and debug for debug...
    queryString = temp;
    system.debug(queryString);
  }
  //set lastSync / lastDelete based on operation
  if(deleting) gcBatchSync.lastDelete__c = system.now();
  else gcBatchSync.lastSync__c = system.now();
  //update our custom setting to preserve latest times
    update gcBatchSync;
  }
  //batch functional method to get next chunk
  global Database.QueryLocator start(
  Database.BatchableContext bc){
    return Database.getQueryLocator(queryString);
  }
  //the execute method where we do our logic for every chunk
  global void execute(Database.BatchableContext bc,
  list<Event> scope){
    //call our handy Google API method to process the events
    //passing in our trusty deleting boolean
    googleCalendar_API.processEventList(scope, deleting);
  }
```

```
//batch functional method when we're done with the entirety of
//the batch; we're going to use this method to cause our batch //to
run infinitely; deletes should run instantly after syncs, //and then
pause before the next sync
  global void finish(Database.BatchableContext bc){
    if(deleting) startBatchDelay(false,5);
    else startBatch(true);
  }
//utility method for starting the batch instantly with //deleting
boolean
  global static void startBatch(boolean d){
    batch_GoogleCalendar_Sync job = new
    batch_GoogleCalendar_Sync(d);
    database.executeBatch(job,50);
  }

  //utility method for starting the batch on a delay
//with deleting boolean; specify delay in whole integer //minutes
  global static void startBatchDelay(boolean d, integer min){
    batch_GoogleCalendar_Sync job = new
    batch_GoogleCalendar_Sync(d);
    system.scheduleBatch(  job,
'GoogleCalendarSync-'+((d)?'del':'upsert'),
  min,50);
  }
}
```

Fairly small, simple batch class. Note that we are setting the job size maximum to 50; as you can recall, that is Google's max limit per batch request callout. We're literally leveraging the same methods we've already seen and used. We have essentially ported over our Execute Anonymous script from our elder days and adapted it to query for events based on last modified and deleted attributes dependent on a Boolean we pass into the class constructor. Pretty nifty eh? Remember how we said that **Custom Settings** are a great way to let the user control what they want to do? Well what if you want to have the batch run more frequently? It's currently hardcoded to 5 minutes; that's too bad! Let's add that to our custom setting. Proceed with the following steps:

1. Go back to **Setup** through to **Custom Settings | GoogleCalendar**.

2. Create a **New** custom field `Frequency(min)`, of type **Number**; no decimals.

3. Save this and go to **Manage**.

4. Set the value to any number, and click on **Save**.

While we're here, let's make this a little easier to look at. You should be at the **GoogleCalendar Manage** screen with the list views. If not, get there by navigating to, **Setup | Custom Settings | GoogleCalendar | Manage**.

Select where it says **View: All** in a drop-down menu. Now proceed with the following steps:

1. Create a **New** view.

2. Name it All for both **View Name** and **View Unique Name**.

3. Add in the **Name, Frequency(min), LastSync, LastDelete** columns.

4. Save and revel in your new spiffy visual of how the batch is configured.

Let's update our batch class to respect this new setting now. We only have to modify the finish method:

```
global void finish(Database.BatchableContext bc){
   //retrieve our custom setting
   GoogleCalendar__c gcBatchSync =
GoogleCalendar__c.getInstance('BatchSync');
   //even no decimal place number fields are decimals in
   //the Salesforce Schema
   decimal delayMin = gcBatchSync.frequency_min__c;
   //If no one set this up, or tried to do a negative #
   if (delayMin == null || delayMin < 0) delayMin = 0;

   if(deleting) startBatchDelay(false,integer.valueof(delayMin));
   else startBatch(true);
}
```

How easy was that? Now you never ever have to go back into the code, compile it, stop the scheduled/running processes (can't modify a batch class if it is in progress or scheduled to be run) and wait for test coverage (*Chapter 9, Test Coverage*) to completely run so that you can deploy a change; all just to alter how often the sync runs. Also, keep in mind that if the sync ever fails for whatever reason, simply changing the date and time of when the last sync/deletion occurred will allow you to backtrack your pushes to Google.

I see a problem, do you? Depending on how busy your organization is, and how many users you have—if we query for 50 events per chunk, then it's possible that each one of them could be owned by someone different! We can only have five different owners per thread remember? (An execute of a batch chunk is considered a thread.) We should really change the job size to five. We'll let you go back and add a field for JobSize to the **Custom Setting** for GoogleCalendar BatchSync and update your code accordingly; it's good practice.

Now that we have a fully running, scalable batch, let's remove those triggers we made earlier so they don't conflict. Also, it's important to note that batches have certain quirks to them. For example, they get queued and can take a few minutes to get rolling. Likewise, scheduled processes can be stuck waiting in line and might not run exactly when you specify. There is a very large slip window that Salesforce clings to (just in case), but we have never seen a delay of more than a few minutes for extremely busy times.

To run the batch instantly, just execute anonymously the following line of code:

```
//start without deleting batch_GoogleCalendar_Sync.startBatch(false);
```

To run it in a few minutes:

```
//start without deleting
batch_GoogleCalendar_Sync.startBatchDelay(false,5);
```

Nifty! I like simple methods that do heavy lifting, don't you?

Summary

Your take away from this chapter should be that the Salesforce1 Platform is awesome. Google is awesome. Put the two together and you get über awesome.

We've shown you how to push all of your data to Google, essentially a one-way sync. I now challenge you to go out there and use this knowledge and Google's documentation (and search engine for Stack Overflow and the likes) to figure out how to sync data from Google into Force.com to create a true bidirectional sync.

Be mindful of limits, and try to think up crazy fun ways of working around them; it's what makes being a Force.com developer fun. While you're at it, try to think of new ideas and things you can do with this integration. For example, many people have more than one calendar that they have access to. How would you go about handling that scenario? You would have to store your tokens differently and identify the matching calendars somehow. What if someone at your organization wanted to use the resources calendar (for rooms, equipment, and so on), those too have to be handled differently.

We hope getting your integration to work takes you less time than it took to write this chapter, and that you'll see just how easy it is to work with the Salesforce1 Platform.

With all that spare time you'll have, you can start reading the next chapter in which we walk you through building a complete working application. It is the pièce de résistance of this book. The chapter to end all chapters (not really, there still is one more after it, but you get the point), the final frontier in these voyages of Force.com development. So grab a fresh cup of coffee, stretch your typing fingers, and engage!

8
Creating a Property Management Application

At this point, we've seen many different aspects of development on the Salesforce1 Platform and should be fairly familiar with both declarative and programmatic solutions to our everyday problems, as well as when to use which solution. In this chapter, we're going to mesh many of the things we have previously learned into a single application on the Salesforce1 Platform after doing a quick analysis run-through.

A big selling point for salesforce.com and the Salesforce1 Platform in general is how transparent the data is and how easy it is to run complex reports using the report builder. Although the process of building a report is outside the scope of this book, it is an important consideration when designing a data model to know your reporting capabilities. You don't want to spend time and effort into designing a perfectly running application that you can't run any meaningful reports on.

So here's the agenda—we're going to discuss what we want to keep track of, who is involved in the process, and what pieces of data are important for us to know about. On top of this, we're going to toss on some functionality to allow for very basic credit card processing (nothing is stopping you from making it more complex and functional!) and present the information in an easy-to-read manner.

Let's get started with using the trusty model of who, what, where, when, why, and how (not necessarily in that order). Note that this will be an overly simplistic model, one that does not account for every little nuance that exists with regard to property management. It is intended to demonstrate the functionality of the Salesforce1 Platform.

Why

Why, exactly, are we trying to do something? That should be the first question you always ask yourself. My typical approach is to gather a high-level overview first; this way, you never lose sight of the big picture. So, at the high-level overview, we want to track rental units, who's renting them, and whether or not they have paid up. Then, you should get into slightly more specific details. On a more in-depth look, we'd also like to know who actually owns the unit, whether or not it's part of a complex system, what additional fees (if any) are accumulated, possibly take a look at vendors who render services to the complex, as well as payment information. Finally, the actual data elements (fields) that we need to collect in order for our app to be as useful as possible and keep the accountants off our backs by offering a high return on investment on licensing/development work. We'll cover fields a little later. For now, let's take a look at the key things and people/entities involved.

What

We're interested in our rental units, right? We also want to be able to aggregate information across the rental units if they are part of a complex to determine the complex's overall performance. Who owns the units can also be a good aggregate piece of information, and let's not forget the actual fees/deposit/rent to be charged as well as their payment status and associated payments.

Who

So we know what we are interested in. Who we are interested in are the owners of the properties, those renting them, any vendors who render services to the property, and any pertinent contact information for each as well as any relationships that might exist related to these.

How

We'll use Accounts and Contacts to handle our *who* including owners, renters (households), as well as vendors. Then, we'll use custom objects to handle our *what* as well as a custom junction object to link our Contacts to rental units.

Although not a topic for discussion, you can set workflows to create tasks as reminders to our staff to calculate monthly dues for our renters, and e-mail reminders to the renters if their bill is due in one day as well as when it becomes past due.

For the payment processing aspect, we will use a very basic, charge-only, Authorize.net integration. We will also allow payments to be saved for cash and check payments via manual entry. More workflows here can send out e-mail notifications to the renter that their bill is now available as well as receipts when it has been paid. For our code in the mix, we'll send the receipts for Authorize.net transactions from Apex.

We'll also show you how to use Apex to do roll-up summaries once you pass the limit (there is a limit on the number of roll-up summaries you can have per object), or want to roll up to the parent of the parent, or there are other limiting factors that prevent you from using the inherent ability of master-detail relationships, which we'll cover. These are all commonplace scenarios in data-intensive organizations.

When and Where

We couldn't just forget about these! Whenever you want and from within Salesforce!

A custom model

No colorful step-by-step instructions here, or pop ups sadly, but we do have pages and pages of text and cryptic code for you! All of it interlaced with the best comments you can have to guide you through to success.

Let's break down all of the objects and data elements (fields) that we need to make this work.

 Review previous chapters for step-by-step instructions on how to create custom fields and settings.

Account (standard object)

These record types will allow us to track Accounts used for different purposes:

- Household (to contain owners/renters)
- Vendor (for all types of vendors)

Contact (standard object)

We want to create these custom fields to track information about each person:

- Total number of properties owned (roll-up summary: COUNT properties)
- Total number of units owned (roll-up summary: SUM property: Total Units)

One thing we have not yet covered is how to create a custom object. It's a fairly straightforward process that should be familiar to you now that you have made other custom data elements on the Salesforce1 Platform. To create a new custom object, perform the following steps:

1. Click on the **Setup** link in the top-right corner of the Force.com GUI.

2. Under the **Create** section, click on **Objects**.

3. Click on **New Custom Object**.

4. Enter in the name (label).

5. Enter in the plural label; usually this just adds an "s" and is used when referencing multiple records of this object.

6. **Object Name** (the API name) is autogenerated from the name.

7. For **Record Name**, determine whether an autonumber or free text is more appropriate.

8. Select **Allow Reports, Activities**, and **Track Field History** as appropriate.

9. Check **Add Notes and Attachments related list** as appropriate (you can always add this later if you decide you want notes/attachments on your object).

10. Check **Launch new Custom Tab Wizard after saving this custom object** to make a tab for your new object. Note that not all objects require a tab.

> Remember that in order to create roll-up summary fields, you will first have to create both the master and detail (parent/child) objects and required fields, and then return to the master object to create the roll-up summary field.

Property (custom object)

The Property object will house the physical location of our property assets, be it an apartment building, a housing complex, or a single unit (in which case, the property will have one and only one rental unit).

When you create an object, you'll be presented with some options; go ahead and configure the Property object as follows:

- **Allow Reports**
- **Allow Activities**
- **Create New Tab**

An object without fields is like a car without wheels; so let's set up some fields:

- Owner (**Master-Detail**: Contact)
- Physical Street (**Text Area** length 255)
- Physical City (**Text** length 255)
- Physical State (**Text** length 2)
- Physical Postal Code (**Text** length 10)
- Laundry Vendor (**Lookup** Account)
- Vending Machines Vendor (**Lookup** Account)
- Phone Vendor (**Lookup** Account)
- TV Vendor (**Lookup** Account)
- Internet Vendor (**Lookup** Account)
- Security Vendor (**Lookup** Account)
- Total Units (**Roll-up Summary** COUNT (rental unit))
- Year Built (**Text** length 4)
- Community Features (Multiselect picklist)
    - Pool
    - Tennis Court
    - Gym
    - Track
    - Basketball Court
    - Community Area
    - Play Area
- Gated (**Checkbox**)

Each type of Property has different attributes; so we're going to set up these record types:

- Apartment Building
- Housing Complex
- Condominium
- House
- Duplex
- Other Multi-tenant Housing

Rental Unit

Rental units will be the actual units for rent. This object will define all of the attributes such as bathrooms, bedrooms, square footage, as well as other information typically collected when renting/owning property.

The Rental Units object should be set up with these options:

- **Allow Reports**
- **Allow Activities**

We have to know more about each unit; so set up these custom fields:

- Unit # (**Text,** length 255)
- Number of Bedrooms (**Number** 2, 0 decimals)
- Number of Bathrooms (**Number** 2, 2 decimals)
- Floors (**Number** 2, 0 decimals)
- Garage (**Picklist**):
    - Attached
    - Detached
    - Assigned Parking
- Number of Parking Spaces (**Number** 2, 0 decimals)
- Laundry (**Picklist**)
    - In-unit hook-ups
    - Community
- Appliances Included (**Checkbox**)
- Furniture Included (**Checkbox**)
- Total Square Feet (**Number** 15, 3 decimals)
- Air Conditioning (**Picklist**)
    - Window Unit
    - Ceiling Fan
    - Central
- Heating (**Picklist**)
    - Forced Air
    - Central

- Pets Allowed (**Checkbox**)
- Utilities Included (Multiselect Picklist)
    - ○ Cold Water
    - ○ Hot Water
    - ○ Gas
    - ○ Electric
    - ○ Sewage
    - ○ Trash

Rental Agreement (custom junction object)

The Rental Agreement will store specific information for the rental term, including the agreed upon rental amount, deposits, and balances for the unique relationship of renter to rental unit.

We hope you're seeing a pattern; we like being able to take advantage of the built-in features such as reporting, so set up these options on this object:

- **Allow Reports**
- **Allow Activities**
- **Track Field History**
- **Show Notes and Attachments Related List**

This is no standard junction object. It serves a very important purpose, so we need to set up these key fields on it:

- Rental Unit (Master-Detail: Rental Unit)
- Renter (**Primary**) (Master-Detail: Contact)
- Pet Deposit (**Currency** 16, 2 decimals)
- Renter Has Pets (**Checkbox**)
- Deposit (**Currency** 16, 2 decimals)
- Rental Amount (**Currency** 16, 2 decimals)
- Total Deposit (**Formula, Currency** 16, 2 decimals)
  Pet_Deposit__c + Deposit__c

- Total Invoiced (**Currency** 16, 2 decimals). This will perform the Apex roll-up of Statement amounts from Statement here

- Total Payments (**Currency**: 16, 2 decimals). This will perform the Apex roll-up of Payments from Statement here
- Balance (**Formula**, **Currency** 16, 2 decimals)

  Total_Invoiced__c - Total_Payments__c

Statement (custom object)

Statements will house our invoices, or in other words, what we expect our renter to pay for this rental property, plus any additional fees incurred.

Here are the options to be set up for the Statement object:

- **Allow Reports**
- **Allow Activities**
- **Track Field History**

Statements are about money; so we need some fields to track it:

- Amount (**Currency** 16, 2 decimals)
- Additional Fees (**Currency** 16, 2 decimals, the default value is 0)
- Total Amount (**Formula**, **Currency** 16, 2)

  Amount__c + Additional_Fees__c

- Rental Agreement (**Lookup**, Rental Agreement)

 You would think this would be a Master-Detail relationship. However, because Rental Agreement is a junction object (with two masters), you cannot set the Statement as a detail object; details of junctions are not allowed on the Salesforce1 Platform.

- Statement Date (**Date**, the default value is *TODAY()*)
- Due Date (**Date**, the default value is *TODAY()+15*)
- Status (**Picklist**)
  - Issued
  - Paid
  - Past Due
- Amount Paid (**Roll-up Summary**: SUM(Payment: Amount), where status= Paid

Payment (custom object)

We'll use the Payment object to store individual transaction information, the type of payment, as well as any relevant authorization codes, and so on. We frequently get into academic debates with peers on this type of object with regards to the payment method. Many argue that this should be a picklist option. However, others such as myself believe that record types fulfill this requirement much better, as they can control the page layout of the Payment record; this allows you to only show fields relevant to that payment method. For example, why would you care to see all the credit card fields if you paid by check or cash?

Of course, we want to be able to report on Payments, so set up these options:

- **Allow Reports**
- **Allow Activities**
- **Track Field History**

We're going to need some record types, as not all payments are the same:

- Credit Card
- Check
- Cash

Here are the custom fields you need to create on the Payment object:

- Amount (**Currency** 16, 2 decimals)
- Statement (Master-Detail: Statement)
- Status (Picklist)
    - Paid
    - Failed
- Payment Date (**Date/Time**)
- Authorize.net Transaction ID (**Text**, length 255; **External Id**)

 By marking the transaction ID as an external ID, it will automatically be indexed for searches, allowing us to quickly find transactions based on this ID.

- `Authorize.net Authorization Code` (**Text** length 255)
- `Authorize.net Response` (**Text** length 255)
- `Billing Name` (**Text** length 255)
- `Billing Street` (**Text Area** length 255)
- `Billing City` (**Text** length 255)
- `Billing State` (**Text** length 2)
- `Billing Postal Code` (**Text** length 10)
- `Check Account Number` (**Encrypted Text** length 128, mask 4)
- `Check Routing Number` (**Encrypted Text** length 128, mask 4)
- `Credit Card Number` (**Encrypted Text** length 16, mask credit card)
- `Credit Card Expiration Month` (**Picklist**)
    - January
    - ...
    - December
- `Credit Card Expiration Year` (**Text** length 4)
- `Credit Card Security Code` (**Encrypted Text** length 4, mask all)

> Even though we are marking some of these fields as encrypted, those without the **View Encrypted Data** permission can still edit these fields to update. The Apex-based functionality is also possible (the code sees the real value).

Let's also create a custom setting while we are in the mindset of clicking around–we will use it later in order to facilitate the Authorize.net functionality; let's make it a public list type setting.

The Authorize.net setting (custom setting)

Remember that custom settings are different from custom objects, but they too have some options:

- **List**
- **Public**

We like to use key-value pairs, so you just need to create one easy field:

- Value (**Text** length 255)

Now that we have our data model set up, let's throw some functionality in.

Paying your dues

We think we can skip the mafia bosses and objects to track broken knees, let's just stick to Authorize.net to process credit cards and the check or cash option via manual entry. Recall from *Chapter 6, Exposing Force.com to the World,* and *Chapter 7, Use Case – Integration with Google Calendar,* everything we said about interacting with external services, their terms, and so on—we're about to put it to good use.

Head on over to developer.authorize.net to sign up for a sandbox account, as shown:

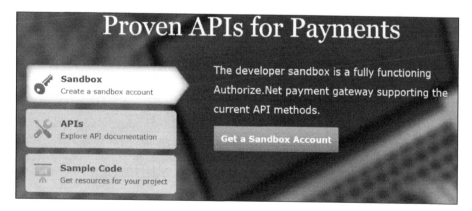

Once you have signed up for an account, you will get an e-mail from Authorize.net confirming your signup, and you can venture over to sandbox.authorize.net to log in. Once you have logged in, proceed with the following steps:

1. Navigate to the **Account** tab; it should be in the rightmost corner.

2. Click on **API Login ID and Transaction Key**; this is highlighted in the following screenshot:

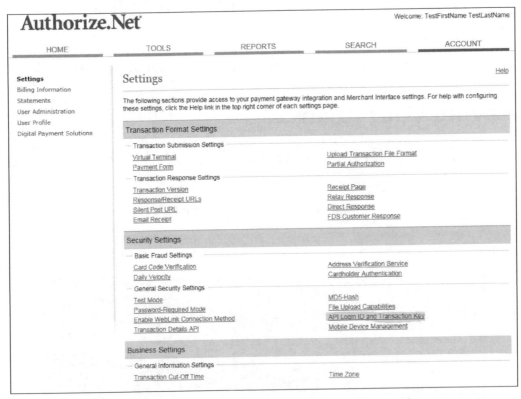

3. Once you are on the next screen, you will have to generate a new transaction key. In order to do so, you need to know your secret answer, as shown in the following screenshot:

API Login ID and Transaction Key

Help

Your API Login ID and Transaction Key are unique pieces of information specifically associated with your payment gateway account. However, the API login ID and Transaction Key are NOT used for logging into the Merchant Interface. These two values are only required when setting up an Internet connection between your e-commerce Web site and the payment gateway. They are used by the payment gateway to authenticate that you are authorized to submit Web site transactions.

IMPORTANT: The API Login ID and Transaction Key should not be shared with anyone. Be sure to store these values securely and change the Transaction Key regularly to further strengthen the security of your account.

For more information about the API Login ID and Transaction Key, please refer to the Reference & User Guides or contact your Web developer.

API Login ID:	37Kt2d6aRg7
API Login ID Last Obtained:	10/08/2014 20:55:36
Transaction Key Last Obtained:	10/08/2014 20:56:00

Create New Transaction Key

* Required Fields

You may obtain a new Transaction Key as often as you wish by providing your Secret Answer. You may choose to disable the old one immediately by checking the **Disable Old Transaction Key(s)** option. If you do not immediately disable the old value, it will automatically expire in 24 hours.

Secret Question: What is your pet's name?

Secret Answer: [••••] *

☐ Disable Old Transaction Key(s)

[Submit] [Cancel]

In fact, it's so secretive that you don't even know what it is! Don't believe me? Try answering, we bet you'll get it wrong. We never actually set this up, so how are we supposed to answer? Well, Authorize.net included it in that sign-up confirmation e-mail for you. It's not indicated in any way, so you'll just have to read through the e-mail for it, as shown here:

log in to the Merchant Interface and click "Account." Then click "API Login ID and Transaction Key." Your A
To do this you will need the Secret Answer to the system-generated Secret Question, which is "Simon".

If you're trying to skim through and are having issues retrieving your transaction key because of your secret answer, read the last paragraph, it will save you loads of head-scratching time.

4. Make sure that you save your transaction key. If you lose it, you will have to generate another, and your old ones will become inactive. (Don't try using the combo shown in the text here, as it has been changed; you need to get your own.)

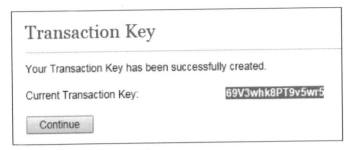

Okay, remember the Authorize.net setting we made earlier? Let's go fill it up:

1. Navigate to **Setup | Develop | Custom Settings**.

2. Click on **Manage** next to the Authorize.net setting.

3. Create an API login record (name) with your API login ID.

4. Create a transaction key record (name) with your transaction key.

Great! Finally, we are done with our point-and-click setup. Now we can look at some code!

 The process to attain your live API login ID and transaction key are identical, except that you would log in at http://www.authorize.net/ instead of the sandbox.

The following slew of code is a complete class for the Authorize.net integration we will be using in this chapter. It has many moving parts, with custom classes (wrappers) declared at the bottom of the class, references to static class variables, and other elements that will be much easier to explain if you follow along with the comments:

```
public class api_AuthorizeDotNet {
   //variables to hold our login credentials
   //these will get set later
   public static string APILOGIN;
   public static string APITRANSKEY;

   //method to process a credit card charge
   //takes in a parameter of authnetreq_wrapper, input
   //returns an authnetresp_wrapper
   //both are declared at the end of the class
   public static authnetresp_wrapper authdotnetCharge
```

```
(authnetreq_wrapper input) {
    //reusable method for setting Authorize.net credentials
    getAuthNetCreds();

    //Construct the request for a charge
    HttpRequest req = new HttpRequest();
    //for testing use the test endpoint
    //otherwise use
    //https://secure.authorize.net/gateway/transact.dll
        req.setEndpoint(
        'https://test.authorize.net/gateway/transact.dll');
        req.setMethod('POST');

    //build message
    Map<string,string> messagestring = new
    map<String,String>();

    //Default Fields
    //See the authorize.net documentation
    //for more information
    messagestring.put('x_login',APILOGIN);
    messagestring.put('x_tran_key',APITRANSKEY);
    messagestring.put('x_version', '3.1');
    messagestring.put('x_delim_data', 'TRUE');
    //specify delimiter character for response
    messagestring.put('x_delim_char', ';');
    messagestring.put('x_relay_response', 'FALSE');
    //The type of transaction
    messagestring.put('x_type', 'AUTH_CAPTURE');
    //Processing credit card
    messagestring.put('x_method', 'CC');

    //Transaction Specific Information
    //card numbers, expiration, security codes
    messagestring.put('x_card_num', input.ccnum);
    //expiration date in the format mmYYYY
    messagestring.put('x_exp_date', input.ccexp);
    messagestring.put('x_card_code', input.ccsec);

    //transaction amount
    messagestring.put('x_amount', input.amt);
    //description of transaction
    messagestring.put('x_description',
    'Your Transaction: '+input.ordername);

    //billing information
    messagestring.put('x_first_name', input.firstname);
```

```
        messagestring.put('x_last_name', input.lastname);
        messagestring.put('x_address', input.billstreet);
        messagestring.put('x_city', input.billcity);
        messagestring.put('x_state', input.billstate);
        messagestring.put('x_zip', input.billzip);

        //encode the message components
        String encodedmsg = '';
        for (string s : messagestring.keySet()){
          string v = messagestring.get(s);
          //fix null values
          if (string.isblank(v)) v='';
          encodedmsg += s+'='+
          EncodingUtil.urlEncode(v, 'UTF-8')+'&';
                //debug message value being added
              system.debug('TRACE: message bit '+s+' added');
        }
        //add message termination
        encodedmsg += 'endofdata';
        system.debug('TRACE: Encoded Message: \n\n'
        + encodedmsg);

        //set the body of the httprequest
        req.setBody(encodedmsg);

        //send and collect response
        Http http = new Http();
         string resp = http.send(req).getbody();
         //debug response
         system.debug(resp);
         //split response by our delimiter
           list<string> responses = resp.split(';');

           //use parsing method to return response wrapper
        authnetresp_wrapper parsedResponse =
        parseIntoResponseWrapper(responses);

        //debug response wrapper
        system.debug(parsedResponse);
        return parsedResponse;
    }

  public static void getAuthNetCreds(){
     //get api login setting value
     //test condition to generate test key
  //during test methods
```

```
    Authorize_net_Setting__c apiloginsetting =
    (test.isrunningTest())?
    (new Authorize_net_Setting__c(name='API Login',
    value__c = 'test')):
    ((Authorize_net_Setting__c.getInstance('API Login')));
    //get transaction key seting value
    //test condition to generate test
//key during test methods
    Authorize_net_Setting__c apitranskeysetting =
    (test.isrunningTest())?
    (new Authorize_net_Setting__c(name='API TransKey', value__c =
    'test')):
    ((Authorize_net_Setting__c.getInstance('API TransKey')));
    APILOGIN = apiloginsetting.value__c;
    APITRANSKEY = apitranskeysetting.value__c;
    }


    /**
    * Method to parse split response into wrapper
* based on appropriate indeces
    **/
    public static authNetResp_Wrapper
    parseIntoResponseWrapper(list<string> input){
      authNetResp_Wrapper temp = new authNetResp_Wrapper();
      temp.responseCode = input[0];
      temp.ResponseSubcode = input[1];
      temp.ResponseReasonCode =input[2];
      temp.ResponseReasonText=input[3];
      temp.AuthorizationCode=input[4];
      temp.AVSResponse= input[5];
      temp.TransactionID=input[6];
      temp.InvoiceNumber= input[7];
      temp.Description= input[8];
      temp.Amount= input[9];
      temp.Method= input[10];
      temp.TransactionType= input[11];
      temp.CustomerID= input[12];
      temp.FirstName= input[13];
      temp.LastName= input[14];
      temp.Company= input[15];
      temp.Address= input[16];
      temp.City= input[17];
      temp.State= input[18];
      temp.ZIPCode= input[19];
      temp.Country= input[20];
      temp.Phone= input[21];
      temp.Fax= input[22];
```

```
       temp.EmailAddress= input[23];
       temp.ShipToFirstName= input[24];
       temp.ShipToLastName= input[25];
       temp.ShipToCompany= input[26];
       temp.ShipToAddress= input[27];
       temp.ShipToCity= input[28];
       temp.ShipToState= input[29];
       temp.ShipToZIPCode= input[30];
       temp.ShipToCountry= input[31];
       temp.Tax= input[32];
       temp.Duty= input[33];
       temp.Freight= input[34];
       temp.TaxExempt= input[35];
       temp.PurchaseOrderNumber= input[36];
       temp.MD5Hash= input[37];
       temp.CardCodeResponse= input[38];
       temp.CardholderAuthenticationVerificationResponse= input[39];
       temp.AccountNumber= input[40];
       temp.CardType= input[41];
       temp.SplitTenderID= input[42];
       temp.RequestedAmount= input[43];
       temp.BalanceOnCard= input[44];
       return temp;
    }


    /**
     * The request wrapper. Holds all information
     * needed by Authorize.net to process a transaction
     * regardless of operation: charge, void, auth, refund
     **/
    public class authnetReq_Wrapper {
      public string ordername {get;set;}
      public string ccnum {get;set;}
      public string ccexp {get;set;}
      public string ccsec {get;set;}
      public string amt {get;set;}
      public string firstname {get;set;}
      public string lastname {get;set;}
      public string billstreet {get;set;}
      public string billcity {get;set;}
      public string billstate {get;set;}
      public string billzip {get;set;}
      public string transid {get; set;}
      public string routingnumber {get; set;}
      public string accountnumber {get; set;}
      public string bankaccounttype {get; set;}
      public string bankname {get; set;}
```

```
    public string bankaccountname {get; set;}

    public authnetreq_wrapper(){}
 }
 /**
   * Response wrapper. Holds the full Authorize.net response
    * in an easy to use object variable
    * Attributes are listed by return index rather than
 * alphabetically
 **/
 public class authNetResp_Wrapper{
    // value, index in split string list
    public string responseCode {get;set;} //0
    public string ResponseSubcode{get;set;} //1
    public string ResponseReasonCode{get;set;} //2
    public string ResponseReasonText{get;set;} //3
    public string AuthorizationCode{get;set;} //4
    public string AVSResponse{get;set;} //5
    public string TransactionID{get;set;} //6
    public string InvoiceNumber{get;set;} //7
    public string Description{get;set;} //8
    public string Amount{get;set;} //9
    public string Method{get;set;} //10
    public string TransactionType{get;set;} //11
    public string CustomerID{get;set;} //12
    public string FirstName{get;set;} //13
    public string LastName{get;set;} //14
    public string Company{get;set;} //15
    public string Address{get;set;} //16
    public string City{get;set;} //17
    public string State{get;set;} //18
    public string ZIPCode{get;set;} //19
    public string Country{get;set;} //20
    public string Phone{get;set;} //21
    public string Fax{get;set;} //22
    public string EmailAddress{get;set;} //23
    public string ShipToFirstName{get;set;} //24
    public string ShipToLastName{get;set;} //25
    public string ShipToCompany{get;set;} //26
    public string ShipToAddress{get;set;} //27
    public string ShipToCity{get;set;} //28
    public string ShipToState{get;set;} //29
    public string ShipToZIPCode{get;set;} //30
    public string ShipToCountry{get;set;} //31
```

```
public string Tax{get;set;} //32
public string Duty{get;set;} //33
public string Freight{get;set;} //34
public string TaxExempt{get;set;} //35
public string PurchaseOrderNumber{get;set;} //36
public string MD5Hash{get;set;} //37
public string CardCodeResponse{get;set;} //38
public string
CardholderAuthenticationVerificationResponse{get;set;} //39
public string AccountNumber{get;set;} //40
public string CardType{get;set;} //41
public string SplitTenderID{get;set;} //42
public string RequestedAmount{get;set;} //43
public string BalanceOnCard{get;set;} //44
public authnetresp_wrapper(){}
    }
  }
```

As can be seen after reading through this class, the wrappers are much more involved than they have to be for the credit card charge method. We've included the exploded versions of these wrappers, not to confuse the reader, but to give those reading this book a leg up in their ambitions to develop the missing methods to address the other functions available through Authorize.net such as electronic checks, refunding, voiding, and simple authorizations.

Forgetting something, are we? Yes, indeed we are. We need to authorize the endpoints in order for us to be able to communicate to Authorize.net. Head on over to **Setup | Security Controls | Remote Site Settings** and add these:

- **Live**: https://secure.authorize.net/gateway/transact.dll
- **Test**: https://test.authorize.net/gateway/transact.dll

Mine, all mine

Now that we have a payment processing solution available, let's put it to good use by creating an interactive Visualforce page that will allow us to collect credit card information for processing. We'll make this page and its extension fairly dynamic, because we will make this one single page available internally as an embedded page within the Statement record view page and as a standalone page overriding the **New** button for payments; we will make it available as an external page that will allow users to pay without logging into Salesforce! We will be using concepts from *Chapter 5, Visualforce Development with Apex*, and *Chapter 6, Exposing Force.com to the World*, extensively, so refer to those if the need arises.

Black magic

First steps first. We'll be using the standard controller for `Statement__c`, and we'll need a custom extension called `payments_Extension` that contains a `Payment__c` record variable. Go ahead and create this extension now in Eclipse by right-clicking and navigating to **src | New | Apex Class**. Your extension class should look like this:

```
public with sharing class payments_Extension {
  //Payment__c record variable to hold payment information
public Payment__c thisPayment {get;set;}
  public payments_Extension(ApexPages.StandardController scon) {
    thisPayment = new Payment__c();
    // our handling logic will go here.
  }
}
```

We'll also need our embedded Visualforce page; let's call it `statement_payment`. To create a new Visualforce page in Eclipse, just right-click on the `src` folder and navigate to **New | Visualforce page** and save it as this:

```
<apex:page standardController="Statement__c"
  extensions="payments_Extension" sidebar="false"
  showHeader="false">
  <!-- rest of page content -->
</apex:page>
```

We now have a blank page, which we can embed on our `Statement__c` view page as well as expose it on a Force.com site for the guest user to see. The next step is to add all of the relevant payment fields and details about the statement and also ensure that these details are only displayed when a guest user is viewing the page (otherwise, the page is being viewed internally on the statement view page and we don't need statement details in this case). So in our extension, let's determine whether the current user is a guest by adding the following method:

```
//by naming this method with the get prefix, we avoid
//having to declare this as a class variable
//this is known as a getter method
public boolean getIsGuest(){
  //query for profile based on current user's (userinfo) profile
  //userType on the profile determines the license type
  //return true/false of comparison to 'Guest'
  return [
      select id, userType
      from Profile
      where id = :userInfo.getProfileId()
    ].userType == 'Guest';
}
```

Although you can use queries to retrieve information about users, there are more efficient ways that do not use up SOQL query calls. For example, the following line of code has the same effect:

```
return UserInfo.getUserType() == 'Guest';
```

There are different ways to define a getter in Apex such as declaring a class variable and setting it in the constructor, but the previous example works well for what we are trying to accomplish and demonstrates a simple getter method.

Getters are regarded as transient and do not impact your view state, which becomes important once you have complex pages or pages with large amounts of data.

We can now simply use `{!isGuest}` on our Visualforce page to instantly know which type of user is accessing the page. Here is the complete embedded page:

You will need to save the extension (shown in the following snippet) before your page compiles.

```
<apex:page standardController="Statement__c"
  extensions="payments_Extension" sidebar="false"
  showHeader="false">
  <apex:sectionheader title="Statement"
  subtitle="{!Statement__c.name}" rendered="{!isGuest}"/>
  <apex:pageblock mode="maindetail" title="Statement Details"
  rendered="{!isGuest}">
    <apex:pageblocksection columns="1">
      <apex:outputfield
      value="{!Statement__c.statement_date__c}"/>
      <apex:outputfield
      value="{!Statement__c.balance__c}"/>
    </apex:pageblocksection>
  </apex:pageblock>
  <apex:form>
    <apex:pageblock title="{!IF(isGuest,'Payment
Details','Quick Payment')}" mode="edit">
<!--pageblockbuttons automatically arrange our buttons-->
      <apex:pageblockbuttons location="bottom">
<!--we only want this button to show at the bottom of our page-->
        <apex:commandbutton value="Save Payment"
        action="{!savePayment}" disabled="{!success}" />
      </apex:pageblockbuttons>
```

```
<!--pagemessages allow us to show feedback to the user-->
    <apex:pagemessages/>
    <apex:pageblocksection id="paymentSection" columns="1">
      <apex:selectlist label="Payment Method"
      value="{!thisPayment.recordtypeid}" size="1"
      disabled="{!isGuest}">
<!--getter method to retrieve our record types for payment__c-->
<!-- only payment method available for guests -->
        <apex:selectOptions value="{!paymentRecordTypes}"/>
<!--actionsupport allows us to call ajax rerenders-->
<!--or controller / extension methods using the-->
<!--action attribute on events-->
        <apex:actionsupport event="onchange"
rerender="paymentMethodDetails"/>
      </apex:selectlist>


<!--amount defaulted to statement amount in extension-->
<!--editable if not guest-->
        <apex:inputfield
value="{!thisPayment.amount__c}" rendered="{!NOT(isGuest)}"/>
<!--if guest, not editable-->
        <apex:outputfield
value="{!thisPayment.amount__c}" rendered="{!isGuest}"/>


<!--generic billing information-->
<!--autopopulated in extension if not guest from renter-->
<apex:inputfield
value="{!thisPayment.billing_name__c}"/>
<apex:inputfield value="{!thisPayment.billing_street__c}"/>
<apex:inputfield value="{!thisPayment.billing_city__c}"/>
<apex:inputfield value="{!thisPayment.billing_state__c}"/>
<apex:inputfield value="{!thisPayment.billing_postal_code__c}"/>
    </apex:pageblocksection>
<!--section to contain check/card details-->
<!--the id will allow us to ajax rerender this section-->
    <apex:outputpanel id="paymentMethodDetails">
<!--check fields-->
      <apex:pageblocksection columns="1"
      rendered="{!thisPayment.recordtypeid != null &&
      recordTypeMap[thisPayment.recordtypeid]=='Check'}">
<apex:inputfield value="{!thisPayment.check_account_number__c}"/>
<apex:inputfield value="{!thisPayment.check_routing_number__c}"/>
      </apex:pageblocksection>
<!--card fields-->
```

```
            <apex:pageblocksection columns="1"
            rendered="{!thisPayment.recordtypeid != null &&
            recordTypeMap[thisPayment.recordtypeid]=='Credit Card'}">
    <apex:inputfield value="{!thisPayment.credit_card_number__c}"/>
    <!-- using pageblocksectionitem requires only 2 child elements -->
    <!-- of pageblocksectionitem. By nesting components in an -->
    <!-- outputpanel, we can get around that restriction -->
            <apex:pageblocksectionitem>
                <apex:outputlabel value= "Credit Card Expiration"/>
                <apex:outputpanel layout="none">
                    <apex:inputfield
                    value="{!thisPayment.credit_card_
                    Expiration_month__c}"/>
                    <apex:selectlist
                    value="{!thisPayment.credit_card_
                    Expiration_year__c}" size="1"> <apex:selectoptions
                    value="{!expirationYears}"/>
                    </apex:selectlist>
                </apex:outputpanel>
            </apex:pageblocksectionitem>

    <!--inputsecret keeps the value masked during input-->
            <apex:inputsecret
            value="{!thisPayment.credit_card_security_code__c}"/>
        </apex:pageblocksection>
      </apex:outputpanel>
    </apex:pageblock>
  </apex:form>
</apex:page>
```

As mentioned, in order to get the page to save, you'll need the following extension. You can ask yourself why it is being presented in this weird out-of-order manner. The answer is simple: it's cleaner and easier to understand if everything is kept chunked like this rather than adding a couple of lines of code every few sentences and never providing you with the big picture. This extension will handle our error checking, success flagging, payment processing through the Authorize.net API and creation of Payment__c records from our embedded page, Force.com sites page, and soon our payment_Edit override page:

```
public with sharing class payments_Extension {
    //Payment__c record variable to hold payment information
    public Payment__c thisPayment {get;set;}
    public Statement__c thisStatement {get;set;}
    public map<id, string> recordTypeMap {get;set;}
```

```
//boolean to determine if payment was successful
public boolean success {get;set;}

public payments_Extension(ApexPages.StandardController scon) {
  if (scon.getRecord() instanceof Statement__c)
  thisStatement = [select id, name,
  Rental_Agreement__r.renter__c,
  Rental_Agreement__r.renter__r.email, balance__c from
  Statement__c where id = :scon.getid()];
  success = false;
  recordTypeMap = new map<id,string>();
  //query for all payment record types
  //populate map
  for (RecordType r : [select id, name from RecordType where
  sobjecttype='Payment__c']){
    recordTypeMap.put(r.id,r.name);
  }

  //instantiate payment
  thisPayment = new Payment__c();
  if (scon.getRecord() instanceof Statement__c){
    thisPayment.Statement__c = scon.getid();
    thisPayment.Amount__c = thisStatement.balance__c;
  }

  //if guest user, preset type to credit card
  if (getIsGuest()){
    for (id i : recordTypeMap.keyset()){
      if (recordTypeMap.get(i) == 'Credit Card'){
        thisPayment.recordtypeid = i;
        break;
      }
    }
  }
  //if not guest, populate billing details from renter
  else if (scon.getRecord() instanceof Statement__c){
    Contact renter = [select id, firstname, lastname,
    mailingstreet, mailingcity,mailingstate,mailingpostalcode
    from Contact where id
    =:thisStatement.Rental_Agreement__r.renter__c];
    thisPayment.Billing_Name__c = renter.firstname+'
    '+renter.lastname;
    thisPayment.Billing_Street__c = renter.mailingstreet;
    thisPayment.Billing_City__c = renter.mailingcity;
    thisPayment.Billing_State__c = renter.mailingstate;
```

```
        thisPayment.Billing_Postal_Code__c =
        renter.mailingpostalcode;
     }
  }

  //this method will process and save our payment
  //or report any errors in the attempt
  public pagereference savePayment(){
     success = false;
     string paymentType =
     recordTypeMap.get(thisPayment.recordtypeid);
     //check if all fields filled out
     if (validateFields(paymentType)){
       //process credit card payments
       if (paymentType == 'Credit Card'){
          //create a request wrapper for authorize.net
          api_AuthorizeDotNet.authNetReq_Wrapper req = new
          api_AuthorizeDotNet.authNetReq_Wrapper();

          //set wrapper values
          req.amt = string.valueof(thisPayment.Amount__c);
          req.firstname = (thisPayment.Billing_Name__c.contains('
          '))?thisPayment.Billing_Name__c.substringbefore('
          '):thisPayment.Billing_Name__c;
          req.lastname = (thisPayment.Billing_Name__c.contains('
          '))?thisPayment.Billing_Name__c.substringafter('
          '):thisPayment.Billing_Name__c;
          req.billstreet = thisPayment.Billing_Street__c;
          req.billcity = thisPayment.Billing_City__c;
          req.billstate = thisPayment.Billing_State__c;
          req.billzip = thisPayment.Billing_Postal_Code__c;

          //set wrapper credit card fields
          req.ccnum = thisPayment.Credit_Card_Number__c;
          req.ccexp =
          monthmap.get(thisPayment.Credit_Card_Expiration_Month__c)
          +thisPayment.Credit_Card_Expiration_Year__c;
          req.ccsec = thisPayment.Credit_Card_Security_Code__c;

  //give this request a name
  //querying here for the statement name to accommodate later //
  functionality with payment_Edit
          req.ordername = 'Payment of '+ req.ordername = 'Payment of
          '+[select id,name from Statement__c where id =
          :thisPayment.Statement__c].name;
```

```
        //process authorize.net request
        api_AuthorizeDotNet.authNetResp_Wrapper res =
        api_AuthorizeDotNet.authdotnetCharge(req);

    //authorize.net data regarding the transaction
        thisPayment.Authorize_net_Transaction_ID__c =
        res.TransactionID;
        thisPayment.Authorize_net_Authorization_Code__c =
        res.AuthorizationCode;
        thisPayment.Authorize_net_Response__c =
        res.ResponseCode+'| '+res.ResponseReasonText;

        //if the transaction failed
        if (res.responseCode != '1' || res.ResponseReasonText !=
        'This transaction has been approved.'){
            thisPayment.Status__c = 'Failed';
            ApexPages.addMessage(new
            ApexPages.message(ApexPages.severity.error,'Payment
            Failed'));
            ApexPages.addMessage(new
            ApexPages.message(ApexPages.severity.error,'
            res.ResponseReasonText'));
            return null;
        }
    }


    //successful transactions
    thisPayment.Status__c = 'Paid';
    thisPayment.Payment_Date__c = system.now();
    upsert thisPayment;
    success = true;
    ApexPages.addMessage(new
    ApexPages.message(ApexPages.severity.confirm,'Payment
    Successful'));

        try{
//if there is an email on the contact
//send them a confirmation email
        if (thisstatement !=null &&
        thisstatement.Rental_Agreement__r.renter__r.email !=
        null){
            //construct message
            Messaging.SingleEmailMessage msg = new
            Messaging.SingleEmailMessage();
            //to addresses is a list
```

```
            msg.setToAddresses(new
            list<string>{thisstatement.Rental_Agreement__r
            .renter__r.email});
            msg.setsubject('Payment Confirmation');
//you can set both html and plaintext bodies in case the
//recipient does not receive html
            msg.setHTMLbody('Your payment of
            '+thisPayment.Amount__c+' has been successfully
            processed.<br/><br/>Thank you.');
            msg.setplaintextbody('Your payment of
            '+thisPayment.Amount__c+' has been successfully
            processed.\n\nThank you.');
            //send the email
            Messaging.sendEmail(new
            list<Messaging.SingleEmailMessage>{msg});
        }
      }
      catch(exception e){}
    }
    else {
      ApexPages.addMessage(new
      ApexPages.message(ApexPages.severity.error,'Please fill out
      all fields'));
    }
    return null;
  }

  //verify required fields have been filled out
  public boolean validateFields(string paymentType){
    boolean valid = true;

    //check common fields
    if (thisPayment.statement__c==null) valid = false;
    if (thisPayment.Amount__c==null) valid = false;
    if (string.isBlank(thisPayment.Billing_Name__c)) valid =
    false;
    if (string.isBlank(thisPayment.Billing_Street__c)) valid =
    false;
    if (string.isBlank(thisPayment.Billing_City__c)) valid =
    false;
    if (string.isBlank(thisPayment.Billing_State__c)) valid =
     false;
    if (string.isBlank(thisPayment.Billing_Postal_Code__c)) valid
    = false;
```

```
//check specific fields
if (paymentType  == 'Check'){
  if (string.isBlank(thisPayment.Check_Account_Number__c))
  valid = false;
  if (string.isBlank(thisPayment.Check_Routing_Number__c))
  valid = false;
}
//credit card specific fields
else if (paymentType == 'Credit Card'){
  if (string.isBlank(thisPayment.Credit_Card_Number__c)) valid
   = false;
  if (string.isBlank(thisPayment.Credit_Card_Expiration_
  Month__c)) valid = false;
  if (string.isBlank(thisPayment.Credit_Card_Expiration
  _Year__c)) valid = false;
  if (string.isBlank(thisPayment.Credit_Card_Security
  _Code__c)) valid = false;
}

  return valid;
}


//getter method for guest user determination
public boolean getIsGuest(){
  //match profile based on current user
  return UserInfo.getUserType() == 'Guest';   }


//return select options based on class map
public list<selectoption> getPaymentRecordTypes(){
  list<selectoption> temp = new list<selectoption>();
//select option structure is value, label, disabled (optional)
  temp.add(new selectoption('','Select Payment Method'));
  for (id i : recordTypeMap.keyset()){
    temp.add(new selectOption(i,recordTypeMap.get(i)));
  }
  return temp;
}


//construct select options for this year
//and the next 4 years after that
public list<selectOption> getExpirationYears(){
  list<selectoption> temp = new list<selectoption>();
  for (integer i=0; i<5; i++){
    string y = ''+system.today().addyears(i).year();
    temp.add(new selectoption(y,y));
```

```
    }
    return temp;
}


//map to convert months to 2 digits for authorize.net
public static map<string,string> monthMap = new
map<string,string>{
    'January'=>'01',
    'February'=>'02',
    'March'=>'03',
    'April'=>'04',
    'May'=>'05',
    'June'=>'06',
    'July'=>'07',
    'August'=>'08',
    'September'=>'09',
    'October'=>'10',
    'November'=>'11',
    'December'=>'12'
    };
}
```

In the previous extension, a confirmation e-mail is sent. However, in order to enable e-mails to be sent, the e-mail administration setting must be changed to allow this (**Setup | Email Administration | Deliverability | Access Level | Set to "All Email" | Save**).You can also retrieve `RecordType` (and other schema-related) information using Schema Describes. In our extension, instead of querying for `RecordTypes`, you can also loop through the following to save a query:

Payment__c.SObjectType.getDescribe().getRecordTypeInfos(
)

Now that we have the extension in place and saved, go ahead and save the page as well. We can now test out our embedded page as well as the Force.com site page. To test the embedded page, go to **Setup | Create | Objects | Statement__c | Page Layouts | Edit Statement Layout**. On the page layout editor, drag a new section down and set it to the following:

- Single column
- Width 100%
- Height 475 px
- Show scrollbars (in our case, the page is bigger than we anticipate)

After this, select the **Visualforce Pages** option from **word bank** on the top-left corner and drag the **statement_payment** page into the newly created section. Now, save the layout and you should see the following page:

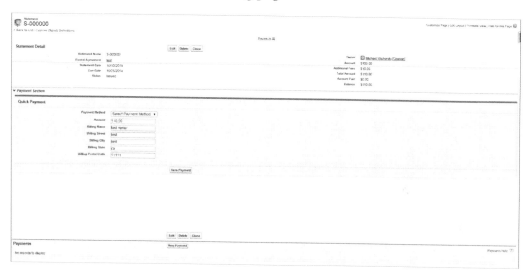

 Keep in mind that embedded pages are only visible on the view page. As such, when you save a new payment, the page will not automatically refresh the entire view page; thus, you will not see the payment in the related list until you refresh the entire page.

The next step is to take a look at our page on the Force.com site. Remember to set all of the relevant Visualforce, Apex class, object, and field permissions for the site guest user profile before attempting this or you will get an error. Here is what the page should look like. Note `id=` `parameter`; this is a `Statement__c` ID and required.

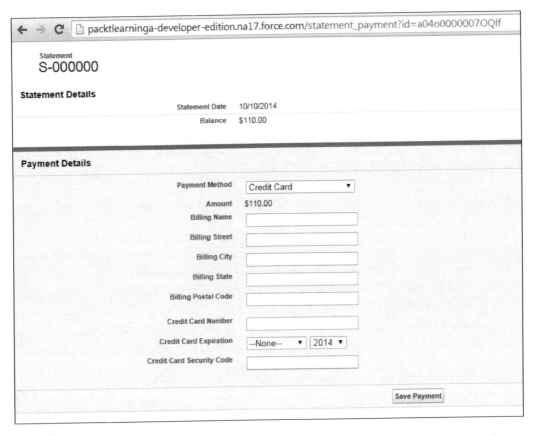

There are, of course, many steps that a developer can take at this point to personalize the experience for backend versus frontend users as explained in previous chapters, but it is easy to see how quickly a single page can be created for use in both worlds.

I did it my way!

The Salesforce1 Platform is a great out-of-the-box user experience; however, for something like our payment processing scenario, the standard *create new page* will not really work. We're now going to create, very quickly, a `payment_Edit` page that we will use to override the standard `Payment__c` new page with. Start by creating a new page called `payment_Edit` and copying in all of the markup from `statement_payment`, but don't save it quite yet. We need to change `standardContro ller="Statement__c"` to:

```
standardController="Payment__c"
```

Next, we will need the ability to set the `Statement__c` field, so let's add `inputfield` for this before the payment method:

```
<apex:inputfield value="{!thisPayment.Statement__c}"/>
```

We also need to remove the initial page block titled `Statement Details` and change `sectionheader` to the following line of code:

```
<apex:sectionheader title="New Payment"/>
```

Also, changing the `showheader` and `sidebar` attributes on the page tag to `true` will make the page feel more like what users are used to seeing. Now, we can compile and save this page and since our extension is already written in a way that conditionally determines what to do based on the standard controller being used, we can override the new `Payment__c` button. Proceed with the following steps:

1. Navigate to **Setup | Create | Objects | Payment__c**.
2. Scroll down to **Buttons, Links, and Actions**.
3. Click on the **Edit** link next to **New**.
4. Select the **Visualforce Page** option with `payment_Edit` for the **Override with** option.
5. The **Skip RecordType Selection Page** should be checked.

Here is a visual; ensure that you check the **Skip RecordType Selection Page** option:

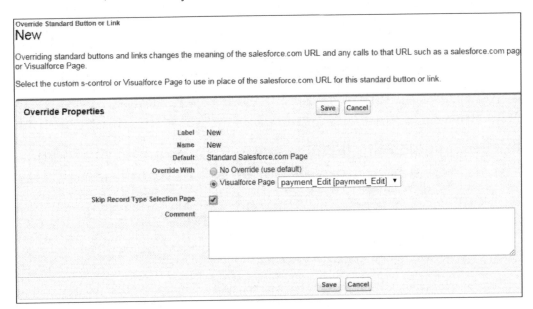

We can test the functionality out by going to any statement and making a new payment using the related list **New** button. You will get a screen similar to the following screenshot:

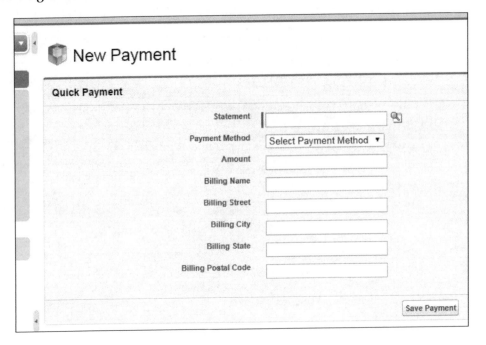

Amazing! How easy it is to reuse our functionality and code to quickly adapt to different scenarios, isn't it? Now, if you are one of those advanced developers reading this book for leisure, you'll probably be saying to yourself that there are more efficient ways of doing certain things that have been covered so far. While this might be true, minifying and optimizing the code, while making it cryptic, is not the goal of this entry-level book; that's something to be covered in an advanced text.

Ain't no mountain

Although Force.com has many different limits on things such as number of fields, number of specific types of fields, and those dictating how custom code should be written and can be used, there are ways to work around many of these limitations. Let's take a look at how to write a roll-up summary formula in a trigger, which we will take advantage of if we have reached the maximum allowed on our object, or want to cross several relationship bridges, or want to mimic the roll-up functionality through a lookup relationship rather than Master-Detail. In order to demonstrate this functionality, we will do two Apex roll-ups using aggregate queries to Rental Agreement; one will be based on `Statement__c` (Total Invoiced) and the other will be based on `Payment__c` (Total Payments). Create the class before the triggers and this time around `rollup_Methods`, as shown:

```
public class rollup_Methods {

    //for rolling up statements to total invoiced
    public static void
    rollupStatementsToRentalAgreement(list<Statement__c> newlist){
      //first we need a set of Rental Agreements involved
      set<id> rentalAgreementSet = new set<id>();
      //loop through every statement and add the related rental
      agreement id
      for (Statement__c s : newlist)
      rentalAgreementSet.add(s.Rental_Agreement__c);

      //list to store our Rental_Agreement__c for update
      list<Rental_Agreement__c> rentalUpdates = new
      list<Rental_Agreement__c>();

      //aggregate query to sum total amount from statement
      //group by rental agreement
      for (AggregateResult ar : [select sum(Total_Amount__c)
      totalInvoice,rental_agreement__c from Statement__c where
      Rental_Agreement__c IN :rentalAgreementSet group by
      Rental_Agreement__c]){
```

```
    //instantiate an update record for each grouped aggregate
    result
    Rental_Agreement__c r = new Rental_Agreement__c(id=
    string.valueof(ar.get('rental_agreement__c')));
    //set value of total invoiced
    r.Total_Invoiced__c =
    double.valueof(ar.get('totalInvoice'));
    //add to update list
    rentalUpdates.add(r);
  }


  //if update list has records, update
  if (!rentalUpdates.isEmpty()) update rentalUpdates;
}


//for rolling up payments to total payments
//note that you can use a map or list from triggers
//use trigger.new and trigger.newmap respectively (same for
'old')
public static void
rollupPaymentsToRentalAgreement(map<id,Payment__c> newmap){
  //since we need to navigate two objects to get to rental
  agreement fields
  //it is best practice to query for the data we need to ensure
  it is available to us
  //triggers do not automatically contain all fields if invoked
  from code actions
  set<id> rentalAgreementSet = new set<id>();
  for (Payment__c p : [select id,
  Statement__r.Rental_Agreement__c from Payment__c where id IN
  :newmap.keyset()]){
    rentalAgreementSet.add(p.Statement__r.Rental_Agreement__c);
  }


  //list to store our Rental_Agreement__c for update
  list<Rental_Agreement__c> rentalUpdates = new
  list<Rental_Agreement__c>();


  //aggregate query to sum total amount from payments
  //group by rental agreement
  for (AggregateResult ar : [select sum(Amount__c) totalPaid,
  Statement__r.Rental_Agreement__c ra from Payment__c where
  Statement__r.Rental_Agreement__c IN :rentalAgreementSet group
  by Statement__r.Rental_Agreement__c]){
//instantiate an update record for each grouped aggregate result
//aliased the rental agreement grouping as 'ra'
```

```
Rental_Agreement__c r = new Rental_Agreement__c(id=
string.valueof(ar.get('ra')));
//set value of total invoiced
r.Total_Payments__c = double.valueof(ar.get('totalPaid'));
//add to update list
rentalUpdates.add(r);
}


//if update list has records, update
if (!rentalUpdates.isEmpty()) update rentalUpdates;
}
}
```

The triggers for these are super easy. They should be upsert triggers (acting on both insert as well as update):

```
trigger payment_Trigger on Payment__c (after insert, after update) {
    if(trigger.isAfter && (trigger.isInsert || trigger.isUpdate))
    rollup_Methods.rollupPaymentsToRentalAgreement(trigger.newmap);
}
```

The other trigger is as follows:

```
trigger statement_Trigger on Statement__c (after insert, after update)
{
    if(trigger.isAfter && trigger.isInsert || trigger.isUpdate)
        rollup_Methods.rollupStatementsToRentalAgreement(trigger.new);
}
```

Easy, right? If anything about the triggers is confusing, refer to *Chapter 4, Triggers and Classes*, for some more in-depth explanations and walkthroughs.

Upgrade to the app status

So far, everything we have created has been a page or class (or trigger), interconnected, yes, but really still standalone. Keeping in line with the chapter's title, we're now going to create an actual app, a collection of tabs, objects, pages, and classes and have it contain our tabs for **Property Management Application**. Proceed with the following steps:

1. Navigate to **Setup | Create | Apps | New**.
2. Select **Custom App** (if prompted to select between **Console** and this).
3. Name the app as App Property Management.
4. Upload a custom logo if you want.

5. Add the following tabs:
    ◦ **Accounts**
    ◦ **Contacts**
    ◦ **Properties**
    ◦ **Rental Agreements**
    ◦ **Reports**

6. Make them visible on the next screen and finalize.

You should now be able to click on the blue bubble (app selector) in the top-right part of the screen and select the **Property Management** app, as shown in the following screenshot:

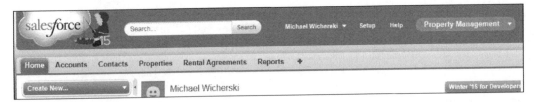

If you want to add any additional tabs, you can; if they are missing, for example, Statements, you can create a tab and then edit the app to add it.

Summary

Hello, are you still there? Did we just blow your mind? Are you feeling confused? Elated? Questioning everything you've ever known? Don't worry; this feeling goes away after a few years. It's hard to believe that in a single chapter of this book, we have walked you through creating a fully functional application that can actually be used for business purposes. Before you run off and try to sell this application, there are some other things to keep in mind. First, you're not the only reader of this book, and we don't want to flood the market with property management applications. Second, in order to package or deploy this app, you're going to need test coverage. So keep reading, because the next chapter is an important one!

In the next and final chapter, we'll review the concept of test coverage. Test coverage is, at the most basic level, code written to run your code to detect errors. However, as professional developers, we tend to strive for functional tests that test your code by simulating actual use cases.

9
Test Coverage

Ah yes, the Achilles heel of developers as a whole. No one enjoys writing test coverage, or extensively testing their functionality against potential end user pitfalls, but it is nevertheless a real requirement. For the Salesforce1 Platform, it is recommended that the developer strive for 100 percent coverage across every class, but only 75 percent average across all classes is required to actually deploy one's code to Production.

There are two schools of writing test coverage, one that is the half-assed approach of just getting lines covered to get the percentage required, and the other, which is the correct approach, of writing test coverage that mimics the business process, which should by its very progression cause your code to be executed and thereby tested. This also means that your test methods should assert that what you expect to have taken place actually did take place. A developer should never simply assume that because the code has lines covered and it ran without errors that everything is as it should be.

The Salesforce1 Platform has several quirks that need to be accounted for during testing, which will be pointed out while discussing test classes and methods for the code that were presented in previous chapters of this text.

@isTest

No, that's not a Twitter handle; this is how a test class is defined as such. This should be the first line of your class, which allows the class to contain test methods and causes the entire class to not be counted against your maximum code storage limit.

 If you are working with an older Salesforce or a Force.com organization, it's possible that you might have classes created prior to API Version 28. Through API Version 27, developers were allowed to place test methods within the class being tested itself. As of Version 28, there must now be a separate class to contain test methods.

The `@isTest` annotation has a parameter that you can pass in to allow the test method to utilize your organization's existing data:

```
@isTest (seealldata=true)
```

In general, this is considered to be bad practice and should only be used if absolutely necessary. Any data you require in order to test your code should be created within the tests themselves. The reason that using real data to fulfill your test coverage is bad is because real data changes, and you might not always have the data your test expects to exist, which would cause your test coverage to fail.

> It is important to note that although using the `seealldata=true` parameter allows test methods to operate on live data, nothing is committed to the database from test methods. Therefore, there is no risk that data you modify/delete/insert in test methods will affect any live data.

Always on my mind

There are several things to keep in mind with regard to test coverage; some are related to actually writing the tests themselves, some are more conceptual, while others are still procedural and how the system handles testing.

The rundown

These are the general requirements for testing and test coverage when deploying to production:

- All classes (including triggers) must compile successfully
- Every trigger must have at least 1 percent test coverage
- All tests will be run during deployment, not just those affecting the components you are deploying
- All tests must run and complete successfully, covering 75 percent of your total code lines for the deployment to succeed

At the parallel

The last bullet of *The rundown* mentions that all tests are run when deploying. This is true, and they are run sequentially. However, when initiating a test coverage run of all tests, they are run in parallel, which might cause you to run into issues. You should try to write your tests in such a way that you do not reuse the same unique index (such as external IDs) for records across your tests. Alternatively, you can disable the feature of running tests in parallel (which for all intents and purposes, just makes your tests complete faster) by performing the following steps:

1. Navigate to **Setup | Develop | Apex Test Execution**.
2. Click on the **Options** button on the screen.
3. In the dialog, check the **Disable Parallel Apex Testing** checkbox.
4. Click on **OK**, as shown in the following screenshot:

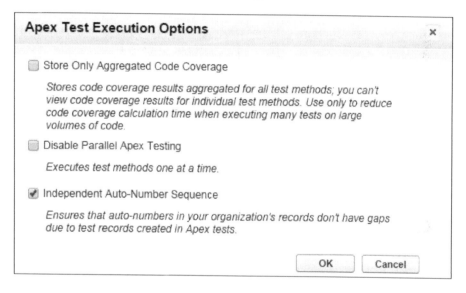

Now you're covered for these situations. Note the other options in the dialog window for testing; they have descriptions and are self-explanatory. However, typically you will want to be able to view coverage percentages for all classes, so leave **Store Only Aggregate Code Coverage** unchecked. As for **Independent Auto-Number Sequence**, this should remain checked; otherwise, the live data is weird and users don't understand why (frankly, I've never understood why this is even an option/possibility, as test methods aren't supposed to affect data).

Products

Testing business flows that included the use of products, such as opportunities with products, used to be a nightmare. You were forced to use the (seealldata=true) parameter in order to allow your test to see standard price book so that a custom price book can be created to add in test products to use. As of API Version 31 (Summer 2014 release), this is no longer an issue! A new method, Test. getStandardPricebookId(), returns the ID for Standard Price Book, without having to use real data. If you are working on a class with products that predate API 31 and you need to write test coverage, we strongly recommend that you explore whether updating the API version of the class would break anything (chances are that this won't happen) and doing so to leverage the new functionality, rather than writing test coverage using seealldata.

Batches and @future

When running tests against batch classes and @future methods, note that they are no longer run asynchronously and instead run in the same thread as everything else in the test method. It makes the testing process slightly more convoluted as you must respect thread limitations as well as additional constraints of why you were using asynchronous processes in the first place. In addition, batch process tests must be able to complete in a single run of the batch—this is typically handled by adding a limit clause to the initial query of limit 1, or ensuring that seealldata is not used and creating only a small amount of test data for the batch to operate on.

Workflows and validation rules

Be mindful of these. Any and all data-related actions you take in your test methods will evaluate validation rules and cause workflows to run; if your test data fails validation rules, either custom ones created by administrators or system ones (such as field max length), the test will fail with a DML exception. You should definitely test to ensure that your workflows are operating correctly by querying for the record that was modified and using an assert statement to verify data is as expected.

Get tested

It's important to get checked out by your doctor on a regular basis. It's just a best practice of life. However, when it comes to writing code, we need to account for many quirks and cover many different avenues of what needs to be tested. There are ways to streamline the process and make our tests more efficient. With that in mind, let's get going!

Helping hands

A good idea to keep you sane while writing test coverage is to create a helper class for yourself that will allow you to quickly insert your test data with the minimum or common fields that should be populated. An example of such a class is shown in the following code. Note that we don't actually insert the record in these methods; this is so that additional fields can be set or modified in the test method using the record before inserting them. This is useful if you are testing a specific attribute of a trigger, validation rule, or workflow. There is a method for each of the sObjects we interact with in our code from *Chapter 6, Exposing Force.com to the World*, through *Chapter 8, Creating a Property Management Application*. There are also additional methods to insert the test record generated, in case we want a quick insert:

```
public class test_helperMethods {

    public static Account generate_TestAccount(){
        Account a = new Account();
        a.name = 'TestAccount';
        return a;
    }

    public static Account insert_TestAccount(){
        Account a = generate_TestAccount();
        insert a;
        return a;
    }

    public static Contact generate_TestContact(id accountid){
        Contact c = new Contact();
        c.firstname ='testfirst';
        c.lastname = 'testlast';
        c.email = 'test@test.com';
        c.mailingstreet = '123 any street';
        c.mailingcity = 'testcity';
        c.mailingstate = 'CA';
        c.mailingpostalcode = '12345';
        if (accountid!=null){
            c.AccountId = accountid;
        }
        return c;
    }

    public static Contact insert_TestContact(id accountid){
        Contact c = generate_TestContact(accountid);
        insert c;
        return c;
```

```
    }

    public static Property__c generate_TestProperty(id ownerid){
        Property__c p = new Property__c();
        p.owner__c = ownerid;
        p.Year_Built__c = ''+system.today().year();
        p.Physical_Street__c = '123 any street';
        p.Physical_City__c = 'testcity';
        p.Physical_State__c = 'CA';
        p.Physical_Postal_Code__c ='12345';
        return p;
    }

    public static Property__c insert_TestProperty(id ownerid){
        Property__c p = generate_TestProperty(ownerid);
        insert p;
        return p;
    }

    public static Rental_Unit__c generate_TestRentalUnit(id
    propertyId){
        Rental_Unit__c r = new Rental_Unit__c();
        r.Property__c = propertyId;
        r.Number_of_Bedrooms__c = 2;
        r.Number_of_Bathrooms__c = 2;
        return r;
    }

    public static Rental_Unit__c insert_TestRentalUnit(id
    propertyid){
        Rental_Unit__c r = generate_TestRentalUnit(propertyid);
        insert r;
        return r;
    }

    public static Rental_Agreement__c
    generate_TestRentalAgreement(id rentalUnitId, id renterId,
    decimal rentAmt, decimal depAmt){
        Rental_Agreement__c r = new Rental_Agreement__c();
        r.Rental_Unit__c = rentalUnitId;
        r.Renter__c = renterId;
        r.Rental_Amount__c = rentAmt;
        r.Deposit__c = depAmt;
        return r;
    }
```

```
public static Rental_Agreement__c insert_TestRentalAgreement(id
rentalUnitId, id renterId, decimal rentAmt, decimal depAmt){
   Rental_Agreement__c r =
   generate_TestRentalAgreement(rentalUnitId, renterId, rentAmt,
   depAmt);
   insert r;
   return r;
}

public static Statement__c generate_TestStatement(id
agreementId, decimal amt){
   Statement__c s = new Statement__c();
   s.Rental_Agreement__c = agreementId;
   s.Amount__c = amt;
   s.Statement_Date__c = system.today();
   s.status__c = 'Issued';
   return s;
}

public static Statement__c insert_TestStatement(id agreementId,
decimal amt){
   Statement__c s = generate_TestStatement(agreementId, amt);
   insert s;
   return s;
}

public static Payment__c generate_TestPayment(id statementid,
decimal amount){
   Payment__c p = new Payment__c();
   p.Statement__c = statementid;
   p.amount__c = amount;
   p.Payment_Date__c = system.now();
   return p;
}

public static Payment__c insert_TestPayment(id statementId,
decimal amount){
   Payment__c p = generate_TestPayment(statementid, amount);
   insert p;
   return p;
}
}
```

 Notice that the class is not defined as a test class and the methods are not test methods. This allows you to gain some extra test coverage, while helping you write more consistent test methods, and speed.

Itchy trigger finger

The first things that should be tested are always your triggers. This ensures that you have tested your triggers for all situations, including data loads, custom pages, and UI data entry. A common approach of those just performing *lines covered* tests is to test their triggers by writing test methods for their custom extensions. Unfortunately, this means that sometimes this causes issues in use due to dataloads or if information is not filled out in the same format through the UI by an end user.

Luckily, testing triggers is easy. They always require a minimum of 1 percent coverage, which is easily attainable by simply performing a DML operation on the sObject. In this case, we will have trigger tests for the `Payment__c` and `Statement__c` objects from *Chapter 8, Creating a Property Management Application*. The methods that these triggers invoke are all in `rollup_Methods`, so go ahead and create a class, `rollup_Methods_TEST`. Test class naming conventions are entirely up to the developer, some people prefix the class with `TEST_`, others add it in the `_TEST` suffix, and still others don't flag it at all. There is really no best practice to speak of here, but we encourage consistency in your own code for readability and consulting with your fellow developers to maintain a clean and unified structure:

```
@isTest
private class rollup_Methods_TEST {

//some records we reuse, so only insert them once
//makes the tests run faster (less DML)
   static Account acct = test_helperMethods.insert_TestAccount();
   static Contact cont =
   test_helperMethods.insert_TestContact(acct.id);
   static Property__c prop =
   test_helperMethods.insert_TestProperty(cont.id);
   static Rental_Unit__c unit =
   test_helperMethods.insert_TestRentalUnit(prop.id);

//test the rollup of statements to agreements
   static testmethod void rollupStatementsToRentalAgreement_test(){
   //inserting the agreement here since it has hardcoded values
   Rental_Agreement__c agree =
   test_helperMethods.insert_TestRentalAgreement(unit.id, cont.id,
   100, 100);
     //indicates the start of our actual test flow
     test.startTest();
       Statement__c statement =
       test_helperMethods.generate_TestStatement(agree.id, 100);
       insert statement;
```

```
      agree = [select id, Total_Invoiced__c from
      Rental_Agreement__c where id = :agree.id];
      //asserting that our trigger ran on insert
  system.assert(agree.Total_Invoiced__c == 100);


      statement.Amount__c = 200;
      update statement;


      agree = [select id, Total_Invoiced__c from
      Rental_Agreement__c where id = :agree.id];
      //asserting that our trigger ran on update
      system.assert(agree.Total_Invoiced__c == 200);
    //indicates the end of our actual test flow
    test.stopTest();
  }


  static testmethod void rollupPaymentsToRentalAgreement_test(){
    Rental_Agreement__c agree =
    test_helperMethods.insert_TestRentalAgreement(unit.id,
    cont.id, 100, 100);
    Statement__c statement =
    test_helperMethods.generate_TestStatement(agree.id, 100);
    insert statement;

    test.startTest();
      Payment__c pay =
      test_helperMethods.generate_TestPayment(statement.id, 50);
      insert pay;
      agree = [select id, Total_Payments__c from
      Rental_Agreement__c where id = :agree.id];
      system.assert(agree.Total_Payments__c == 50);

      pay.Amount__c = 100;
      update pay;
      agree = [select id, Total_Payments__c from
      Rental_Agreement__c where id = :agree.id];
      system.assert(agree.Total_Payments__c == 100);
    test.stopTest();
  }
}
```

In the following sections, you'll learn how to run methods as specific users for the purposes of test coverage. It is best practice to ensure that all users who should be able to use your code can and have the necessary permissions to do so.

Mocking you

Typically, we'd consider testing callouts more advanced than testing a custom controller/extension and would discuss how to cover that first. However, because the extension we are trying to test uses a callout to communicate with Authorize.net, the test would be skipped as callouts are not allowed in test methods. Luckily, we can create a mock responder by implementing `HttpCalloutMock`, which will allow our tests to perform callouts to our mock responder by mimicking the behavior of the real system you are using.

 The easiest way to do this is to copy the result of `HttpResponse` you receive into your mock responder as the response.

The following small class will show you how to set up a mock responder for Authorize.net, assuming a successful transaction. You'll notice it's flagged as a test class and marked global:

```
@isTest
global class mock_AuthorizeDotNet implements HttpCalloutMock{
    //this method MUST be called respond and return
    //HttpResponse
    global HttpResponse respond(HttpRequest req){
        //curiosity killed the cat, what's the request?
        system.debug(req);

        //instantiate the response we'll return
        HttpResponse res = new HttpResponse();
        //usually a good idea to set the status code/value
        res.setStatusCode(200);
        res.setStatus('Ok');

        //construct response body
        string response = '1;1;1;This transaction has been
        approved.;DMPWBZ;Y;2196294662;;Transaction:
        test;10.00;CC;auth_capture;;first;last;;street;
        city;state;billzip;;;;;;;;;;;;;;;;;;449B10456AF4D3B815F828D
        3E82185F5;P;2;;;;;;;;;;;XXXX0002;American
        Express;;;;;;;;;;;;;;;;;;';

        //set response body and return
        res.setBody(response);
        return res;
    }
}
```

We'll also need one of these for our `googleCalendar_API` class so that we can test our `batch_GoogleCalendar_Sync` class:

```
@isTest
global class mock_GoogleService implements HttpCalloutMock{

    global HttpResponse respond(HttpRequest req){
        system.debug(req);

        HttpResponse res = new HttpResponse();
        res.setStatusCode(200);
        res.setStatus('Ok');

        string response = '--batch_WwEGYD6Iy8A_ABl0yltfmbo\nContent-
        Type: application/http\nContent-ID: <response-
        00Uo0000001JynUEAS>\n\nHTTP/1.1 200 OK\nETag:
        "2826236657198000"\nContent-Type: application/json;
        charset=UTF-8\nDate: Sun, 12 Oct 2014 12:52:14 GMT\nExpires:
        Sun, 12 Oct 2014 12:52:14 GMT\nCache-Control: private, max-
        age=0\nContent-Length: 780\n\n{\n "kind": "calendar#event",\n
        "etag": "\"2826236657198000\"",\n "id":
        "1u5fli71vjtmv4tqc5d61lhdu4",\n "status": "confirmed",\n
        "htmlLink":
        "https://www.google.com/calendar/event?eid=MXU1ZmxpNz
        F2anRtdjROcWM1ZDYxbGhkdTQgdGVkd2ljaGVyc2tpQG0",\n "created":
        "2014-10-12T12:52:08.000Z",\n "updated": "2014-10-
        12T12:52:08.599Z",\n "summary": "test",\n "creator": {\n
        "email": "test@test.com",\n "displayName": "Michael
        Wicherski",\n "self": true\n },\n "organizer": {\n "email":
        "test@test.com",\n "displayName": "Michael Wicherski",\n
        "self": true\n },\n "start": {\n "dateTime": "2014-10-
        12T06:00:00-07:00"\n },\n "end": {\n "dateTime": "2014-10-
        12T07:00:00-07:00"\n },\n "iCalUID":
        "1u5fli71vjtmv4tqc5d61lhdu4@google.com",\n "sequence": 0,\n
        "reminders": {\n "useDefault": true\n }\n}\n\n--
        batch_WwEGYD6Iy8A_ABl0yltfmbo--\n';

        res.setBody(response);

        return res;
    }
}
```

Now that we have our mock responders set up, we are ready to write our test classes for the `payment_Extension` and `batch_GoogleCalendar_Sync` classes.

AI – Sans input

When testing custom controllers/extensions, the developer needs to account for the lack of human input. The test method must provide all initial data as well as mimic user input by setting fields to their appropriate values. To mimic button clicks, tests must call the methods a button click would invoke and all getters should be called independently (these are normally called when the page loads when in the UI).

The following class only contains methods to test credit card payments, but when testing, you should always write methods to test every branch of your logic (such as checks). This includes using valid and invalid data, following all logic branches (if statements, including ternary) and causing exceptions to be thrown so that your try-catch methods are used. Furthermore, you'll notice in the following sample test class that the runAs method is used.

The runAs method allows a developer to test the functioning of their code when a specific user is attempting to run it (per profile). In order to run as a user of a specific profile, you must create the user first (but don't have to insert them) before running the test—demonstrated as follows. Also, pay close attention to the use of the test.startTest() and test.stopTest() methods in the following code as well as test.setMock(); their placement is crucial to avoid exceptions:

```
@isTest
private class payments_Extension_TEST {
  //declare all static data
  static Account acct = test_helperMethods.insert_TestAccount();
  static Contact cont =
  test_helperMethods.insert_TestContact(acct.id);
  static Property__c prop =
  test_helperMethods.insert_TestProperty(cont.id);
  static Rental_Unit__c unit =
  test_helperMethods.insert_TestRentalUnit(prop.id);
  static Rental_Agreement__c agree =
  test_helperMethods.insert_TestRentalAgreement(unit.id, cont.id,
  100, 100);
  static Statement__c statement =
  test_helperMethods.insert_TestStatement(agree.id, 100);

  //test system administrator credit card payments
  static testmethod void payments_Extension_Credit_TEST(){
    //start the test and separate DML flow
    test.StartTest();
      //set our mock class for callouts
      Test.setMock(HttpCalloutMock.class, new
      mock_AuthorizeDotNet());
```

```
//instantiate the standard controller for our statement
    ApexPages.StandardController scon = new
    ApexPages.StandardController(statement);
//instantiate the extension based on standard controller
    payments_Extension ext = new payments_Extension(scon);

//test the validate method, without filling in any fields
    ext.validateFields('Credit Card');

    //mimic user input
    ext.thisPayment = fillPaymentFields(ext.thisPayment, 'Credit
    Card');
    //save payment
    ext.savePayment();
  //stoptest
  test.StopTest();
}


//test guest user credit card payments
static testmethod void payments_Extension_Credit_GUEST_TEST(){
  //get the site guest user profile
  Profile p = [SELECT Id FROM Profile WHERE Name='LearningApex
  Profile'];

      //create a guestUser with the site guest user profile
  User guestUser = new User(Alias = 'guest',
  Email='guestuser@testorg.com',
          EmailEncodingKey='UTF-8', LastName='Testing',
          LanguageLocaleKey='en_US',
          LocaleSidKey='en_US', ProfileId = p.Id,
          TimeZoneSidKey='America/Los_Angeles',
          UserName='guestuser@testorg.com');
  //set running user as our guest user
  system.runAs(guestUser){
    //start the test
    test.StartTest();
      //set our mock class for callouts
      Test.setMock(HttpCalloutMock.class, new
      mock_AuthorizeDotNet());
//instantiate the standard controller for our statement
      ApexPages.StandardController scon = new
      ApexPages.StandardController(statement);
  //instantiate the extension based on standard controller
      payments_Extension ext = new payments_Extension(scon);
```

```
    //test the validate method, without filling in any fields
        ext.validateFields('Credit Card');

        //mimic user input
        ext.thisPayment = fillPaymentFields(ext.thisPayment,
        'Credit Card');
        //save payment
        ext.savePayment();
      //stoptest
      test.StopTest();
    }
}


//test getters
static testmethod void payments_Extension_Getters_Test(){
  ApexPages.StandardController scon = new
  ApexPages.StandardController(statement);
  payments_Extension ext = new payments_Extension(scon);

  //test getters
  ext.getIsGuest();
  ext.getExpirationYears();
  ext.getPaymentRecordTypes();

  //although not explicitly used by this extension
  //and therefore not necessary for the test
  //the following demonstrates how to set
  //a page for the current test and how to
  //assign parameters to the page, enabling the
  //apexpages.currentpage().getparameters() call
  //from the test.
  PageReference p = Page.statement_payment;
  p.getParameters().put('param','value');
  Test.setCurrentPage(p);
}

//utility method to populate the payment fields in extension
static Payment__c fillPaymentFields(Payment__c thisPayment,
string paymentMethod){
  thisPayment.Billing_Name__c = 'test';
  thisPayment.Billing_Street__c = 'test';
  thisPayment.Billing_City__c = 'test';
  thisPayment.Billing_State__c = 'ca';
  thisPayment.Billing_Postal_Code__c = '12345';
```

```
        thisPayment.recordtypeid = [select id from RecordType where
        sobjecttype='Payment__c' and name =:paymentMethod].id;
    //check specific fields
        if (paymentMethod  == 'Check'){
          thisPayment.Check_Account_Number__c = '1234567890';
          thisPayment.Check_Routing_Number__c = '1234567890';
        }
    //credit card specific fields
        else if (paymentMethod == 'Credit Card'){
          thisPayment.Credit_Card_Number__c = '4111111111111111';
          thisPayment.Credit_Card_Expiration_Month__c = '01';
          thisPayment.Credit_Card_Expiration_Year__c =
          ''+system.today().addyears(1).year();
          thisPayment.Credit_Card_Security_Code__c = '123';
        }

        return thisPayment;
      }
    }
```

There are system-level restrictions where you cannot perform DML operations before a callout in the same transactional thread. This means that any data you need to create for your test must occur outside of the `test.startTest()` and `test.stopTest()` indicators, which simulate a separate DML flow. Also, note that the mock class needs to be set inside the test flow. The `system.runAs()` method should also be set before the start of the test flow, or you will run into exceptions.

Let's also test our `googleAuthorization` page and the related extension. For this one, we need to use the page parameter trick we mentioned in the previous test class. Remember the flow for this page, we visited and clicked a button to request authorization. After logging into Google and approving the app, we were returned to our page with a code to exchange for the access and refresh tokens. In our test, we can't be redirected or manually accept the app, so we need to fake it. The test class "redirects" after instantiating the controller, then puts parameters onto the page, and runs the authorization methods:

```
@isTest
private class googleAuthorization_Controller_TEST {
  static testmethod void googleAuthorization_Controller_TEST() {
    googleAuthorization_Controller con = new
    googleAuthorization_Controller();
    con.requestAuthorization();

    PageReference p = Page.googleAuthorization;
    p.getParameters().put('state',con.googleEmail);
```

```
      p.getParameters().put('code','testcode');
      test.setCurrentPage(p);

      test.startTest();
        Test.setMock(HttpCalloutMock.class, new
        mock_GoogleService());
        con.doOnLoad();
      test.stopTest();
   }
}
```

Batch tests

Batches can be tested by running their constructor and calling the `system.executeBatch()` method on it as long as the batch does not need to run the execute method more than once, which means that the initial query results must be the smaller of 200 records (which is the default batch size), or the specified batch size when constructing the batch. For our purposes of testing the `batch_GoogleCalendar_Sync` class, we can use our `startBatch()` and `startBatchDelay()` methods. In the following class, we test the delete process; can you see how to test the regular update process?

```
@isTest
private class batch_GoogleCalendar_Sync_TEST {

   static testmethod void batch_GoogleCalendar_Sync_Delete_TEST() {
      //instantiate and insert our event to work on
      Event e = new Event();
      e.subject = 'test';
      e.startDateTime = system.now();
      e.endDateTime = system.now().addhours(1);
      e.description = 'test';
      insert e;
      //delete the event
      delete e;

      //instantiate and insert our sync control setting
      GoogleCalendar__c gcBatchSync = new GoogleCalendar__c();
      gcBatchSync.name = 'BatchSync';
      gcBatchSync.lastSync__c = system.now().addhours(-1);
      gcBatchSync.lastDelete__c = system.now().addhours(-1);
      insert gcBatchSync;

      test.startTest();
```

```
    //set the mock responder
    Test.setMock(HttpCalloutMock.class, new
    mock_GoogleService());
    //run the delete sync batch
    batch_GoogleCalendar_Sync.startBatchDelay(true, 1);
  test.stopTest();
  }
}
```

Note that Event to operate on is inserted within the test method before the
`test.starttest()` through the `test.endtest()` block.

Fruits of our labour

We can run the tests in our organization in several ways through the UI or through
Eclipse. To run the tests through the UI, perform the following steps:

1. Navigate to **Setup | Develop | Apex Test Execution**.

2. Click on the **Select Tests** button.

3. Select which tests you wish to run as follows:

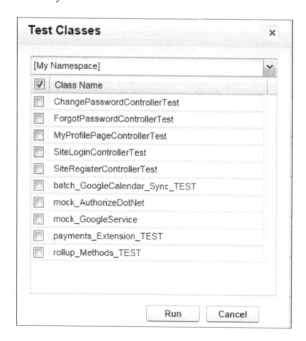

4. Click on **Run**.

The results of the tests will be shown on the following page:

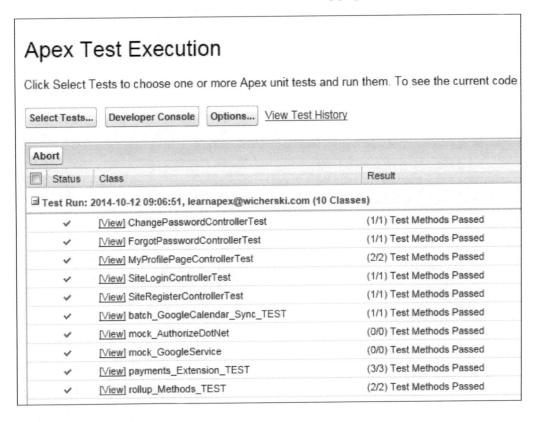

That's about the UI, and as for Eclipse, you would right-click on the folder (or a specific test class), select **Force.com**, and then select the **Run Tests** option, as shown in the following screenshot:

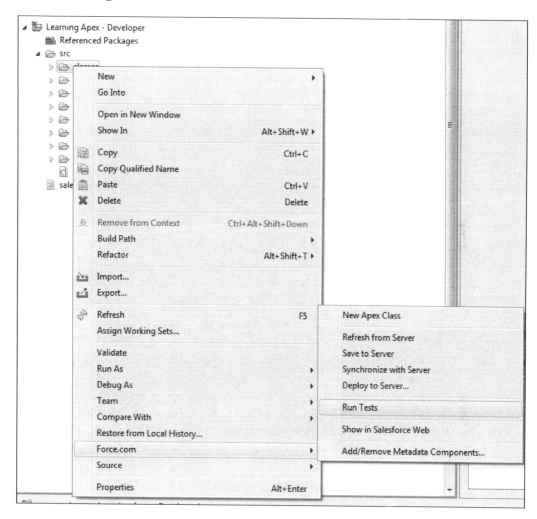

The results of Eclipse test runs are displayed in the **Apex Test Runner** view. If you do not see it, it should open automatically for you when you run a test. Otherwise, you can navigate to **Window | Show View | Apex Test Runner**. The results appear as follows:

You might notice that Eclipse displays a green check next to all classes that are above 75 percent test coverage as well as a debug log of all methods run in the right pane. In the event that there are test failures, or insufficient organization-wide test coverage, there would be another category at the same level as **Code Coverage Results** called **Test Warnings** that indicate any test issues.

The ultimate goal

Everything this book has gone over from start to this point has been with the ultimate goal of deploying our code to a Production environment, and having end users use our fancy-schmancy new code and functionality. Assuming that you have written something useful, with the appropriate test coverage, tested without using `seealldata`, accounting for different user profiles, and using `system.asserts` to ensure that the data is as we expect it to be after our code runs and assuming that you have at least 75 percent average for the instance, we can now go over the process of deploying. You will need your credentials for the Production environment for this. The steps are as follows:

1. Select the components for deployment in Eclipse. These can include pages, components, objects, triggers, and classes.

    You can select the entire directory, for example, the `classes` folder or a single component such as a single class or multiple classes.

    Be aware of dependencies between different components.

    If you try to deploy a page without a referenced extension, the deployment will fail.

    Usually, objects are deployed first, as they are the easiest to deploy, followed by classes, triggers, and pages, assuming that there are no dependencies such as overridden buttons, in which case you have to message the deployment; but this is advanced.

2. With the components selected, right-click on one of the selected components.

3. Navigate to the Force.com menu and select **Deploy to Server…**, as shown in the following screenshot:

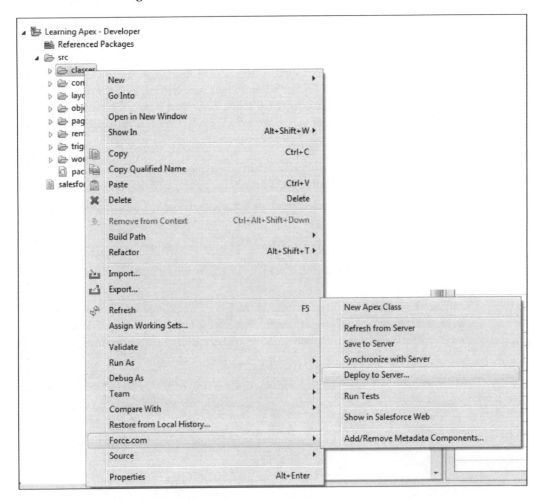

4. A sync check will run automatically for you.

5. The prompt for credentials will appear; log in here as you would to import a new project. Credentials will validate and you will see the following screenshot:

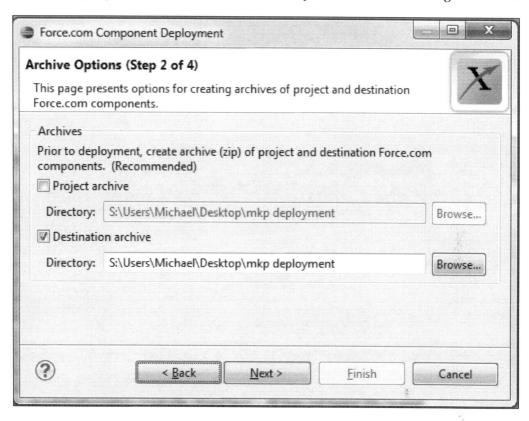

The previous screenshot allows you to create backup archives of the deployment process:

- **Project archive**: This creates a backup that contains the files you are promoting to the server. This is not really that important; you should still have a copy of these locally as your sandbox files. This is useful as a version track of pushes.

- **Destination archive**: This creates a backup of the files you are replacing. This is strongly recommended. If your deployment succeeds, but you discover an error or things go crazy in the live environment, you can use these files to roll back your changes.

 Always create a **Destination archive** backup; it will save your life one day.

6. A deployment payload comparison will run (this compares what you are deploying to production files). You are now presented with a deployment plan, shown as follows:

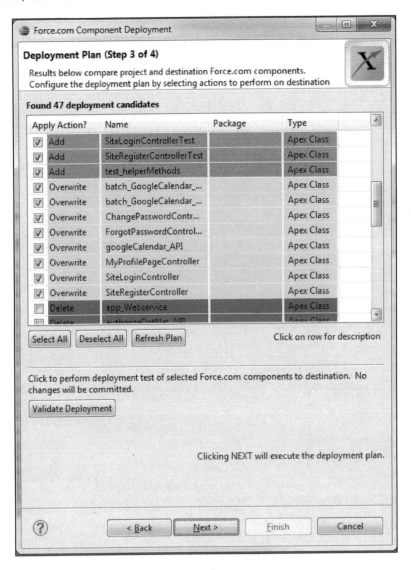

Note the color coding. Green indicates that this component is brand new and to be added. Yellow means that the component exists and will be updated. Red indicates that it exists already in production and is not in whatever source you are deploying for.

7. Select (or rather confirm) what you are deploying.

8. The **Validate Deployment** button will run all tests and attempt to deploy without actually committing and should be run before the actual deployment is attempted.

9. Clicking on **Next** will begin the deployment process, which, like the **Validate** option, will run all tests and attempt to commit the changes to the server. The next screen will notify you of success/failure:

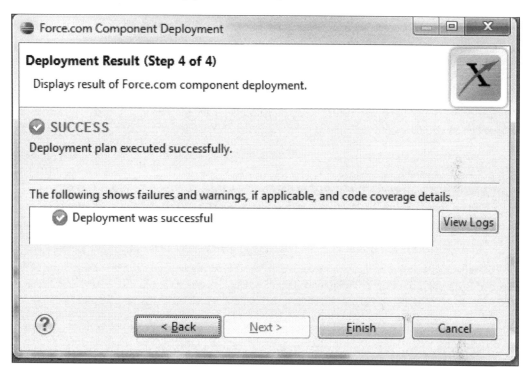

10. At this point, you can click on **Finish** and close the deployment window.

Go get a cold one and hope no one calls saying something broke.

Summary

Test coverage is the bane of every new Force.com developer. You can spot a newbie by the red mark on their foreheads caused by banging their heads on their desks. For experienced developers though, test coverage is an utter pleasure to work on. Test coverage requirements aren't decided by business users, so they don't change much. Also, how often in life are you given a calculated score on your performance? Test coverage gives us the validation that all good programmers need. Nothing cheers you up like seeing a big 100 percent on your test results.

If you can master test coverage, then your deployments will be easy and painless. Over time, you can even leverage more advanced tools such as ANT to automate the process with scripts. Regardless of how you deploy, it's important to have a documented process that is followed and to keep backups of your deployed and overwritten components.

Well, it seems like we just started this journey but it's hard to believe how far we've come. We told you this was unlike any other book, but we can't take all the credit. Everything we've shown you is only possible because of the ingenious folks at salesforce.com. They've built an amazing platform that enables you to focus on the fun and exciting stuff.

You are now armed with the knowledge to expand upon the Salesforce1 Platform with custom development, including the ability to write required test coverage for your enhancements; you're able to interact with services external to your Salesforce instance as well as have the capability to allow external services to interact with you.

It has been mentioned before that Salesforce has frequent updates with three major releases each year. The most recent big feature that has been announced, and is currently in beta, is Lightning Components. Lightning Components are scalable UI components built on the Aura framework that allow the developer to utilize client-side processing more efficiently across different platforms. They can utilize JavaScript as well as any other web-enabled language and can interact with Apex controllers as well, just like normal components. The most extensive example of Lightning Components in action right now is the Salesforce1 mobile app, which is built using these components. This is definitely a new feature to keep an eye on as it progresses towards general release.

We hope you've enjoyed reading this text as much as we've enjoyed writing it. We wish you the best of luck in your development efforts and hope that you will continue to explore the possibilities on and capabilities of the Salesforce1 Platform to drive your business digitally and effectively.

Thank you.

Index

Symbols

A

B

protected access modifier 80
public access modifier 80

Q

queries
  defining 44
query limits
  avoiding 42, 43

R

records
  performing 39-41
  processing 38
relative limit, in space 37
Remote Site Settings
  configuring 167
Rental Agreement object 219, 220
Rental Units object 218, 219
REST
  about 148-154
  cons 163
  limits 164
  pros 163
REST Console extension
  URL 153
RestContext, properties
  RestContext.Request.Headers 154
  RestContext.Request.httpMethod 154
  RestContext.Request.params 154
  RestContext.Request.remoteAddress 154
  RestContext.Request.requestBody 154
  RestContext.Response.headers 154
  RestContext.Response.responseBody 154
  RestContext.Response.StatusCode 154
REST GET method
  testing 169
roll-up summary formula
  writing, in trigger 247-249
runAs method 262

S

Salesforce
  URL 164
Salesforce1 Platform
  about 8, 9, 141

data, storing 23
  Eclipse, linking to 17-19
  Force.com sites, enabling 142-148
  installing 10
  metadata, storing 23
  public facing page, exposing 142
  working 19-22
Salesforce calendars
  sending, through Google calendar 184, 185
Salesforce Limits Quick Reference Guide
  URL 59, 66
Salesforce Object Query
        Language (SOQL) 43
sandbox account
  signup 223
s-con 96-98
simple sales deal
  process 47
Snippet
  starting 15
SOAP
  about 155-161
  cons 163
  pros 163
SOAP API, Salesforce1 Platform
  using 52
SOAP UI
  URL 160
sObjects
  implementing 84-86
  triggers, defining for 76-78
  working with 61
sObject variables
  trigger.isAfter 76
  trigger.isBefore 76
  trigger.isDelete 77
  trigger.isInsert 77
  trigger.isUndelete 77
  trigger.isUpdate 77
Software as a Service (SaaS) 7
speed limit, transaction
  obeying 32
Statement object
  about 220
  options, setting up 220
static resources 123, 124

System.scheduleBatch() method, parameters
  Apex class 62
  batch size 63
  job name 62
  minutes from now 63

T

tags, Visualforce
  <apex:actionFunction> 109
  <apex:actionPoller> 109
  <apex:actionSupport> 109
  <apex:column> 103
  <apex:commandButton> 109
  <apex:commandLink> 109
  <apex:dataTable> 102
  <apex:inputField> 102
  <apex:inputText> 102
  <apex:outputField> 102
  <apex:outputPanel> 103
  <apex:outputText> 102
  <apex:page> 101
  <apex:pageBlock> 101
  <apex:pageBlockSection> 102
  <apex:pageBlockTable> 102
  <apex:pageMessages> 103
  <apex:repeat> 102
  <apex:selectCheckboxes> 102
  <apex:selectList> 102
  <apex:selectOption> 102
  <apex:selectOptions> 102
  <apex:selectRadio> 102
technology
  considerations 163
Terms of Service (ToS) 177
test
  running 253
  running, through UI 267-270
test coverage
  requirements 252
testing
  requirements 252
time limit, in space 37
triggers
  about 70, 71
  creating 75, 76
  defining, for sObject 76-78

executing 72-74
history 69, 70
pulling 71
testing 258, 259
trigger variables
  trigger.new 77
  trigger.newMap 77
  trigger.old 77
  trigger.oldMap 77
  trigger.size 77

U

UI
  tests, running through 267-270

V

validation rule 254
values
  passing, to controller 112-114
variables
  using 106-108
Visualforce
  components 130-132
  limits 45, 46
Visualforce page
  creating 99, 100
  example 100, 101

W

web service providers
  API key authentication 178
  basic authentication 178
  no authentication 178
  no authentication but rate/hit limit
    by IP address 178
  OAuth 178
  session ID 178
**Web Services Description Language
  (WSDL) 156**
with sharing keyword 80
workflow rule 254

Thank you for buying
Learning Apex Programming

About Packt Publishing

Packt, pronounced 'packed', published its first book, *Mastering phpMyAdmin for Effective MySQL Management*, in April 2004, and subsequently continued to specialize in publishing highly focused books on specific technologies and solutions.

Our books and publications share the experiences of your fellow IT professionals in adapting and customizing today's systems, applications, and frameworks. Our solution-based books give you the knowledge and power to customize the software and technologies you're using to get the job done. Packt books are more specific and less general than the IT books you have seen in the past. Our unique business model allows us to bring you more focused information, giving you more of what you need to know, and less of what you don't.

Packt is a modern yet unique publishing company that focuses on producing quality, cutting-edge books for communities of developers, administrators, and newbies alike. For more information, please visit our website at www.packtpub.com.

About Packt Enterprise

In 2010, Packt launched two new brands, Packt Enterprise and Packt Open Source, in order to continue its focus on specialization. This book is part of the Packt Enterprise brand, home to books published on enterprise software – software created by major vendors, including (but not limited to) IBM, Microsoft, and Oracle, often for use in other corporations. Its titles will offer information relevant to a range of users of this software, including administrators, developers, architects, and end users.

Writing for Packt

We welcome all inquiries from people who are interested in authoring. Book proposals should be sent to author@packtpub.com. If your book idea is still at an early stage and you would like to discuss it first before writing a formal book proposal, then please contact us; one of our commissioning editors will get in touch with you.

We're not just looking for published authors; if you have strong technical skills but no writing experience, our experienced editors can help you develop a writing career, or simply get some additional reward for your expertise.

Force.com Development Blueprints

ISBN: 978-1-78217-245-1   Paperback: 350 pages

Design and develop real-world, cutting-edge cloud applications using the powerful Force.com development framework

1. Create advanced cloud applications using the best Force.com technologies.

2. Bring your cloud application ideas to market faster using the proven Force.com infrastructure.

3. Step-by-step tutorials show you how to quickly develop real-world cloud applications.

Force.com Developer Certification Handbook (DEV401)

ISBN: 978-1-84968-348-7   Paperback: 280 pages

A comprehensive handbook to guide Force.com developers through important fundamentals and prepare them for the DEV401 exam

1. Simple and to-the-point examples that can be tried out in your developer org.

2. A practical book for professionals who want to take the DEV 401 Certification exam.

3. Sample questions for every topic in an exam pattern to help you prepare better, and tips to get things started.

4. Full of screen-shots, diagrams, and clear step-by-step instructions that cover the entire syllabus for the exam.

Please check **www.PacktPub.com** for information on our titles

Force.com Tips and Tricks
ISBN: 978-1-84968-474-3   Paperback: 224 pages

A quick reference guide for administrators and developers to get more productive with Force.com

1. Tips and tricks for topics ranging from point-and-click administration, to fine development techniques with Apex and Visualforce.

2. Avoids technical jargon, and expresses concepts in a clear and simple manner.

3. A pocket guide for experienced Force.com developers.

Force.com Enterprise Architecture
ISBN: 978-1-78217-299-4   Paperback: 402 pages

Blend industry best practices to architect and deliver packaged Force.com applications that cater to enterprise business needs

1. Build your own application from start to finish, making use of unique tools and platform features.

2. Learn how to use the platform to build a truly integrated, scalable, and robustly engineered application to design, develop, package, and support an application focusing on enterprise-level customer demands.

3. Build the first iteration of your own ready-to-install packaged application with the help of a mix of step-by-step, worked examples and tips and tricks that discuss and answer key architectural questions.

Please check **www.PacktPub.com** for information on our titles

Made in the USA
San Bernardino, CA
08 March 2016